Yale Agrarian S

JAMES C. SCOTT, SERIES EDITOR

The Agrarian Studies Series at Yale University Press seeks to publish outstanding and original interdisciplinary work on agriculture and rural society—for any period, in any location. Works of daring that question existing paradigms and fill abstract categories with the lived experience of rural people are especially encouraged.
—James C. Scott, *Series Editor*

For a complete list of titles in the Yale Agrarian Studies Series, visit yalebooks.com/agrarian.

REALITY OF DREAMS

POST-NEOLIBERAL UTOPIAS IN THE ECUADORIAN AMAZON

• • •

JAPHY WILSON

Yale
UNIVERSITY PRESS
New Haven and London

Yale University Press books may be purchased in quantity for educational,
business, or promotional use. For information, please e-mail sales.press@
yale.edu (U.S. office) or sales@yaleup.co.uk (U.K. office).

Set in Gotham & Adobe Garamond type by IDS Infotech Ltd.,
Chandigarh, India.
Printed in the United States of America.

Library of Congress Control Number: 2020952830
ISBN 978-0-300-25342-9 (paper : alk. paper)

A catalogue record for this book is available from the British Library.

This paper meets the requirements of ANSI/NISO Z39.48–1992
(Permanence of Paper).

10 9 8 7 6 5 4 3 2 1

For Molly

It seems to me I am trying to tell you a dream—making a vain attempt, because no relation of a dream can convey the dream-sensation, that commingling of absurdity, surprise, and bewilderment . . . that notion of being captured by the incredible which is of the very essence of dreams.

Marlow, in Joseph Conrad's Heart of Darkness

Contents

Acknowledgments

This book is not the meticulously executed outcome of a rationally organized research project. Instead, it has drifted into existence through the meandering pursuit of vague hunches, bewildering perplexities, and unanticipated possibilities. Its improbable reality is due in large part to the generosity, inspiration, and companionship of others. First in this regard is Manuel Bayón, my *compañero de lucha* at the Centro Nacional de Estrategia para la Defensa del Territorio (CENEDET), the institute at which we conducted a good chunk of the research on which the book is based. Manu and I spent much of 2015 in the Ecuadorian Amazon, exploring deserted highways, inhabiting half-abandoned towns, and infiltrating militarized extraction zones. Many of the ideas developed in this book were first discussed on these gonzo wanderings. I am immensely grateful to all those who contributed to our research during this period, many of whose names appear in the text, and many more of whom have necessarily remained anonymous. Thanks especially to Angus Lyall for sharing his contacts along the Aguarico, and to Natalia Valdivieso for sharing her Millennium House on the Napo, both of which were crucial to our solution of a particularly intractable mystery.

I will always be grateful to Tom Purcell, the assistant director of CENEDET, for inviting me to join the team, and for being my staunch ally and drinking partner throughout the brief period of its existence, along with my firm friends and committed colleagues

Estefanía Martínez and Jhanilka Torres. I would also like to thank the directors of CENEDET, David Harvey and Miguel Robles-Durán, for giving me the opportunity to participate in the project, and my other fellow team members, Lisset Coba, Henar Diez, Nora Fernández, Verónica Morales, Jeremy Rayner, and Carla Simbaña, with whom I was fortunate to share the short and wild ride. My close comrades during this time also included David Chávez, David Suárez, Vanessa Barham, Gerard Coffey, Milagros Aguirre, and Sofía Jarrín, whose knowledge and friendship repeatedly infused a confusing and volatile experience with insight and laughter.

Following the conclusion of the CENEDET experiment, I spent six months researching the remarkable recent history of the Ecuadorian Amazon, which unfolded in front of my eyes as if I were traveling through the pages of the book I had yet to write. Much of this history was related to me by some of its key protagonists, including José Miguel Goldáraz, Enrique Morales, Donald Moncayo, Guadalupe Llori, Humberto Piaguaje, Julio González, Pablo Gallegos, Ángel Sallo, Jhon Rosero, and Diocles Zambrano. I learned a huge amount from the vivid memoirs of the oil worker Jorge Viteri and the *colono* pioneer Jorge Añazco, and I was fortunate to conduct interviews with Viteri in his twilight years, and with Añazco's son, Carlos, who founded Lago Agrio alongside his father. I discovered a further indispensable resource in the extraordinary anthropological works produced by the radical priests of the Capuchin mission in Coca, printed on their own press and sold in the little office of the mission—a haven of peaceful greenery hidden within the concrete overgrowth of Coca.

The argument of the book was developed in conversation with many good friends and insightful interlocutors. My most inspirational experience in this regard was a visit to Neil Brenner's Urban Theory Lab at Harvard. My theoretical approach was dramatically advanced by discussions at that seminar, and by further conversations with Neil, Mazen Labban, and Martín Arboleda. Martín also offered very encouraging and perceptive comments on early drafts of the initial chapters, and Mazen provided an incredibly helpful review of the first draft of the manuscript. Thanks also to Bob Catterall, Richard Christian, Carl Death, Rob Fletcher, Alex Loftus, Estefanía Martínez (again), Richard Peet, Tom Purcell (again), Erik Swyngedouw, and Ioanna Tantanasi, all of whom provided invaluable reflections at various critical points in the evolution of the text. I am grateful to Jean Thomson Black at Yale for convincing me to ditch a lot of pedantic ballast; to Elizabeth Sylvia and Joyce Ippolito for their additional editorial insights; to Ann Twombly for her meticulous revisions; to Nick Scarle for the map; and to an anonymous reviewer, whose comments were truly wonderful, and whose style is so distinctive that it could be only one person! And thanks to Jimmy Marshall at Boulevard 251 in Iquitos, for providing the perfect garret in which to write the final draft.

Above all, thank you Ioanna. For your constant love and support while the book was being researched and written. For being my kindest and most forensic reader. And for being the beautiful and courageous mother of our little Molly, who you fought so hard to bring into the world and who, like this book, was conceived in the Amazon. Only dreamers move mountains!

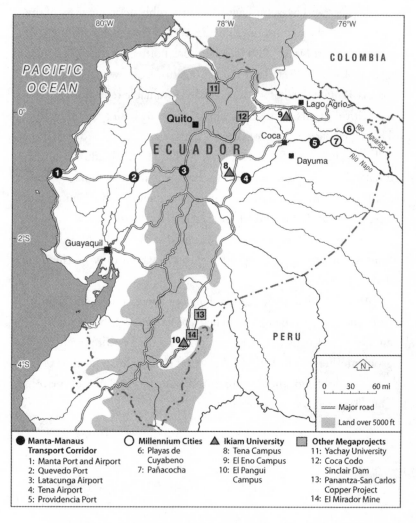

Amazonian megaprojects of the Citizens' Revolution and other related projects and locations in Ecuador.

INTRODUCTION

Fantastical Materializations

Dreams are transformed into reality with the Citizens' Revolution.

Roadside billboard, Ecuadorian Amazon, 2015

The Aguarico River cascades out of the Ecuadorian Andes before snaking slowly eastward through the Amazon toward the border with Peru. We traveled downstream for over three hours from the end of the last road, past endless tangled foliage, occasional thatched huts, and the discrete port of the Pañacocha oil field. As the canoe rounded a long curve in the river, a different reality emerged. Beneath towering storm clouds, set against the dark green jungle, a white city glowed in the evening sun. This was Playas de Cuyabeno, the first of two hundred Millennium Cities that would be built throughout the Ecuadorian Amazon to ensure that its indigenous population would finally benefit from the oil beneath their territories. In stark contrast to the poverty and abandonment that had long been the fate of the region, the Millennium Cities appeared as magical embodiments of modernity. Each house was filled with plush furnishings and gleaming appliances, and the orderly streets were set around schools, health centers, and sports facilities. In the words of President Rafael Correa Delgado, at the inauguration of the second Millennium City in 2014, "This is a dream in the heart of the jungle . . . where beforehand there was nothing."[1]

Correa had been elected in 2006 on a radical economic platform, which promised an end to the deepening poverty, widening inequality, and unbridled ecological destruction that had characterized the disastrous neoliberal experiment of the previous twenty-five years. His election marked a further victory for a wave of post-neoliberal governments sweeping to power across South America in response to the continental crisis of free market capitalism, which included the regimes of Hugo Chávez in Venezuela, Evo Morales in Bolivia, Néstor Kirchner in Argentina, and Luis Inácio Lula da Silva in Brazil. Following his election, Correa joined Chávez and Morales in the construction of a "twenty-first-century socialism," which would not only overcome neoliberalism, but also challenge the very structures of the global capitalist system. A new constitution was ratified in 2008, becoming the first in the world to enshrine the rights of nature. The constitution was centered on the *Kichwa* indigenous principle of *sumak kawsay*, or *buen vivir*—good living—which rejected capitalist development as a neocolonial imposition inconsistent with indigenous practices and cosmologies.

Over the course of the following decade, these principles would inspire an economic project that aimed to overcome the nation's socially and environmentally catastrophic dependence on Amazonian oil reserves. By reclaiming control of its natural resources from transnational corporations, Ecuador would mobilize the bonanza of a global commodities boom to catalyze a transition from the "finite resources" of the oil industry to the "infinite resources" of a collective knowledge economy, based on the unparalleled biodiversity and genetic wealth of the country's Amazonian ecosystems. Cities were planned throughout the region to incorporate the local population into this "Citizens' Revolution." A state-of-the-art university would be constructed in the depths of the rain forest to research the genetic diversity of the Amazon and develop its biotechnological applications. And an interoceanic transport corridor would integrate the region into a brave new world of global production networks. To quote Correa again: "There is a radical transformation under way in our Amazon."[2]

The grand scale and transformative vision of these projects recalled the era of heroic modernism eulogized by Marshall Berman, which was based on "immense construction projects . . . bridges and highways . . . new towns and cities" and devoted to the "long-range development of the productive forces."[3] These epic schemes were emblematic of the "construction of mass utopia," which Susan Buck-Morss has described as "the dream of the twentieth century."[4] This dream had long since been consigned to a time before the fall of communism and the "end of history." According to Jacques Rancière, under conditions of neoliberal hegemony, such dreams had been replaced with "the theme of objective necessity, identified with the constraints and caprices of the world market."[5] As Fredric Jameson has concluded, our political horizon was now defined by "our constitutional inability to imagine utopia itself . . . as the result of the systemic cultural and ideological closure of which we are all prisoners."[6]

Within this desert of shattered dreams and empty futures, the Citizens' Revolution shimmered on the horizon like a utopian oasis. According to one of its architects, "The socialism of *buen vivir* is the most beautiful utopia possible in the twenty-first century."[7] The national development plan envisaged "the execution of a project, of a dream: the society of *buen vivir*." This dream was cast against the nightmare of "capitalism . . . which destroys everything in its path, generating poverty and inequality . . . and the accelerated deterioration of the environment." In contrast to this dystopian scenario, the socialism of *buen vivir* was envisioned by the Correa administration as "the utopia that allows us to walk . . . in an emancipatory direction toward the transformation of existing social relations," including "the dismantling of the bourgeois state," "the egalitarian redistribution of resources," and the inclusive participation of the indigenous peoples of Ecuador, who would finally cease to be "objects of 'civilization,' indoctrination, and colonial subordination."[8]

But what appears as an oasis is sometimes a mirage. After rounding the long curve of the Aguarico, we began to cut across the river toward the Millennium City of Playas de Cuyabeno. Seen from a distance, the city sparkled with all the promise of a post-neoliberal utopia. But as the canoe neared the dock, I could see that the iron retaining wall had been grotesquely distorted by the weight of the rushing water. Huge sandbags had been heaped onto the exposed bank but were collapsing into the river. I scrambled ashore and was confronted not with a thriving modern city, but with the eerie emptiness of a ghost town. As I wandered the streets in the following days, it became clear that this "dream in the heart of the jungle" was not the material embodiment of a socialist revolution. In reality, it was a mere facade of modernity—schools without teachers, clinics without doctors, roads without cars—which was being abandoned by its inhabitants and consumed by the ravenous encroaching vegetation.

This book is about the reality of dreams, in two senses of the term. It explores the role of utopian dreams in the production of social space, as constitutive dimensions of material reality. And it traces the ways in which such dreams are distorted and inverted in the process of their implementation, through which their reality emerges as something very different from their utopian vision. Tales of failed utopias, of course, are nothing new. In *Seeing Like a State*, James C. Scott has dissected the multiple hubristic follies of "authoritarian high modernism" in socialist and postcolonial regimes.[9] According to Scott, spatial utopias such as those of the Citizens' Revolution are driven by the state's desire for territorial legibility and social control, abstracting from the multiple complexities of living places in the production of reductive plans that are then projected back onto these places, which results in the destruction of preexisting lifeworlds and the ruination of the plans themselves. Scott's anarchist analysis has much in common with Henri Lefebvre's Marxian critique of capitalist spatial planning, according to which technocratic representations of space are concretized on the representational spaces of everyday life, which generates the alienated dominion of an "abstract space."[10] And James Ferguson adopts a similar position from a Foucauldian perspective, arguing that development—in both its capitalist and socialist variants—functions as an "anti-politics machine" that systematically misrepresents its objects of intervention in ways that fail to achieve their stated objectives while simultaneously functioning to enhance the bureaucratic power of the state.[11]

Despite their diverse theoretical inspirations, these critiques of utopian social engineering share a vision of totalizing master plans, which are subverted by their violent collision with complex lived realities that they fail to comprehend. My experience of the deserted Millennium City seemed to correspond to this vision. Like the ill-fated utopian city of Brasília in James Holston's seminal analysis, *The Modernist City*, the Millennium City would appear to provide yet another example of "the delirium of power in master planning, which itself creates conditions over which the planners stumble and consequently conditions for its own subversion."[12] Reluctantly, I abandoned my initial faith in the radical vision of the Citizens' Revolution and began to approach its transformation of the Amazon in these more jaded terms. But as my research progressed, it became increasingly evident that something else was going on. Like Playas de Cuyabeno, the second Millennium City that I visited resembled an abandoned movie set, in which the water didn't work and raw sewage ran down the road. The fluvial section of the interoceanic corridor turned out to be unnavigable, and the corridor was not a technocratic master plan, but the half-baked scheme of a silver-tongued con man on the run from trouble downriver in Brazil. A new airport had been built in the middle of the jungle. It was maintained in immaculate condition but received no flights. An enormous suspension bridge had been erected across a mighty river, but the road on the other side remained a single-lane death trap. And the state-of-the-art biotech university had international scientists but no laboratories. Meanwhile, the oil frontier was rapidly expanding, and mining concessions were being granted to transnational capital. And all along the overgrown roadsides, between the tangled oil pipelines and the blackened gas flares, the tattered billboards repeated the same utopian promise: "Dreams are transformed into reality with the Citizens' Revolution."

This perplexing situation presented me with an unanticipated theoretical challenge: *how to make sense of things that don't make sense.* According to the dominant critical approaches to social engineering exemplified by Scott, Ferguson, and Lefebvre, such grandiose state plans invariably fail both despite and because of the scale of their ambition. But in the case of the Citizens' Revolution, *there was no plan.* The Millennium Cities were delivered to their inhabitants without a development plan or a management structure, and the biotech university had been launched in the absence of a national technology strategy or a local territorial plan. A team of technocrats at the planning ministry was supposedly working on a master plan for the Amazon. But when I asked them about the fluvial port that would complete the Ecuadorian section of the interoceanic corridor, and that was under construction at the time, they looked at each other blankly. *They had never heard of the project.* These apparently monolithic plans weren't failing because of their totalizing abstraction from local particularities, as the critical literature on such projects had led me to assume. They weren't really plans at all. And the cities and highways produced in their name weren't strategies of top-down domination. They were modernist mirages, spectacular fakeries, absurdist incongruences grafted onto the overwhelming material dynamics of the Amazon.

This book documents my attempts to come to grips with this baffling scenario. What could explain this immense surge of utopian visions and projects? How could I make sense of the farcical extent of their failure? What lessons did this hold for the possibility of post-neoliberal and post-capitalist transformation? And what might all this tell us about the relationship between dreams and reality in the capitalist production of space? These remain the central questions that animate the book. But as my perplexity increased over the course of my research, I gradually concluded that the quest to get a grip on a nonsensical reality, and to make sense of the senseless, was precisely the temptation to be resisted. Too often, in our eagerness to explain the world, we set aside the most incongruous elements of our findings and emphasize those that fit our frameworks. We make sense, in other words, of things that don't make sense. In doing so, we unwittingly perform the task of the ideological state apparatus by retroactively projecting greater coherence onto social reality than it in fact possesses. In this book, I have ended up taking a different approach, by seeking to *make sense of the fact that things don't make sense*, and by attempting to make room for the fantastical and nonsensical within the space of explanation. As Michael Taussig has argued, we need to "reject the familiar fantasy of a reassuringly real and motivated order," which is nurtured by the state and "its strange facility of seeming to make sense," and commit ourselves to the alternative project of revealing "the massive degree of uncertainty, deception, bluff, and ignorance on which such gargantuan enterprises as the ship of state rest."[13]

This task demands a theoretical approach that is attentive to the phantasmatic and absurd dimensions of the transformation of social reality under conditions of global capitalism. Such an approach, as Rosemary Jackson has noted, "subverts dominant philosophical assumptions, which uphold 'reality' as a coherent entity," and cuts against the grain of critical theories that hold that "fantasy . . . is not serious, not material, too flighty and hence not worth bothering about."[14] The Marxian tradition, in particular, has tended to dismiss fantasy as an ideological irrelevance in comparison to the stern materiality of the dialectical process. But a handful of errant Marxists have challenged this assumption. China Miéville has pointed out that "'real" life under capitalism *is a fantasy* . . . an absurdity which is true, but no less absurd for that."[15] And David McNally has similarly argued that "invisible powers—market forces—are . . . *fantastically real*," and that critical theory accordingly requires "an armory of defamiliarizing techniques, a set of critical-dialectical procedures, that throw into relief its fantastic and mysterious processes."[16]

The remainder of this introduction draws together a set of techniques and procedures of this kind, in sketching the outline of a *fantastical materialism*, which is developed over the course of the subsequent chapters. It introduces three related concepts, *phantasmagoria*, *social fantasy*, and *the fantastic*, before concluding with some thoughts on form and method.

Toward a Fantastical Materialism

Walter Benjamin's *Arcades Project* can be regarded as a pioneering work of fantastical materialism. A vivid compendium of notes and quotations compiled between 1927 and 1940, it explores the arcades of nineteenth-century Paris as an embodiment of the fantasy space of an emergent consumer capitalism in which "a new dream-filled sleep came over Europe."[17] The conceptual inspiration for the *Arcades Project* was provided by the phantasmagoria—a technology of illusions invented in the late eighteenth century that conjured spectral presences for the terrified delight of Parisian elites.[18] In contrast to the traditional Marxist depiction of ideology as a camera obscura that projected inverted images of the external world onto the walls of a darkened room, the alternative metaphor of the phantasmagoria suggested an understanding of ideology not as the distortion of an objective material reality, but as a constitutive element of reality itself.[19]

In developing his concept of the phantasmagoria, Benjamin fused Marx's theory of the fetishism of commodities with the surrealist theory of dreams. According to Marx, under capitalist social relations, the value of a commodity is abstracted from its use value and determined solely by the socially necessary labor time expended in its production. In the production of commodities, workers are paid the full value of their labor power—the cost of its reproduction—in the form of wages. But the equality of this monetary transaction conceals the fact that their labor power is put to work for longer than is necessary to cover this cost. The resulting surplus value is then realized as an ostensibly miraculous profit in the exchange of the commodities produced for money in the market. The origin of profit in exploitation is thus obscured, and value acquires an apparently autonomous power in the form of money, which seems to make the world go round.[20] As Marx observed, the social relations between people involved in the production of use values throughout the global economy thus assume "the fantastical form of relations between things."[21]

From this perspective, capitalist social reality is both phantasmatic and absurd: phantasmatic because its social relations systematically produce their own misrepresentation; and absurd because its agents remain in thrall to their own powers as if they were an external force. This understanding of capitalism resonates with the Freudian understanding of the dream as a displaced expression of a repressed wish, which is phantasmatic in its illusory wish fulfillment and absurd in its distorted form.[22] The close relationship between reality and dreams was noted by the early surrealists. In the 1924 *Manifesto of Surrealism*, André Breton claimed that Freud's identification of the unconscious as a repressed dimension permeating both dreams and waking life demanded the conceptual fusion of "dream and reality, which are seemingly so contradictory, into a kind of absolute reality, a *surreality*."[23] Benjamin sought to apply this principle to the study of social phenomena, noting that "it is one of the tacit suppositions of psychoanalysis that the clear-cut antithesis of sleeping and waking has no value," and suggesting that this principle "need only be transferred from the individual to the collective."[24] This led him to interpret the world of commodity fetishism as a domain of utopian dreams that fulfilled the emancipatory desires of the proletarian masses in the displaced form of commodity-filled arcades and modern urban infrastructures—spaces in which "the phantasmagoria was rendered in stone."[25] As the organizer of such "spatial phantasmagorias," the state was endowed with the magical capacity to stage a collective dream of social progress and mass abundance without the need for revolution.[26]

Benjamin's concept of the phantasmagoria can be combined with Slavoj Žižek's concept of social fantasy, which likewise draws on psychoanalytic theory in developing a critique of ideology that replaces the division between appearance and reality with a materiality permeated by fantastical elements. Žižek's approach is based on the conceptual schema of Jacques Lacan, who took inspiration from surrealism in his reinterpretation of Freudian theory. According to Lacan, our experience of reality is composed of three registers: the Symbolic—a differential network of signifiers; the Imaginary—a compendium of phantasmatic images of wholeness and order; and the Real—an unsymbolized dimension of repressed drives and unresolved antagonisms. The phenomenal world of everyday life is woven together of Symbolic and Imaginary elements and structured to exclude the Real, the presence of which is nonetheless discernable in the distorted form imposed on this structure by the weight of its exclusion and in traumatic moments of the return of the repressed.[27]

According to Žižek, under conditions of global capitalism, the Real excluded from our spontaneous experience of social reality is primarily the Real of capital itself. Capitalism, of course, is very much a part of symbolically structured reality, appearing in the form of individuals and institutions, discourses and practices, images and things. But *capital* is absent from this symbolic universe, existing only as value-in-motion—a process of constant metamorphosis that imperceptibly animates the objects through which it circulates in pursuit of its own expanded reproduction, as the surplus value realized as profit in commodity exchange is repeatedly thrown into the production of still more surplus value. It is here, Žižek argues, that "we encounter the Lacanian difference between reality and the Real: 'reality' is the social reality of the actual people involved in . . . the productive process, while the Real is the inexorable "abstract" spectral logic of capital that determines what goes on in social reality."[28]

The exclusion of the Real of capital from our symbolic universe is ensured not only by the enchantment inherent in the fetishism of commodities, but also by the ideological production of a symbolic order structured by a web of social fantasies, through which the constitutive antagonisms of capitalist society are erased from our spontaneous experience of social reality and replaced with reassuring visions of social harmony and natural order. Utopian socialism can be regarded as a fantasy of this kind, which was derided by Marx and Engels for painting "fantastical pictures of future society" and for expecting "historically created conditions of emancipation to [yield to] fantastical ones."[29] Utopian socialists seek to eradicate the symptomatic expressions of capitalist dynamics—poverty, inequality, economic crises, environmental destruction, and so on—while "leaving intact the essence of capital," which "through the play of its internal determinations, continues to produce . . . the very phenomena they had claimed to eliminate."[30] Just as fantasy structures reality to exclude the Real, so utopian socialism stages a reproduction of capitalist reality that has apparently been cleansed of its internal contradictions. As such, it is just one of multiple utopian fantasies, through which the Real of capital is not confronted but occluded by a vision of society that, in Žižek's terms, is "not split by an antagonistic division, a society in which the relation between its parts is organic, complementary."[31]

But that which is repressed is destined to return. This brings us to the fantastic, as a further conceptual dimension of fantastical materialism. In diametrical opposition to phantasmagoria and social fantasy, the meaning of the fantastic is "to make visible or manifest."[32] In his influential work on the subject, the literary critic Tzvetan Todorov has defined the fantastic as the experience of a situation in which everyday reality is radically disrupted by traumatic or seemingly impossible events, and we are confronted with the question: "Reality or dream? Truth or illusion?"[33] This definition of the fantastic resonates with Žižek's attention to those rare moments in which the Real disrupts a reality structured by fantasy and "the immanent social antagonism . . . erupts on the social surface."[34] Such apparently unintelligible events should not be ignored or explained away in the rush to make sense of things that don't make sense. On the contrary, as Mladen Dolar has argued, "the retroactive imposition of sense on what didn't make sense . . . *is precisely the moment of obfuscation.*"[35] This conviction was shared by Marx, for whom moments of economic crisis and systemic breakdown were not "simple deviations, contingent deformations and degenerations of the 'normal' functioning of society [but] the points at which the 'truth,' the immanent antagonistic character of the system, erupts."[36]

Benjamin captured the political significance of such moments with his concept of awakening, which he contrasted to the phantasmagorical dreamworld of everyday life in capitalist modernity. Abandoning the traditional Marxist faith in progress, which he regarded as ideologically complicit with the productivist logic of capital, Benjamin sought to reformulate historical materialism, not as a theory of the dynamic overcoming of a social order by the progressive forces contained within it, but as a theory of rupture, which unearths those fleeting moments in which a social order trapped in a nightmare of endless repetition is torn open by an act or event that brings it to a sudden stop. For Benjamin, such moments constitute "the now of recognizability . . . the moment of awakening."[37]

Žižek locates an insurgent utopian kernel in such moments of awakening, which is radically opposed to the wishful dreams and optimistic plans of utopian socialism, and which "is not an exercise in free imagination. . . . It's something to be immediately enacted when there is no other way."[38] An insurgent utopia surges up from below rather than being imposed from above, and it is rooted in the urgency of immediate necessity rather than in fantasies of perfect social order. In contrast to utopian fantasies, insurgent utopias embody "a *politics of traversing the fantasy*: a politics which does not obfuscate social antagonisms but confronts them, a politics which aims not just to 'realize an impossible dream' but . . . which touches/disturbs the Real."[39] Through their violation of the phantasmatic coordinates of social reality, insurgent utopias acquire an incandescent dimension that Miguel Abensour has called "the utopian fantastic."[40] Like the medieval carnival celebrated by Mikhail Bakhtin, the utopian fantastic directly realizes a carnivalesque inversion of the established order, in which "life [comes] out of its usual, legalized and consecrated furrows and enter[s] the sphere of utopian freedom."[41]

Fantastical Materialism as Form and Method

Fantastical materialism approaches global capitalism as a world saturated with phantasmagorias, sutured by social fantasies, and shattered by the fantastic, in an attempt to make sense of the fact that things don't make sense and to bring the phantasmatic and the absurd within the horizon of materialist critique. But this way of looking at the world poses certain challenges when it comes to writing about it. How can a fantastical materiality be conveyed in words? How can unseen dimensions of reality be represented? And how can such an approach circumvent the abstraction of academic discourse without becoming complicit in the fantasies and fetishes it seeks to deconstruct?

The progenitors of fantastical materialism have developed a variety of strategies in response to such questions. The surrealists took inspiration from Freud's method of free association in advocating the technique of automatic writing to give direct expression to unconscious processes.[42] Benjamin deployed the method of montage—assembling a kaleidoscope of dissociated fragments "to effect 'the cracking open of natural teleology.'"[43] Taussig has developed a methodology that he calls "fictocriticism"—a combination of documentary and fiction through which he seeks to convey "how truly strange is our own reality."[44] And Marx appealed to gothic metaphors to capture the Real of capital as an apparently autonomous force, describing it as "an animated monster" with a "werewolf-like hunger," which "lives only by sucking living labor, and lives the more, the more labor it sucks."[45]

These methods all seek to express what Jameson has called "the content of the form."[46] According to Jameson: "A work has content. It has raw material. . . . And the content already has a form inside it. . . . The writer does not impose a form on it. The writer draws the form out of the very content itself."[47] In attempting to draw the form of this book from its material content, I have again taken inspiration from *The Arcades Project*, in which Benjamin combined "Marxist method with a heightened sensuous emergence of presence."[48] I have sought to synthesize this approach with one of the key elements of the fantastic as a literary genre, which Todorov has identified as "an ambiguous perception shared by the reader and one of the characters," who "is himself amazed by the extraordinary phenomena that sur-round him."[49] The narrative deconstructs the utopian fantasies of the Citizens' Revolution and unearths the insurgent utopias that they conceal. But rather than immediately dismantling the elaborate retinue of spatial phantasmagorias explored in the book—the Millennium Cities, the biotech university, the interoceanic corridor—I have tried to capture the enchantment of their immediate appearances, to convey my bewilderment when confronted with their farcical dimensions, and to unfold the contorted process of their failure in ways that trace the path of my own perplexed investigations.

This approach inverts the standard structure of academic argumentation, in which conclusions are set out in advance, illusions are immediately debunked, incongruencies are swept under the carpet, and the confusions of the research process are replaced by a rational sequence of events reported by an objective observer in neutral scientific prose. As such, it has much in common with the "nonfiction novel" pioneered by Hunter S. Thompson, who developed gonzo journalism on the principle that "reality itself is too twisted" to be accurately captured by putatively objective research methods.[50] From Thompson's perspective, the relentless sense making of "journalistic [and academic] order is a farce . . . the signature of complicity in a desperate plot to maintain the social superstructure in spite of the crumbling foundation."[51] Fantastical materialism, by contrast, shares Thompson's commitment to "infuse his prose with the characteristics of the . . . 'truer reality' he senses: chaos, violence, disintegration, proliferation of inhuman proportions, absurdity."[52]

Gonzo journalism demands direct involvement in the events being reported and requires "going out and getting into the weirdness of reality."[53] The research for this book was undertaken in something approaching a gonzo style in this regard. Most of it was conducted from within the institutional machinery of the Citizens' Revolution, and I was therefore directly involved in the reality that I was investigating. From September

2014 to December 2015, I worked for the National Center of Strategies for the Right to Territory (CENEDET), a state-funded research institute directed by the Marxist geographer David Harvey, which was established by members of the Correa administration with the stated aim of providing policy advice to the planning ministry, training civil servants in radical social theory, and contributing to the construction of the "socialism of *buen vivir*." My location within the ideological state apparatus ensured unprecedented access to politicians, bureaucrats, and planners, as well as internal reports, memos, and plans, and facilitated my exploration of the "weirdness of reality" in the remote spatial utopias and militarized extraction zones of the Ecuadorian Amazon.

Much of this research was conducted in collaboration with my comrade at CENEDET, Manuel Bayón. We must have made a strange sight for the unsuspecting inhabitants of municipal offices and indigenous communities. Two scruffy, bearded foreigners showing up in a chauffeur-driven SUV with government plates was odd enough. Then, in contrast to other representatives of the state, we wanted to hear the truth about the Citizens' Revolution, instead of expecting them to conspire in simulations of its success. But any initial suspicions were invariably replaced by an avalanche of information from people eager to finally tell their side of the story. In the following chapters, whenever I speak in the first-person plural, I am referring to experiences that Manu and I shared.

My position at CENEDET provided a unique perspective on the unfolding of a utopian experiment, which I have sought to capture through close attention to the quotidian complexities of the dialectical process. My objective throughout the book has been to allow theory to breathe through the narration of events, rather than forcing the empirical material into a framework that has been established in advance. Theoretical reflections are scattered across the text, arguments are often ambiguous, and conclusions are not always clear. From the perspective of a fantastical materialism, it is through intricate descriptive detail, rather than dense theoretical argumentation, that the phantasmatic and absurd dimensions of capitalist social reality can most effectively be expressed.

This approach has less in common with conventional academic writing than with the literary tradition of fantastic realism, which is defined by the conviction that "real life is more singular and more fantastic than anything else, and all a writer can do is present it as 'in a glass, darkly.'"[54] Fantastic realism is exemplified by Joseph Conrad's account of colonial brutality and illusion in *Heart of Darkness*, in which "the insistence on the details" serves not to faithfully reproduce a familiar reality but, rather, to disrupt the self-evidence of reality itself.[55] Werner Herzog's *Fitzcarraldo* tells a comparable tale of colonial fantasy and farce, which was filmed on the principle of "trusting your eyes, trusting what you see there. I knew that by doing this, things would emerge, and reality would set in the strangest way."[56] J. G. Ballard composed fine-grained descriptions of abstract urban landscapes as a means of drawing out their surreal dimensions, on the basis of the premise that "Freud's classic distinction between the manifest and latent content [of the dream] now has to be applied to the outer world of reality."[57] And Joshua Oppenheimer's *The Act of Killing* deploys intense documentary detail to bring a hidden entanglement of fantasy and violence to the surface of everyday reality, in the creation of "a kind of nonfiction fever dream. It's nonfiction in the sense that everything in it is real. But much of what is real are the fantasies through which the characters, and the whole political regime understands itself. . . . And these real fantasies have terribly real consequences."[58]

This book is a dream of this kind.

1

Enchanted Forest

The whole landscape was compounded of illusion, the
hulks of fabulous dreams drifting across it like derelict galleons.

J. G. Ballard, Vermilion Sands

The Amazon has long been a land of fever dreams and a place
where utopias come to die. The river itself was first "discovered" by
Spanish conquistadors in search of the fictitious realm of El Dorado,
and since then the region has inspired countless quixotic escapades by
knights and scientists, priests and criminals, states and corporations.
The jungle is littered with the ruins of hubristic modern follies, such
as the Madeira-Mamoré railway, constructed with Brazilian capital to
access Bolivian rubber reserves, and finally abandoned in 1912 after
ruining great fortunes and costing thousands of lives.[1] Werner Herzog's film *Fitzcarraldo* depicts a nineteenth-century Peruvian rubber
baron who drags a steamship over an Amazonian mountain in a futile
attempt to exploit an inaccessible rubber reserve, and Herzog himself
was driven to attempt this feat in his own elaborate and destructive
"conquest of the useless."[2] Even Henry Ford, the very personification
of rational industrial capitalism, was inspired to build the utopian city
of Fordlandia, a doomed re-creation of small-town USA, which was
constructed in the 1920s to house the workers on his rubber plantations in the Brazilian Amazon. In his study of Fordlandia, Greg Gran-

din has noted: "The Amazon is a temptress . . . a metaphysical testing ground, a place that seduces man to impose his will only to expose that will as impotent."[3]

What explains the persistent framing of the Amazon as a fantasy space in the modern colonial imaginary? The sheer physical extent and biological exuberance of the region are enough to establish it as a place apart. It is, after all, "the largest river in the world, running through the largest forest," covering over three million square miles and containing a quarter of all the freshwater on the planet.[4] It is a place of unparalleled biodiversity and extraordinary vitality, which Herzog experienced as "the harmony of overwhelming collective murder, . . . overwhelming fornication, overwhelming growth, and overwhelming lack of order."[5] The landscape is constantly remade by the shifting courses of its immense rivers, forming huge islands, washing entire communities away, and flooding vast extensions of forest in a ceaseless process of creative destruction. Writing in the early twentieth century, the Brazilian explorer Euclides da Cunha described the Amazon as "ever disorganized, turbulent, vacillating, tearing down, building up, rebuilding and levelling, devastating in an hour what it spent decades building."[6] In the words of another adventurer, the Amazon is "an orgy of forms, an unimaginable surfeit of climbing plants, a tragic disorder of trunks, of branches, of carpets of greenery and parasites, of mortal combat among trees and species. In the South American forests, one sees man imprisoned in a labyrinth of demented vegetation."[7]

The original colonial name of the Amazon was *Marañon*, which means "entanglement or plot."[8] The name referred to the dense network of rivers and forests of the region. But it is also reflected in the overgrowth of dreams that the Amazon has provoked. These dreams have been inspired less by the poetry of the landscape than by the infinite profits that it seems to promise to those who might seize control of its resources. A nineteenth-century promotional campaign for the region depicted vast reserves of "silver, iron, coal, copper, quicksilver, zinc, tin, gold, diamonds and precious stones, . . . drugs of virtues most rare, spices of aroma most exquisite, gums and resins of the most useful properties, dyes of hues the most brilliant, with cabinet and building woods of finest polish and most enduring texture."[9] Such visions have always fired the utopian imagination. Gold inspired the conquistadors in their search for El Dorado, while Fordlandia, the Madeira-Mamoré railway, and the story that inspired *Fitzcarraldo* were all driven by the "hypnotic effect" of the rubber boom.[10]

The endless accumulation of capital depends on the constant opening of new frontiers,[11] and the utopian fantasies that frame the Amazon as a space of impossible wish fulfillment are profoundly entangled with this material dynamic, which repeatedly reinvents the region as a primary commodity frontier, and thus as a potential source of incredible instant wealth. This chapter explores this entanglement in the case of the Ecuadorian Amazon. Focusing on three subaltern utopias that flourished in the context of the discovery of oil, it traces the ways in which these fantasies unconsciously produced a space of unbridled capital accumulation that shattered the dreams themselves, sowing the seeds of an insurgent utopia that would contribute to the emergence of the Citizens' Revolution.

Land of Beasts and Savages

The role of utopian fantasies in the production of the Ecuadorian Amazon began with the myth of El Dorado. The conquest of the Incan Empire in 1533 had provided the Spanish Crown with immense quantities of gold. By the end of that decade, however, the riches of the Incas had been plundered, and further discoveries were demanded from the pioneers of the New World. Tantalizing rumors began to circulate of an indigenous king who dwelt in the unexplored continental interior that lay to the east of the Andes. This king's name was *El Dorado*—The Gilded One—and his wealth of gold was said to be so great that he dressed in nothing but a coating of gold dust, which was applied anew each day.[12] In February 1541 the conquistadors Gonzalo Pizarro and Francisco de Orellana embarked on an expedition in search of the kingdom of El Dorado. The expedition included two hundred Spaniards accompanied by four thousand *indígenas* and departed from the Andean city of Quito, which would later become the capital of Ecuador. It took them ten months to reach the foot of the densely forested mountains, by which time their supplies had been exhausted, death and disease were rife, and El Dorado was still nowhere to be found. In desperation, Pizarro sent Orellana down the Coca River with a small party in search of supplies. Soon their raft reached the mighty Napo, the main Ecuadorian tributary of the Amazon. After traveling for several days downriver Orellana resolved not to return. Instead, he forged on for over 2,000 miles, reaching the Atlantic coast in August 1542.

Following the discovery of the Amazon, the exploration of the region focused on the Spanish territories of what is now Peru and the Portuguese territories of what is now Brazil, while the Spanish Crown's pursuit of precious metals shifted to the silver mines of Potosí in the Bolivian highlands. Meanwhile, the Ecuadorian Amazon returned to its earlier condition of colonial abandonment. Following its establishment as an independent republic in 1830, Ecuador was too weak to contemplate the integration of its Amazonian territories, and apart from its territorial designation on maps of the continent, the region was excluded from the new Ecuadorian nation. In the cities of the sierra and the coast, the "*Oriente*" was known only as a perilous and inaccessible realm of "*fieras y aucas*"—beasts and savages.[13]

This began to change with the rubber boom that got under way in the late 1870s. Rubber had been discovered during a scientific expedition to the Amazon in the eighteenth century. It was now a crucial component of the rapidly expanding automobile industry, and the Amazon was its main source. The rubber boom led to the amassing of vast fortunes by international rubber barons, who developed extensive networks of wild latex extraction along the Amazon and its tributaries, radiating from the jungle cities of Manaus in Brazil and Iquitos in Peru. Rubber was collected by *indígenas*, who were hunted in jungle raids and held in appalling conditions under a system of debt slavery, in which they were forced to work indefinitely to pay off false debts that were never cleared.[14]

At the time of the rubber boom, the Ecuadorian Amazon remained entirely isolated from the rest of the nation. The region was therefore incorporated into the rubber trade not via the Ecuadorian coast, but as the outer periphery of a vast fluvial system stretching westward from Iquitos in Peru. This peripheral location, and the relatively small quantities of wild latex in the region, led it to be ignored by the larger rubber barons. Instead, its riverbanks were settled by smaller traders originating from Peru, Colombia, and Brazil, as well as European countries, including Spain, Italy, and Portugal. These rubber traders were heavily indebted to the trading houses in Iquitos, and many sold slaves as well as rubber to cover their debts. The search for both these commodities was undertaken on excursions into the jungle interior, in which *indígenas* were either seized or murdered, which resulted in the decimation and fragmentation of the indigenous peoples of the region.[15]

Reports of the foreign rubber trade being freely conducted in the Ecuadorian Amazon eventually reached the major highland and coastal cities of Quito and Guayaquil. "The rubber fever reactivated the imaginary of the great riches of the *Oriente*" among national elites, leading to the incipient colonization of the southern Amazon.[16] The more extensive and inaccessible northern Amazon, however, remained entirely isolated, despite numerous governmental plans for its colonization.[17] These included a utopian proposal made in 1876, in which the fantasy of El Dorado was rekindled, and the Amazon was framed once again as a promised land of infinite wealth:

> The doors of this Eden have remained closed, and its treasures hidden. Our adventurous future lies in the opening of a road to the *Oriente*. In these rich and vast expanses, we will improvise towns that will soon become capitals of the first order that will catch the attention of the world. . . . There can be no doubt that these regions abound with gold mines as rich as the renowned mines of California. . . . In this enchanting paradise we will establish numerous towns . . . and along the riverbanks we will construct great factories that will be visited by ships from around the world.[18]

Like the other state proposals for the region inspired by the rubber boom, this vision was eventually revealed as nothing more than "a bubble of vibrant discourses, a castle of dreams that collapsed."[19] An assessment of the progress of various schemes for the development of the northern Ecuadorian Amazon, issued in 1928 by the Ministry of Public Works, concluded, "In this immense region, there are no roads or communications, and the only official reports deform reality with their deficiency, inaccuracies, and fantasies."[20] By this time, the rubber boom was over, and the region had been abandoned once again. The few remaining rubber traders retained the system of debt slavery developed during the boom, but they shifted from rubber extraction to the production of sugar, rice, and cattle on remote riverside haciendas, from which these commodities were floated downstream on rafts and sold at the Peruvian border to steamships coming upriver from Iquitos. The most lasting effect of the rubber trade on the region was inflicted on its indigenous peoples. Some had been sold as slaves in

Iquitos to pay off the debts of the ruined rubber traders, and the rest either worked as peons on the haciendas or survived in small, dispersed groups hidden in the depths of the jungle.

Meanwhile, however, a new dream was emerging of another El Dorado. Oil had been discovered in small quantities on the Ecuadorian coast in the 1920s, and in 1937 a 25-million-acre concession was issued to the Anglo-Dutch multinational Royal Dutch Shell for the exploration of the northern Ecuadorian Amazon. The American corporation Standard Oil had been granted a similar concession in Peru. In 1941 Peru took advantage of the effective absence of the Ecuadorian state from its Amazonian region to launch an invasion of this contested territory, advancing up the Napo virtually unchallenged and seizing large stretches of the Ecuadorian Amazon. A peace agreement was signed in 1942, which ceded almost half of Ecuador's entire territory to Peru. Peru then granted a large concession to Standard Oil in the land that it had gained from Ecuador, fueling suspicions that the conflict had been a proxy war between Standard Oil and Royal Dutch Shell over control of prospective Amazonian oil reserves.[21]

Following the war with Peru, an incipient colonization program was developed for the northern Ecuadorian Amazon to create "living frontiers" that could repulse any future invasion. But this was a very limited exercise, and the region continued to be physically isolated from the rest of the country. The decline of the region that had followed the end of the rubber boom was deepened by a further loss of trade downriver with Peru, and in 1949 Royal Dutch Shell abandoned what remained of its concession, claiming that its explorations had revealed that there was no oil in the region. The Ecuadorian president, Galo Plaza Lasso, reported this apparently conclusive discovery in a somber address to the nation, announcing, "It has been definitively established that there is no oil in the *Oriente*." He concluded his address with a weary rejection of the utopian fantasies that had haunted the region for over four centuries and that had never amounted to anything: *"El Oriente es un mito"*—"The Amazon is a myth."[22]

The Discovery of El Dorado

In 1963 the dream of El Dorado was ignited once again when the American oil consortium Texaco-Gulf was granted a forty-year concession for the exploration and potential exploitation of 7.5 million acres of the northern Ecuadorian Amazon. Two years later, Jorge Viteri Toro, an unemployed man from the impoverished lowland province of Los Rios, arrived in the capital city of Quito in search of work. Perusing the classified section of the local newspaper, Viteri saw an advertisement for the post of administrative assistant for Geophysical Service Incorporated (GSI), the exploration company contracted by Texaco-Gulf to hunt for oil in the Amazon. He had always been captivated by "the marvelous bewitchment and enchantment" of this unknown region, and he was convinced that the job was his destiny, deciding at that moment: "I had to enter the *Oriente*! It became such a great obsession that it was like a magnet for me."[23] Viteri got the job and was put on a military flight to Santa Cecilia, the site of the first exploration camp, in the depths of the Texaco concession. It was a beautiful day, and he recalls: "I could admire, entranced and absorbed, all the majesty and beauty of the jungle that never ended, and the rivers that I spied like fine white threads, one after the other."[24] Then, at last, "for the first time in the long path of my life, my feet touched the blessed and ancient land of God they call the *Oriente*, filled with fantasies and mysteries."[25]

The exploration led by GSI was far more extensive than the operation previously conducted by Royal Dutch Shell. There was still no road access to the Ecuadorian highlands; construction materials and heavy machinery had to be brought by river from Colombia, and groups of workers were dropped by helicopter into isolated reaches of the jungle. They would set up camp before cutting geometrical grids

through the dense foliage, along which explosive charges were detonated; teams of engineers analyzed seismographs for signs of oil buried as much as two miles underground. Exploratory wells would then
be drilled at promising sites. This was dangerous and exhausting
work, undertaken in extremely inhospitable terrain and involving frequent accidents and illnesses. But the workers were motivated not
only by their individual need for wages, but also by a collective vision
of national salvation, according to which the discovery of oil would
end the poverty and suffering of the Ecuadorian people. In Viteri's
words, "We were fighting for a single cause and dreaming of a shared
ideal . . . a more dignified and sovereign nation, in which one day the
sun of justice would shine on everyone."[26]

The initial results were promising, and the first exploratory wells
were soon being drilled. On March 29, 1967, a siren wailed at Santa
Cecilia, confirming that oil had been struck. Over the two-way radio,
Viteri was told that the workers were bathing in the oil, embracing
each other, and singing the national anthem. He rushed to join them,
and he later recalled the ecstasy of the moment: "The miracle had
been granted. The blessed Lord had heeded the supplications of the
entire *pueblo*. 'Oil! Oil!' we shouted, and lost ourselves in a single embrace. . . . Those hours that I lived and that I felt so deeply in my soul,
together with a handful of Ecuadorians, were something indescrib-
able, one of the most beautiful things that could happen to anyone."[27]

The Amazon was a myth no longer. As Michael Watts observes,
"El Dorado had been located, and it was in an oil well."[28] According
to Viteri, "Now everyone had only one thought, and everyone's gaze
was fixed in a single direction: toward the *Oriente*, where the oil
flowed that would provide work, money, well-being . . . the solution
to their problems."[29]

Oil was struck again and again. All but one of the thirty-seven
wells drilled in 1967 proved positive, and similar results were achieved

in the following years.[30] A region that had been abandoned for centuries was suddenly transformed into a vast construction site. The rivers were filled with barges carrying vehicles, building materials, and drilling equipment; the sky teemed with helicopters flying to oil wells and exploration sites; the ground was shaken by dynamite; the forest was torn down for oil platforms, stations, pipelines, and camps; the air reverberated with the constant snarl of chainsaws and the steady beat of rotor blades; and a road was rapidly constructed through the mountains from Quito, along which a 300-mile pipeline was assembled, which would transport 250,000 barrels of oil per day over the Andes and down to the Pacific coast at the port of Esmeraldas.

The Trans-Ecuadorian Pipeline (SOTE) was completed on June 26, 1972, and the beginning of its operation was marked by an official state ceremony. A newsreel reporting on the festivities, shown in cinemas around the country, conveys the phantasmagorical power of oil in the national imaginary of the time. Footage of the SOTE and the oil installations on the coast is accompanied by a voiceover describing the pipeline as a "titanic work," rising from "the guts of the *Oriente*," crossing "the imposing Andes, . . . overcoming rivers and abysses," deploying "the most modern engineering techniques and vast financial resources" and "representing a significant and decisive contribution to the accelerated economic and social development of Ecuador. All thanks to the oil that arrives today." The Ecuadorian president then turns a spigot, from which thick black crude flows luxuriantly into "the first barrel of oil"—a ceremonial wooden barrel bound with iron straps, which is surrounded by excited local people who plunge their hands into the oil and wave them at the camera, while the narrator announces that "the people cannot contain their emotion. Their hands hardened by labor are stained with the black gold of their dreams." The scene then shifts to Quito, where the little wooden barrel arrives in a grand procession, mounted on the back of a tank surrounded by a motorcycle escort, which drives sedately through thronging crowds, followed by military top brass in full regalia. Behind them comes a parade of "beautiful ladies" dressed in white and waving Ecuadorian flags to the rhythm of a marching band. They are followed by groups of workers, students, and highland *indígenas* in traditional clothing. People are covering their hands and clothes in the "black gold" dispensed from a military vehicle and waving joyfully at the camera. The little wooden barrel, sitting on a sumptuously cushioned chair, is carried by four guardsmen to the middle of a red carpet, where it is saluted by a line of army generals. It remains seated there alone, presiding over the parade that marches in its honor.[31]

At the end of this collective veneration of the commodity fetish, the minister of defense solemnly places the first barrel of oil "in the custody of the military," and the barrel is escorted into the army headquarters, to mark "the beginning of a new era of prosperity in our country." In February 1972, just four months before the oil began to flow, a coup had deposed President José María Velasco Ibarra and installed a "revolutionary" military junta led by Guillermo Rodríguez Lara, which pledged to manage the oil for the benefit of all Ecuadorians. Claiming to represent popular aspirations for national development, such as those that had inspired Viteri and his fellow oil workers, the military regime renegotiated oil contracts, joined the Organization of the Petroleum Exporting Countries (OPEC), and expanded the operations of the state oil company. These actions coincided with the "oil shock" of the early 1970s, when OPEC engineered an unprecedented spike in international oil prices. Ecuador suddenly became an "oil nation," in which oil rents consistently constituted at least 50 percent of state revenues.[32] These rents were channeled into the construction of roads, dams, schools, and hospitals and the promotion of national industrial development. Annual GDP growth averaged over 6 percent from 1972 to 1980, compared to an average of 2 percent over the previous two decades. Economic output more than doubled during this period, and government expenditure increased at an average of 12 percent per year.[33] The Amazon may no longer have been the myth dismissed by Galo Plaza Lasso. But amid this booming industrial economy, fueled by a bonanza of magical petrodollars, "a new myth emerged, that of the virtually never-ending oil fields of the *Oriente*."[34] Ecuador was now fatefully immersed in the fantastical materiality of oil wealth described by Ryszard Kapuściński: "Oil kindles extraordinary emotions and hopes. . . . It is a filthy, foul-smelling liquid that squirts obligingly up into the air and falls back to earth as a rustling shower of money. . . . Oil creates the illusion of a completely changed life, life without work, life for free. . . . The concept of oil expresses perfectly the eternal human dream of wealth achieved through lucky accident, through a kiss of fortune. . . . In this sense oil is a fairy tale and, like every fairy tale, a bit of a lie."[35]

The Conquest of the Promised Land

Jorge Añazco Castillo was listening to the news on the radio when he heard the first reports of the discovery of oil. He was running a small business in Quito at the time, producing brooms in a family workshop and selling them in the coastal lowlands. But the news rekindled old ambitions. As a young man, Añazco had served in the Ecuadorian military and had been dispatched to the Amazon to build "living frontiers" after the war with Peru. Ever since that time, he had been obsessed with the notion of creating a city in the depths of the jungle. As his son recalls: "He had the idea of founding a *pueblo* in his head for his entire life. . . . He was one of those men who dream."[36] This dream had been reawakened by the reports on the radio. Añazco foresaw that, with the discovery of oil in the Amazon, a system of roads would be opened through the jungle, connecting Quito, the new oil fields, and the nearest riverports and border crossings. He believed he could predict the point at which these roads would intersect. This point, he reasoned, would inevitably become a new population center. There, before the roads arrived, he resolved to found his city.

Añazco was born in Loja, an agricultural region in the highlands of southern Ecuador. In the late 1960s, the region was afflicted with a severe drought that forced many of its peasant farmers to migrate to the coastal lowlands in search of work. The drought, however, coincided with the collapse of the banana boom that had sustained the coastal economy throughout the 1950s. Work was scarce, and conditions on the lowland haciendas were highly exploitative. During his frequent journeys to the lowlands to sell his brooms, Añazco got to know many of his fellow *Lojanos*, and he saw that "the destiny or future of every family appeared opaque and hopeless."[37] One evening he called a group of them together. By candlelight, and over many cups of *aguardiente*, he told them of his utopian vision of forging a new life together in the Amazon: "I told them about the Ecuadorian *Oriente*, which for them was an unknown and distant world. And so it was that, one drink after another, a project emerged for the colonization of the northeast, where oil had been found, and where there were millions of acres of unclaimed lands, with room for thousands of landless peasants."[38] Drawing on his old military connections, Añazco arranged a meeting with a high-ranking officer of the armed forces, whom he convinced to support his project as part of the ongoing campaign to reinforce the national presence in the region. The officer agreed to provide the impoverished *colonos* (colonizers) with free military flights to the Santa Cecilia oil camp, from which they would have to make their own way to the site that Añazco had identified, several miles deeper into the jungle.

The first group of twenty-five men, women, and children flew to Santa Cecilia on December 3, 1969. Most of them had no idea what to expect from the *Oriente*, which they knew only as a mythical land of "beasts and savages." In his memoir, Añazco recalls the moment: "I could see the excitement of my friends, who from this point were entering the unknown. As the airplane devoured the horizon, they could contemplate for the first time the breadth of the jungle and the quantity of virgin lands where they would have their own plot, to secure the survival of their family. They knew, as well, that they were the first group of organized *colonos* prepared to found a *pueblo* in the oil sector of the northeast. . . . So far everything was rosy [*Hasta aquí todo color de rosa*]."[39]

On their arrival in Santa Cecilia, the group rented a canoe and headed down the wild Aguarico. They pitched camp on the riverbank, before cutting their way through the jungle to the place designated by Añazco. Over the following months they cleared the land and planted their first crops, setting aside five hundred acres for the construction of their city and plotting the location of the "avenues, streets, church, plaza, schools, etc. Dreaming costs nothing . . . and so we kept our fantasy alive, pestered by our empty guts."[40]

The group called their city Nueva Loja, in memory of the region from which they all originated. In February 1970 a second group of thirty *colonos* arrived, and further groups followed over the course of that year. Small shops began opening to cater to the oil workers, and the construction of the town accelerated, as weekend *mingas* (days of collective labor) soon attracted over a hundred people at a time. In 1971 the road from Quito reached Nueva Loja. Añazco's prediction had proven correct—the town was located at the center of the new road network, and now it began to boom.

Meanwhile, the Ecuadorian government began to promote the *Oriente* as "a land without people for a people without land." In 1964, faced with agrarian tensions and threatened by the Cuban Revolution and the growing power of the communist movement throughout Latin America, the government had created the Ecuadorian Institute of Colonization and Agrarian Reform (IERAC) to implement a process of land reform. A new law designated the majority of the Ecuadorian Amazon as *tierras baldías*—state lands that were regarded as uninhabited and that could be claimed by landless peasants from the highlands and the coast. The opening of the region by the oil roads was now seen as a convenient means of avoiding social conflict without engaging in the redistribution of land and power in other parts of the country.[41] This strategy proved successful, and the new Amazonian roadsides were quickly settled by thousands of *colonos* from the sierra and the coast—"landless peasants and itinerant laborers . . . who had accepted the challenge of life and were waging their battles in the northeast."[42]

Despite being encouraged by the government, the colonization of the region took the form of a chaotic land grab. The *colonos*, however, ensured that they were operating within the legislative framework of the state, forming cooperatives of between fifty and one hundred members in advance, and constructing their *fincas* (farms) to conform with IERAC regulations: each family would claim a 124-acre (50-hectare) parcel measuring 800 by 6,600 feet (250 by 2,000 meters), with the narrow side facing the road. Provided these conditions were met, and 80 percent of the land on the *finca* was cleared, their titles would be granted retroactively by IERAC. Subsequent "lines" of *fincas* were often built behind the initial parcels, sometimes reaching as many as ten lines—over twelve miles—from the roadside into the jungle, and each cooperative would designate a space for a primary school and a community meetinghouse. Through this process, the wild reaches of the northern Ecuadorian Amazon were rapidly transformed into a patchwork of thriving settlements, driven by a collective vision of the future described by Añazco as "the conquest of the vital space needed for human survival . . . the promised land of the *Oriente*, equipped only with machete, axe, and hope."[43]

The utopian dimension of this process is evident in the names that the *colonos* gave to their new towns, through which they inscribed their hopes, dreams, and struggles into the daunting landscape of the *Oriente*: *Nuevo Paraíso* (New Paradise); *Nuevo Mundo* (New World); *Luz y Vida* (Light and Life); *El Porvenir* (The Future); *Bella Esperanza* (Beautiful Hope); *Pioneros del Oriente* (Pioneers of the East); *Luz de América* (Light of America); *Nuevos Horizontes* (New Horizons); *Tierra y Libertad* (Land and Freedom); *Trabajadores Libres* (Free Workers); *El Triunfo* (Triumph); *Nueva Libertad* (New Freedom); *Nueva Delicia* (New Delight); *El Esfuerzo* (The Endeavor); *El Sudor* (Sweat); *El Progreso* (Progress); *Nueva Esperanza* (New Hope); *Selva Alegre* (Joyful Jungle); *Nueva Vida* (New Life); *Unidos Venceremos* (United We Shall Overcome); *Sol Naciente* (Rising Sun); and, of course, *El Dorado*.

In the early years of colonization, the dreams captured by these names must have seemed to have been realized for many of the *colonos* who had followed the new roads into the *Oriente*. They had escaped drought, hunger, and relations of domination on the haciendas; their lands were abundant and filled with precious timber; the jungle soils were initially highly productive; market prices for export crops such as coffee were rising; and trade and employment opportunities were plentiful in the booming oil industry. As one *colono* recalls of his arrival in the region as a landless peasant in 1978: "At first it was a beautiful abundance. There was a lot of forest, an incredible biodiversity of every kind. . . . It was a marvel."[44] In the words of a Carmelite missionary: "To arrive here from Loja, after a drought that had lasted so many years, and to see so much green, so much rain, so much water— it was a paradise. They had fish, they had wild game, everything that they planted grew. So it was marvelous for them. Everything was new. Everything was virgin."[45]

In 1979 a new canton called Lago Agrio was created in the region, named after the first oil field, and Nueva Loja was designated its municipal capital. For Jorge Añazco, "the fiction had been converted into a reality."[46] In the space of ten years he had gone from making brooms in Quito to completing the city he had always dreamed of building in the depths of the jungle. Not only that, but the entire northern Amazon was now being rapidly colonized. Surveying this radically altered reality, Añazco paid tribute to "the struggle of the *colonos* who . . . are overcoming all barriers to create a new society, more just and humane, produced by a combination of the popular cultures of every province of Ecuador."[47] At the inauguration of the new municipal capital, he delivered a triumphant speech in which he declared the historical fulfillment of the colonizing mission that had been launched by the conquistadors with the discovery of the Amazon: "The establishment of the canton of Lago Agrio as the governing center of the new *pueblos* consolidates the task of Orellana and constitutes the civilized vanguard of the occupation of our frontiers. . . . Nature and geography favor us. We are at the geographical center of a vast field of minerals, forests, and agriculture, served by a network of roads that converge on Nueva Loja. . . . Thousands of years of continental solitude have finally come to an end."[48]

The Creation of Edén

In 1971 a young Catholic priest called José Miguel Goldáraz arrived at the confluence of the Coca and the Napo—the fateful point that Orellana had passed before deciding to forge on to the Atlantic. He had come to work at a Capuchin mission in the town of Francisco de Orellana, which had been named in honor of the conquistador, although everyone called it Coca. From this point, the Napo ran east for 140 miles to the border with Peru, through a region still controlled by the handful of *hacendados* who had survived the demise of the rubber trade and the Peruvian invasion, and who continued to dominate the local *Kichwa* population through the system of debt slavery developed during the rubber boom. On the far side of the Napo, the jungle was inhabited by the *Huaorani*, who had escaped enslavement by the rubber traders and had since survived in "voluntary isolation." In Coca, the *Huaorani* were known and feared by the *colono* population as *aucas*—savages—and were notorious for living naked and for murdering those who threatened their territory.[49]

Like so many others before him, Goldáraz had come to the Amazon driven by a dream. He came from the Basque Country in northern Spain, where he had been inspired by the region's long struggle for autonomy. Goldáraz's dream was to liberate the *Kichwa* people of the Napo from slavery on the haciendas and to create an autonomous indigenous nation in the *Oriente*. In his words, "The dream of constructing a nation of free, independent *indígenas*—that was the utopia."[50]

Coca had been founded by the mission in 1958 as a handful of thatched huts built around a school, a clinic, and a general store. But by the time that Goldáraz arrived, this remote settlement had exploded into an oil city. Oil had recently been struck on the far side of the Napo, and Coca was now the new boom town, located at the cutting edge of the petroleum frontier. A trader who had left the town in 1969 and returned in 1974 recalls the seemingly miraculous nature of this transformation: "They had built a road from Quito. They had built a bridge [across the Napo] where beforehand there was nothing. And now there were buses transporting people from here to Quito. It was an incredible thing. I couldn't believe it. Lots of *colonos* were grabbing land, creating *fincas*, lots of people were coming and going, doing business. It seemed incredible to me, impossible that it could have happened. But that's the power of oil. Everything was completely different. Unrecognizable."[51]

These radical transformations posed an imminent threat to Goldáraz's dream of an autonomous indigenous nation. The utopias of the oil workers and the *colonos* were both expressive of the desires of some of the poorest members of Ecuadorian society. But these utopias were also profoundly racist, in the sense that their visions of this society excluded the indigenous population of the *Oriente*. From their perspective, the Amazon was just the "jungle guts" from which the wealth of the nation would be removed, and a "land without people" to be claimed by a people without land. In fact, the region was inhabited by no fewer than eight indigenous peoples: the *Achuar, Cofán, Huaorani, Kichwa, Secoya, Shuar, Siona,* and *Zápara*. To the extent that their existence was acknowledged at all, these peoples were crudely divided into *aucas*—the "savages" who had escaped enslavement during the rubber boom by fleeing deeper into the jungle and who were seen as little more than wild beasts—and *indios*—the supposedly "domesticated" peons of the haciendas. None of them were national citizens, and none possessed any legal rights over the land they occupied or the resources beneath the soil.[52]

The dreams of the oil workers and the *colonos* were therefore being materialized through the dispossession and displacement of the indigenous population.[53] Rather than attempting to oppose this process directly, however, Goldáraz decided that its internal contradictions could be harnessed in the realization of his own utopia of indigenous liberation and territorial autonomy. He had heard that an oil exploration company was looking for a site on the Napo to station a new base camp. Instead of resisting this incursion, Goldáraz invited the company to make use of the mission's facilities seventy miles east of Coca, in the tiny settlement of Pañacocha. He did so, however, on condition that the company employ *Kichwa* men from the nearby *haciendas* for the cutting of the seismic grids. The loss of their workforce quickly pushed the last surviving *hacendados* into ruin, and by the end of the 1970s, debt slavery on the Napo had finally been abolished. As Goldáraz himself wryly observes, "The economic liberation of the *indígenas* was achieved by the oil companies."[54]

Goldáraz combined this strategic alliance with the oil industry with a campaign to incorporate the indigenous population into the process of land reform under way in the region. In 1937 the Ecuadorian government had passed a law that sought to regulate indigenous land claims in the highlands through the establishment of *comunas* (communes)—territories held in common by a given indigenous community, in which land could not be divided, bought, or sold.[55] Goldáraz saw that the colonization of the Amazon under the auspices of IERAC had opened the possibility for the indigenous communities of the region to legally constitute themselves as *comunas*. Throughout the 1970s and early 1980s, he traveled the rivers and oil roads, encouraging these communities to organize *comunas* on the abandoned haciendas and on the lands designated by the state as *tierras baldias*. One of his *Kichwa* allies of the time recalls their struggle: "Together we began to organize my brothers to defend the land. . . . We had to defend ourselves from the *colonos*, the companies, the roads. . . . Father José Miguel and I went from house to house, talking to our companions, convincing them. . . . That's how we began, on foot, sleeping wherever night fell . . . exhausted and hungry. . . . Putting heart and soul into the struggle. Those were difficult times. But I was convinced that we had to organize ourselves or we would lose everything."[56]

The most utopian of these *comunas* was called Edén. Goldáraz remembers visiting Pañacocha in the early 1970s with some of his *Kichwa* companions and discussing the jungle that stood on the far side of the Napo: "I told them that those were great lands, that it was like an Eden, because it was a beautiful region over there."[57] The decision was made to create a *comuna* in those lands, and to call it Edén. Other *comunas* along the Napo had been formed by small groups of liberated slaves on the grounds of the ruined haciendas in which they had been exploited. But the jungle opposite Pañacocha would form the basis for a more universal community of the dispossessed, composed of all the ex-slaves of the region who still remained landless, and conceived as a society of "self-management . . . based on their own aspirations."[58] The *comuna* was established in 1975 and was granted 57,000 acres of land by IERAC in 1982.[59] As one of the founders of Edén later recalled, "At that moment we were no longer tied to the landowners, and it was we ourselves who now determined how each of us would control his destiny."[60]

By the time that Edén was granted its land, Goldáraz had organized the legalization of over twenty *comunas* in the Napo region, and he was now focused on the construction of a broader movement for indigenous autonomy.[61] In 1978 the Native Union of the Ecuadorian Amazon (UNAE) was formed to advance the territorial claims of the indigenous communities of the northern *Oriente*. In 1979 the election of Jaime Roldós as president of Ecuador signaled the end of the military dictatorship and the return of representative democracy, which led to a flourishing of social movements and political organizations. In 1980 the Confederation of Indigenous Nationalities of the Ecuadorian Amazon (CONFENIAE) was formed, incorporating all the indigenous peoples of the region, who now defined themselves as "nations," reflecting an increased emphasis on political rights and territorial autonomy.[62] And in 1984 the UNAE was transformed into a larger and more formal organization, the Federation of United Native Communes of the Ecuadorian Amazon (FCUNAE), which was created to "defend indigenous territories and promote the autonomous economic development of its *comunas*."[63]

Goldáraz could now claim that his project was complete. Since his arrival in the Amazon thirteen years previously, he had led the defeat of a system of debt slavery that had lasted for almost a century and had helped the liberated indigenous population create a network of *comunas* with political and territorial rights, organized in a confederation of autonomous "nations." He recalls the establishment of the FCUNAE as the conclusion of a struggle in which he had "borne witness to a vertiginous transition from a state of servitude and slavery to . . . the organization and constitution of *comunas* and cooperatives under a regime of territorial self-management [*autogestión*]."[64] Like Viteri's vision of a black gold El Dorado, and Añazco's dream of a city in the jungle, Goldáraz's seemingly impossible utopia had apparently been realized.

Bonfire of the Fantasies

This chapter has narrated the colonization of the northern Ecuadorian Amazon as a process infused with powerful utopian visions, each of which was committed to the liberation or deliverance of a sector of the poor and dispossessed: the utopia of the oil workers was devoted to discovering the oil that would end the poverty of the Ecuadorian majority; the utopia of the *colonos* was based on claiming the land and building the cities that would feed and house the landless workers of the sierra and the coast; and the utopia of the missionaries was founded on the rupture of master-slave relations and the construction of indigenous territorial autonomy. Unlike the broken dreams and wild chimeras for which the Amazon is notorious, these utopias met with remarkable initial success. El Dorado was discovered in an oil well, and the nation was propelled into industrial modernity; great cities were constructed in the jungle, and there was land enough for every landless peasant; and the indigenous population was liberated from slavery and granted territorial autonomy.

None of these utopias was conceived in terms of the establishment of capitalist social relations or the expanded reproduction of capital. Yet all were animated by the dynamics of transnational capital accumulation unleashed by the discovery of oil, and all functioned to deepen these dynamics. The developmentalist utopia of the oil workers was made possible by multinational corporations and opened the Ecuadorian Amazon to foreign exploitation. The frontier utopia of the *colonos* was enabled by the opening of oil roads and served to reinforce the structures of agrarian capitalism by creating a vast new land market and displacing rebellious peasantries from the rest of the country. And the territorial utopia of the missionaries was facilitated by the oil industry's demand for cheap labor and functioned to proletarianize the indigenous population of the region, while incorporating them into the juridical frameworks and territorial delimitations of the capitalist state.

This demonstrates the profoundly dialectical relationship between utopian fantasies and the Real of capital, in which fantasy not only conceals the Real, but is unconsciously animated by it, while simultaneously "creating what it purports to conceal, its own 'repressed' point of reference."[65] The capitalist production of space tends to be conceptualized as a top-down process imposed on subaltern populations, which Lefebvre has described as "a product of administrative and repressive controls, a product of relations of domination and strategies decided at the summit of the state."[66] In the case of the Ecuadorian Amazon, however, this space was largely a product of the utopian fantasies of the subaltern populations themselves, who unconsciously enacted the logic of capital. It is through obscure, unplanned, and unintentional processes such as these, as much as through the meticulous technocratic machinations of state power, that capital "comes to represent itself in the form of a physical landscape created in its own image, created as use values to enhance the progressive accumulation of capital on an expanding scale."[67]

The outcome in this case, however, was not an abstract space of geometrical networks and regulated flows, but what Karl Polanyi would have described as a "stark utopia" of totally unbridled capital accumulation, which "could not exist for any extended period of time without annihilating the human and natural essences of society."[68] By the early 1980s, the northern Ecuadorian Amazon had been transformed into an apocalyptic labyrinth of seismic grids, oil platforms, and rusted pipelines. Oil comes to the surface mixed with water and gas, which are then separated from the crude. In the absence of regulation, millions of gallons of highly toxic "formation waters" were discharged into streams and rivers from hundreds of unlined waste pits, and billions of cubic feet of gas were burned off by grimy gas flares. An estimated 17 million gallons of oil were spilled in the region between 1972 and 1990.[69] The toxic muds that lubricated the drilling rigs were released directly into the environment, and waste pits would sometimes catch fire, raging for days and producing towering clouds of smoke that fell back to earth as "black rain." During the dry season, the oil companies would spread thick waste crude on the dusty gravel roads. Rain turned these roads into treacherous oil slicks, causing horrific accidents and washing the oil into the rivers in which the people bathed and from which they took their water. One *colono* recalls: "People had no idea of the dangers of oil. They didn't know because the oil companies and their functionaries devoted themselves to telling them that oil was good, that oil was fertilizer for plants, that oil was medicine for rheumatism, [that it was good] for your hair. The workers who joined the industry were even [thrown] in a pit of oil. You came out totally covered, and now you had been baptized as a *petrolero*."[70]

The opening of the oil roads soon led to the establishment of a network of illegal logging mafias and the concession of vast palm oil plantations to agroindustrial companies. These factors, combined with the frenzied expansion of the oil industry and the equally rapid colonization of the region, resulted in the highest deforestation rate in Latin America. Contamination of the soil, air, and rivers accelerated the disappearance of wildlife and led to increased rates of miscarriages, skin diseases, respiratory ailments, nerve damage, birth defects and multiple forms of cancer.[71] The social landscape has been described "a distinctly Creole version of the epic conquest of the North American West," in which thousands of itinerant oil workers mixed with peasant adventurers, displaced *indígenas*, opportunistic con men, and fugitive criminals.[72] Violent crime was widespread in the unlit streets of the new frontier cities, and the near-total absence of schools and clinics stood in contrast to the greatest concentration of brothels in the country.[73] At night, thieves would steal redundant oil pipes, cutting them loose under the dark glow of the gas flares. Sometimes they would cut through a live pipe by mistake, and the pipe would whip and flail like a snake, killing anyone in its path.

This catastrophic panorama gradually eroded the utopian fantasies of the oil workers, landless peasants, and radical missionaries. The oil workers had been convinced that they were "forging a bright future for the nation," but they had produced a space dominated by foreign corporations, in which the *gringo* managers and engineers lived in luxury in their oil camps, while the workers lived in miserable conditions and risked their lives in the oil fields.[74] Texaco was deploying obsolete technology with few safety controls, and accidents were frequent and often fatal. The jungle also claimed lives, as workers were sucked into whirlpools and consumed by anacondas. And tensions with the "*aucas*" intensified, as the exploration teams were forced to push ever deeper into *Huaorani* territory in search of new oil fields. Most of the *Huaorani* were gradually assimilated into the "Wild West" society, and the men were soon working for the oil companies, getting drunk, and visiting the local brothels. But two subgroups, the *Tagaeri* and the *Taromenane*, refused all contact and continued to resist. In 1977 an attack was launched by the *Tagaeri*, in which three oil workers were killed. Jorge Viteri organized the mission to retrieve their corpses. In his words, "The oil that they extracted was mixed with the blood of our workers. We always asked God to help us find oil. That was our wish as Ecuadorians. But it was tough. The oil had its cost in blood."[75]

Furthermore, the discovery of oil had not produced the national salvation that Viteri and his fellow workers had anticipated. Inequality increased dramatically during the oil boom, and industrialization ground to a halt when the boom came to an end in the early 1980s.[76] Over the course of the 1970s, oil rents had proven increasingly inadequate to finance the development of the country, and the gap had been covered by foreign debt, which increased from $209 million in 1970 to $4,167 million in 1980.[77] Now, in the absence of these rents, the debt could no longer be sustained. In 1981, following the suspiciously convenient death of the progressive president Jaime Roldós in an airplane accident,[78] his replacement, Osvaldo Hurtado, immediately declared: "We neither can nor should continue to resort to eternal indebtedness. . . . The age of petroleum prosperity has come to an end. It is necessary to begin an age of austerity."[79] He soon announced the first of several structural adjustment programs that Ecuador would be obliged to sign with the International Monetary Fund (IMF) over the following decades, and neoliberal reforms began, including the further privatization of the oil industry.[80]

The oil price continued to fall throughout the 1980s. Growth rates collapsed, poverty increased, and transnational capital strengthened its control over national oil rents through the liberalization of oil contracts and in the form of debt repayments. The developmentalist utopia of Viteri and his fellow oil workers lay in ruins. In his memoir, Viteri reflects on the ecstatic moment when oil had first been struck, and he and his comrades had bathed in black gold and sung the national anthem: "How far I was, at that moment, from imagining that this discovery in our Amazon, which we received as a gift from heaven, would later cost tears, sorrows, and disappointments, mixed with the blood of the workers, pilots, and engineers who left their lives there. I feel a bitter taste in my mouth when I remember [that moment], because it shames me to see how our people, once bewitched by that magic word *oil*, are now trapped in poverty and misery."[81]

The great expectations of the *colonos* had also been dashed by subsequent events. Despite being founded on a collective vision of land

and freedom, their settlements were organized not on the basis of communal landholdings, but in the form of individual parcels. The establishment of private property rights throughout the Amazon unleashed the dynamics of an unregulated land market, including violent dispossessions, the fragmentation and concentration of landholdings, and the extensive "trafficking" of land, in which false titles were sold to landless peasants who would arrive in the Amazon to discover that their dream had been a lie. Those who did find land were confronted with the pollution caused by oil spills and forced to "drink contaminated water and breathe air poisoned by the gases burned in hundreds of oil wells."[82] The coffee market collapsed in the 1980s, and despite their initial fertility, the thin soils of the Amazon were rapidly exhausted, which resulted in high levels of poverty and malnutrition and led many *colonos* to return to their places of origin. Meanwhile, the autonomous urbanization of the region was confronting severe limitations. Electricity was scarce and intermittent, water and sewage systems were nonexistent, and the minimal health and education services of the missions, which had been designed to attend to the sparse indigenous population of the region, had been utterly overwhelmed by the sudden arrival of over 200,000 impoverished peasants. As Jorge Añazco was forced to conclude: "To possess land with abundant water, and to live surrounded by infinite horizons, was not sufficient to weave the web of happiness [*tejer la felicidad*]. Despite everything that had been achieved, we lacked . . . the integral development of society."[83]

In March 1987 an earthquake destroyed the SOTE oil pipeline and the road from Quito, spilling vast quantities of crude into the Amazonian ecosystem and cutting communications between the northern *Oriente* and the rest of the country. The earthquake also blocked the flow of the Coca and Aguarico rivers, and "all that descended was a gelatinous mass of thick mud that . . . slid like an immense, injured boa. Huge fish and cattle came down with it, dead and rolling in the clay."[84] No official records exist, but it is estimated that one thousand *colonos* lost their lives in this disaster, and twenty thousand had their homes destroyed.[85] Rather than attending to the needs of the population, however, the state focused its resources on the oil infrastructure. Oil began to be pumped again in May of the same year, but the road remained unrepaired for months, and the increasingly destitute population continued to be ignored.

The pressure to increase oil output intensified in the aftermath of the earthquake. The killing of the oil workers in 1977 had not halted the advance of the frontier into *auca* territory, and this process now accelerated. Fearing another deadly confrontation with the *Tagaeri*, Jorge Viteri requested the assistance of the bishop of the Capuchin mission, Alejandro Labaka, who had previously mediated between the oil companies and the *Huaorani*. In July 1987 Labaka and the Capuchin nun Inés Arango attempted to establish contact with the *Tagaeri*. It did not go well. They were murdered at the moment of their initial encounter, and José Miguel Goldáraz participated in the recovery of their bodies.[86] The incident further illustrated the ambiguous relationship between the mission and the oil companies. Like Goldáraz, Labaka had been committed to a utopian vision of indigenous autonomy, which he had sought to achieve through constructive engagement with the oil industry. Commenting on the killings, a representative of CONFENIAE now argued that the missionaries had been "criminally used by the oil transnationals . . . that are mining our territory."[87]

Goldáraz had also cooperated with the oil companies in his struggle against the *hacendados*. But now the relationship that he had established between the companies and the *Kichwas* was undermining his own utopia of indigenous autonomy. In the early 1980s, the oil companies responded to increasing levels of indigenous organization by forming teams of "community relations officers," whose objective was to "facilitate the operations of the companies . . . through the anticipation and mitigation of local conflicts."[88] Their strategies included the bribing of community leaders to sign exploration and exploitation agreements; the division of communities through the selective distribution of employment opportunities; and the delivery of symbolic development projects that littered indigenous communities with absurdist pastiches of modernity: classrooms without teachers, toilets without water, refrigerators without electricity.

In many cases, the autonomous and indivisible nature of the *comunas*, which Goldáraz had imagined as the basis of territorial autonomy, functioned to facilitate the operation of the oil companies. In contrast to operating among the fragmented private plots of the *colonos*, which required multiple negotiations, in the *comunas* the companies required only the signing of a single agreement to gain access to thousands of acres of land, which could then be turned into a privatized, securitized enclave. This is precisely what happened in Edén, the most utopian of the *comunas* founded by Goldáraz. In 1995 the American corporation Occidental discovered vast oil deposits in Edén. The majority of the *comuna* initially resisted exploitation, having witnessed the destruction caused by the oil industry elsewhere. The community relations officers of Occidental, however, used all their powers of persuasion to gain the *comuna*'s consent, including offers of employment and community development projects. Realizing that an agreement was inevitable, Goldáraz worked with lawyers and community members to ensure that the deal was negotiated on the best possible terms. The community relations officers, however, invited the leaders of the *comuna* to secret negotiations in the bars and brothels of Quito, where an alternative agreement was signed behind the backs of Goldáraz and the rest of the community. Edén was rapidly transformed into a maze of oil roads, pipelines, and processing plants, closed to public access, filled with surveillance cameras, and patrolled by private security guards. Soon, from a network of over 150 oil wells, 100,000 barrels a day were being extracted, accompanied by frequent oil spills and all the social and ecological consequences of contamination. A huge gas flare was installed in the center of the territory; its fifty-foot flame roared for twenty-four hours a day and caused black rain to fall on the homes and fields of the region. At night a demonic glow could sometimes be seen from far away, thrown against low, dark clouds by the fires of Edén.

By the end of the 1980s, the utopian fantasies of the oil workers, *colonos*, and radical missionaries had been destroyed by the Real of capital that they had both concealed and enhanced. But these fantasies seemed to burn with even greater intensity in the moment of their annihilation. In 1989 a new province called Sucumbíos was created in the northern Amazon, and Nueva Loja was designated as the provincial capital. By this time, the city had come to be known to its inhabitants by the more appropriate name of the local oil field and canton: Lago Agrio—"Bitter Lake." But for Jorge Añazco it would always be Nueva Loja, and this moment marked the final transformation of his dream into "a vibrant reality: the burnished chalice of a new society."[89] A huge parade was organized to mark the occasion, in which "Nueva Loja pulsated [*vibraba*] with joy and emotion."[90] Even the oil companies participated in the festivities by spreading a thick coat of waste crude on the dirt streets to keep down the dust. The sun shone strongly on the day of the parade. The black roads melted, and the delirious city bathed in oil, as one participant recalls: "There was still no consciousness in those days. We didn't have the capacity to assimilate what was happening. . . . We paraded with bands and music, marching through the city and stomping in petroleum. Our trousers were soaked in oil up to our knees. . . . That afternoon there was a rainstorm and by the end of the day our trousers were black, and our shirts were ruined. But that is how the people lived."[91]

2

The Politics of Awakening

Dreams are the guardians of sleep, and not its disturbers.

Sigmund Freud, The Interpretation of Dreams

For Donald Moncayo, it was a day like any other. He was a peasant farmer, eking out a living in the stark surroundings of the Lago
Agrio oil field. He had taken the afternoon off and was cycling to the
local volleyball court, which had been constructed by an oil company
as a token of modernity to gain acceptance from his community for
the extraction of the oil beneath their lands. Moncayo was content
with this arrangement. "I wasn't interested in struggles, in what was
going on," he recalls. "I lived a quiet life, I didn't have any consciousness."[1] Suddenly, he awoke:

It was in 2000 that my way of thinking was shaken. There was
an oil spill. I was on my way to play volleyball. We had arranged to meet at the court at 4 p.m. I set out about 3 p.m. And
the river was black with oil. The ducks and chickens were
catching the fish. Because with the oil, it's like the fish went
crazy. They started jumping, and the ducks became like bears
catching salmon, like you see on TV. And at that moment
someone showed up from [the oil company] to compensate the
family [for livestock lost to the oil spill]. . . . There were loads

of chickens in the yard. Some of them were already dead. Others were still moving, but they were covered in oil. [The man from the company] said, "Hey, this one is alive." Then [the mother of the family] said, "But no, they're all going to die." Then he said, "Of course they're not going to die! Wash them with a bit of soap and they'll be fine." Damn it, and that's when it struck me. Like, "This son of a bitch, what's his problem? They come here and contaminate your rivers, they kill your animals, and then they tell you to go to hell over the ones that haven't died yet." It struck me. And it's like it's still rooted in me now. It's like something that shakes you. And that shook me.

This was not an awakening from sleep into a familiar everyday reality. Instead, it was an awakening from everyday reality into a fantastic world in which things had ceased to make sense, where death could be washed off with soap, and ducks hunted fish like bears in a river running thick and black with oil. The experience changed everything for Moncayo. "I didn't know anything at that time," he recalls, "but afterwards I kept thinking, 'This is bad, this is bad. I have to do something. Because this is bad, this is not okay.' So I started talking with people to see what we could do, because what happened was . . . well, it really hit me, it moved me."[2] Over the following years he would come to play a leading role in a wave of insurrectional struggles spreading like wildfire throughout the northern Ecuadorian Amazon, fueled by many similar moments of awakening, in which the *colono* fantasy of abundant agriculture and petroleum prosperity finally disintegrated into the apocalyptic wastelands of an oil-ravaged Amazon. In the words of three leaders of this emergent movement: "The people were desperate, and they couldn't take it anymore"; "The situation was brought to the point of total rupture"; "There were many, many problems, and we could see no way out."[3]

This collective awakening was soon followed by a different wake-up call. In 2006 Rafael Correa launched his presidential campaign by calling on the Ecuadorian people to awaken from "the long neoliberal night."[4] But his election manifesto promised to build "the nation that we dream of,"[5] and his campaign song was titled "Dreams."[6] This seductive invitation to *awaken into a dream* contrasted with the more radical awakening already under way in the Amazon. The tension between these two forms of awakening is the focus of this chapter, which traces the relationship between utopian fantasies and insurgent utopias in the emergence of post-neoliberalism in the Ecuadorian Amazon and the subsequent rise of the Citizens' Revolution.

An Immense Unease

Donald Moncayo's situation was not unusual. Like countless other *colonos*, his family had come to the Amazon with great hopes, which had been gradually undermined by the socioecological consequences of an unregulated oil industry in the context of a deepening national crisis exacerbated by a seemingly endless barrage of neoliberal reforms. Following the collapse of the oil price in the early 1980s, the IMF had imposed a series of structural adjustment programs involving the withdrawal of subsidies, the reduction of the public sector, and the liberalization of trade and investment, in exchange for balance of payments support in the context of soaring debt obligations. In 1990 the resulting impoverishment and instability led the indigenous social movements of the highlands and the Amazon to form the Confederation of Indigenous Nationalities of Ecuador (CONAIE), which began organizing a national campaign of marches and blockades to demand the abandonment of neoliberalism. Further reforms, however, continued throughout the 1990s. In 1998 President Jamil Mahuad responded to the failure of four private banks by transferring $6 billion to the banking sector—23 percent of the annual

GDP. The bailout was financed by further cuts in social spending, which was reduced by 50 percent in 1999 alone. Mahuad then announced the replacement of the national currency with the U.S. dollar. This symbolic capitulation to imperial power provoked a national uprising led by the CONAIE, which forced Mahuad out of office on January 21, 2000. But Vice President Gustavo Noboa then assumed the presidency and completed the dollarization of the Ecuadorian economy, while maintaining the neoliberal reform program, in exchange for a further loan package from the IMF.[7]

The entire period of economic crisis and neoliberal reform was underpinned by a persistently low oil price. And yet throughout this period, the oil extracted from the northern Amazon continued to contribute between 45 and 50 percent of the national budget, while only 2–3 percent of that budget was reinvested in the region.[8] In 2000 the poverty rate in the province of Sucumbíos stood at 84 percent, compared to 55 percent at the national scale.[9] This inequality was thrown into sharp relief by the proximity of the squalid Amazonian cities to the luxurious oil camps. As one *colono* recalls, the oil camps had "bowling alleys, telephone services, a menu with five options, huge modern installations, daily flights to Quito. The shock of the contrast was constant. As the population [of the cities] grew, people began to ask: 'Why do they have everything, and we have nothing?'"[10]

For the indigenous communities of the region, this question was being posed in equally stark terms. Their dream of territorial autonomy had been destroyed by the depredations of the oil industry, and the CONFENIAE, which had represented the highpoint of indigenous organization in the region in the 1980s, had been weakened by internal divisions and corruption scandals.[11] Lands that had been granted to indigenous nationalities were being included in new oil blocks, and decades of contamination were beginning to result in a proliferation of cancers and other diseases.[12] As Humberto Piaguaje of the *Secoya* recalls:

> We watched, without any information, when down the River Aguarico, down the River Shushufindi, down the River Eno, there came huge quantities of oil. We bathed in those rivers. We took water from them to cook and to drink. And we grabbed the fish that died [in the oil spills] as well, to cook and to serve at the table. But as time passed, after ten, eleven, twelve years, sicknesses like cancer began to appear. First my grandfather died of stomach cancer. I had to take him to [the hospital in] Quito. We came back and a week later he died. Then my thirty-nine-year-old cousin died, also of cancer. His daughter died of leukemia. And then my cousin Adelia died of cancer at thirty-two years of age. Cancer of the uterus. Then my brother-in-law got cancer. It came out of his throat and he had terrible tumors all over his body by the time he died. And that's when we started to say: "How is it possible that we are living in our sacred lands, and then some companies come . . . and deceive us and leave us here to die?"[13]

Like Moncayo, Piaguaje responded to this awakening by taking political action. The decline of the indigenous movement, and the failure to maintain their territorial integrity against the advance of the oil frontier, led Piaguaje and other indigenous leaders to consider allying themselves with the *colonos* who were beginning to organize against the oil industry: "How could we work with our *compañeros colonos*, who were also invaders, who had come here to rob us of our territories? How could we be comrades? We discussed this, and we decided that we could find unity, that it existed. It makes no sense to speak of difference, if we are pursuing the same objective of defending ourselves against the big companies that have done so much damage to human life."[14]

The movement that began to emerge in the northern Amazon thus combined the forces of the most historically marginalized and dispossessed sectors of Ecuadorian society: the landless peasants of the sierra and the coast, who represented the majority of the *colono* population of the region, and the indigenous communities of the Amazon that the *colonos* had initially dispossessed. The central strategy of this nascent movement was the paralyzation, "*el paro.*" In its simplest form, the *paro* involved the barricading of a road with rocks, rubble, and tree trunks as a means of obstructing the everyday activities of the oil industry, to ensure the fulfillment of an agreement signed with an oil company, or to enforce the payment of compensation for an oil spill. Ever since the 1970s, the population of the region had launched *paros* to assert their demands. From the early 1990s onward, however, these occasional, fragmented *paros*, spontaneously executed by isolated communities, became increasingly frequent and integrated. As one activist later explained: "We managed to convince political and religious authorities, communities, and lots of other isolated groups from here and there to join up. We were cooking up something that was getting really hot! *Paro* in the municipality! *Paro* in the parish! *Paro* in the community! *Paro* on the access road! *Paro* at the oil well! And now the *paros* would last two days, three days, a week. Now the mayors were involved, the communities, the social movements. . . . And so, an immense unease began to grip the province."[15]

This process culminated with the creation of the Bi-Provincial Assembly of Orellana-Sucumbíos (ABP), which combined the two provinces of the northern Amazon in a single movement.[16] The first assembly was held in January 2001. According to a self-published history of the ABP, the meeting concluded that the desperate conditions of the two provinces "left us with only one option: to fight. And so we decided to embark on the first bi-provincial paralyzation."[17] The scale of the struggle, the experience acquired over decades of *paros*, and the increasing radicalization of the population led to a *paro* of unprecedented strength, which forced the government to enter negotiations with the ABP. The resulting accords committed the government to a list of projects, including the construction of a paved road across the northern Amazon, the incorporation of the region into the national grid, and the construction of state schools and public hospitals.[18]

In the words of the ABP, the first *paro biprovincial* had demonstrated "that no government will attend to our needs unless we make them hear our voice, and that this can be achieved only through the paralyzation of petroleum production."[19] Yet following the signing of the accords, and the resumption of oil production, the abandonment of the region continued. Further *paros* were organized by the ABP in 2002 and 2004, resulting in further accords that also remained largely unfulfilled.[20] Meanwhile, a new oil pipeline was constructed, and the oil price finally began to recuperate after a twenty-year slump. But the neoliberalization of the oil industry implied that the vast majority of profits were now claimed by foreign companies, and IMF conditionalities ensured that most of the public revenues flowing along the pipeline were diverted to the payment of the external debt.[21] The restive inhabitants of the northern Amazon were thus confronted with an increasingly stark discrepancy between their own abjection and the glut of petrodollars being funneled from their territories into the coffers of foreign banks and oil companies. One leading member of the ABP recalls: "We could see that the entire neoliberal project had served to rob us of our oil. And the oil price kept rising. And the private oil companies were taking everything and were leaving us with nothing."[22]

It was under these circumstances that the ABP resolved to launch a fourth *paro biprovincial*, which was scheduled for June 21, 2005. The announcement was made in the context of a deepening crisis of the neoliberal project at the national scale. Just two months previously the Ecuadorian president, Lucio Gutiérrez, had been forced out of office by another popular revolt. Elected in 2003 on a left-populist platform that promised an end to neoliberalism, Gutiérrez had subsequently agreed to a further structural adjustment program with the IMF and had opened negotiations for a free trade agreement with the United States, which provoked a spontaneous uprising that became known as the Outlaw Rebellion.[23] Gutiérrez had been replaced by his vice president, Alfredo Palacio. The weakness of the new government led Palacio to open negotiations with the ABP on June 18, just before the *paro*, in an attempt to prevent its taking place.[24] The chief negotiator for the government was the newly appointed minister of economy and finance, a charismatic young economist named Rafael Correa. In stark contrast to previous finance ministers, Correa was fiercely opposed to neoliberalism. Before joining the government, he had participated alongside members of the ABP in a series of meetings on energy sovereignty and was regarded by them as a uniquely honest broker. According to Donald Moncayo, who was present at the negotiations, Correa ensured that things "went smoothly. He was very intelligent and willing to negotiate."[25] As another member of the ABP, although other ministers resisted their demands, "Correa guaranteed that all our petitions were met."[26]

The *paro* was postponed, pending the outcome of a further meeting between the government, the foreign oil companies, and the ABP, scheduled for August 2. The oil companies, however, did not show up to the meeting.[27] Instead, they published a full-page statement in the national press, which complained that "the oil industry is being unjustifiably harassed [by] the Eastern provinces," while reminding the Ecuadorian government of its responsibility "to guarantee the established order [and] ensure the public tranquility required for the oil companies to execute their activities."[28]

The ABP responded to this betrayal of the negotiations by declaring that the *paro* would now indeed take place. This announcement was accompanied by a bold new set of demands that went far beyond those of all previous accords, including the redirection of 25 percent of the corporate income tax paid by all foreign oil companies to the provincial governments of Orellana and Sucumbíos; the presence of ABP delegates at the signing of all contracts with foreign oil companies; and the reform of the Hydrocarbons Law to ensure that "the resources that are now exported abroad with impunity serve instead to construct schools and hospitals."[29] These new demands marked a radical shift in the political horizon of the ABP. As one leader observes: "Now we were fighting not only for ourselves, but for all Ecuadorians. And now the battle was explicitly over the oil."[30]

The ABP prohibited further negotiations before the planned launch of the *paro* on August 15, to ensure that, this time, the *paro* would go ahead. As Donald Moncayo recalls: "Now it was out of the government's control. No government could have prevented it. . . . The *pueblo* couldn't take it anymore. They had reached their limit. Absolutely everyone was mobilized."[31] In the words of the self-published history of the ABP: "The grievances felt by the masses . . . brought about a massive and overwhelming paralyzation. . . . *The paro was converted into a popular uprising!*"[32]

Carnival of Rage

The fourth *paro biprovincial* began one day earlier than scheduled, in order to get a jump on the security forces that had been steadily amassing in the region. On the night of August 14, the roads leading into Coca were blocked with tree trunks, rubble, earth, and vehicles. The bridges over the Napo and Payamino rivers were closed, several oil wells were seized by protesters, and hundreds of people occupied the Coca airport.[33] The next morning, the Lago Agrio airport was taken over by a handful of demonstrators led by Donald Moncayo:

> When we arrived at the airport, a group of soldiers was already there. Once seventy or so people had arrived, I told them: "You know what? We declare this airport occupied!" . . . And before I knew what was happening there weren't seventy people anymore. In less than ten minutes, five hundred people had arrived. I mean, the soldiers couldn't do anything. There were only about forty soldiers there. . . . And then the municipal dump trucks began to arrive, loaded with stones, to block the arrival and departure of airplanes, and to block the arrival of more soldiers as well.[34]

Meanwhile, an attempt to occupy the installations of the American oil company Occidental was met with military violence, in which a woman was shot. Another group of demonstrators blocked the access road to the installations of the Canadian company Encana and were also violently dispersed. But the security forces were unable to contain the scale of the protests, in which 85 percent of the population of the northern Amazon are estimated to have taken part.[35] One member of the ABP recalls it as a moment of collective awakening: "In that moment, *an immense solidarity was awakened in the people.* They prepared food for everyone in the nearest houses [to the barricades]. They provided water. And it was because they had reached their limit. They learned to defend their rights. They threw themselves into the struggle."[36]

By the end of the first day of the *paro*, the roads and rivers of both provinces had been blockaded. Both regional airports were occupied, dozens of wells had been seized, and pitched battles were under way for control of the infrastructures of transnational capital. The economic impact was immediate and severe: the flow of oil out of the Amazon fell from 400,000 barrels a day to under 200,000 barrels on the first day of the uprising.[37] In a press release issued that evening, the ABP announced, "We have shut down the majority of the oil production of the country."[38]

On August 16 more wells were occupied across the region, and the Lago Agrio pumping station was seized by protesters. The army attempted to retake the installations, which led to violent confrontations that resulted in over sixty injuries and more than one hundred arrests. Thousands of people took to the streets. Police vehicles were overturned and torched, and two members of the security forces that had infiltrated the protests were taken hostage and exchanged for the release of twelve demonstrators.[39] Running street battles were under way in Coca, where the military opened fire on the headquarters of the municipal government, from within which the ABP dispatched a defiant message to the nation: "The army is firing on us. . . . Nothing can justify the state firing on an unarmed population. We repeat: our struggle is to change the oil politics of our country, so that Ecuador will be a sovereign nation, instead of puppets in the hands of foreign interests."[40]

Despite the intensifying repression, the *paro* continued to tighten its control over the oil installations and transportation infrastructures of the region, and national oil production on August 16 was reduced to 155,000 barrels. On the following morning, the government agreed to open negotiations with the ABP in Lago Agrio. The meeting, however, was canceled after the oil companies again refused to participate, denouncing the *paro* as "an expression of aggression and intolerance, including criminal acts and terrorist tendencies."[41] The people on the streets of Lago Agrio responded by attacking the central government offices, hurling stones and Molotov cocktails, overpowering the police guard, and burning the offices to the ground.[42] Confronted by this repudiation of state authority, and with oil production continuing to dwindle, Palacio declared a state of emergency and imposed a curfew across the two provinces.[43] The population of Lago Agrio responded by parading through the city in a motorized caravan as the curfew came into force, mocking the state of emergency, and chanting slogans against the government and the oil companies.[44]

The *paro* held firm, and national oil production was reduced to just 23,000 barrels on August 17. The next day, the mayor of Lago Agrio and fifteen other leading figures in the ABP were arrested under the state of emergency legislation.[45] People took to the streets again, and "the battle extended to the most far-flung barrios of the city. . . . No street corner lacked a barricade, a burning tire, the flag of the province, and the red flags of the popular organizations."[46] Lago Agrio was "transformed into a battleground between citizens, military, and police. Stones, tear gas, and Molotov cocktails fell like rain."[47] By 2 p.m., however, the army had reestablished control over the city. According to one account, "The atmosphere was heavy. The air had been contaminated by hundreds of tear gas canisters . . . and barricades of burning wood and tires smoldered in the suffocating heat."[48] In Coca the army retook the airport, and all that remained in the abandoned streets was "garbage, burning tires, and mountains of stones piled on the street corners."[49] But outside the cities, the roads and oil wells remained under popular control, causing oil production to fall to just 10,500 barrels on August 18. These straitened circumstances forced the government to take the unprecedented decision to suspend the oil exports on which the economy depended. The following day, Palacio claimed that $570 million of revenue had been lost because of the *paro*.[50] An article published in the national press stated, "Ecuador is experiencing the greatest oil crisis in its history . . . owing to the *paro biprovincial* of Orellana and Sucumbíos."[51]

Over the next few days, an eerie calm descended on the Ecuadorian Amazon. The cities were under military lockdown, but the wells remained occupied, and the oil was still not flowing.[52] A report issued during this hiatus by an American political risk agency emphasized the severity of the situation: "If Ecuadorian President Alfredo Palacio cannot quell the strike and restart oil production quickly, Ecuador will likely suffer a financial crisis . . . that could aggravate social tensions. Provincial strike leaders, however, appear determined to press their demands. If neither side makes concessions, the chances are high that more clashes between Ecuadorian troops and civilian protesters will occur in coming days as the government struggles to regain control of the oil industry."[53]

A truce was finally called on August 21, and negotiations were opened in Quito. An agreement was signed between the government and the ABP four days later, on the understanding that the oil companies would sign the following day. The *paro* and the state of emergency were lifted, amnesty was granted to all those involved in the uprising, and oil production resumed. The signatures of the oil companies, however, were not forthcoming. Instead, on August 28 they presented their own watered-down version of the accords. Effigies of government ministers and oil executives were burned on the streets during furious demonstrations in Coca and Lago Agrio, and the ABP announced that the *paro* would be reinstated in forty-eight hours if the original agreement was not signed by the companies. Two days later, faced with the imminent resumption of the *paro*, and under pressure from a government desperate to avoid economic collapse, the companies signed the accords in their entirety.[54]

The ABP Accords of August 2005 included the fulfillment of many of the seemingly impossible demands issued before the *paro*, including the direct transfer of 16 percent of corporate income tax revenues from the foreign oil companies to the two provinces (negotiated down by the government from the original demand of 25 percent); the creation of a fund financed by the oil companies for the paving of 160 miles of roads in the region; the preferential hiring of local labor and the purchase of local goods and services; and the progressive elimination of outsourcing, through which oil companies had avoided the legal obligation to pay employees 15 percent of their local profits. A faded facsimile of the agreement concludes with the scratchy signatures of the representatives of ten transnational oil companies, including Encana, Petrobras, Perenco, Repsol, and Occidental.[55]

Unlike previous *paros*, the August Uprising not only gained promises from the national state, but also forced concessions directly from transnational capital. And on this occasion many of the agreed-on reforms were swiftly implemented, resulting in the paving of major roads and city centers, the distribution of profits to workers in the oil sector, and a significant increase in the budgets of the provincial governments.[56] These achievements demonstrated the possibility of a developmental alternative to neoliberalism, in which the oil revenues appropriated by capital would be reclaimed by the state. As the ABP noted: "Our struggle made the oil transnationals tremble, [because] *the consciousness of the Ecuadorians was awakened* to the necessity of nationalizing the oil. . . . It constituted the greatest economic blow against imperialism and its oil companies that has yet been achieved by the Ecuadorian people."[57]

The trajectory of the ABP traced the arc of an insurgent utopia, which emerges "when the situation is so without issue, without a way to resolve it within the coordinates of the possible, that out of the pure urge of survival you have to invent a new space."[58] It began with a process of radical awakening in the northern Amazon, in the context of the deepening socioecological crisis of the region, which shattered collective fantasies of petroleum prosperity, abundant lands, and indigenous autonomy, confronting the population with the violence of capital in the form of despoiled landscapes, ruined livelihoods, rampant diseases, and vast disparities of wealth and power. The recognition of a common struggle against seemingly impossible odds transcended the differences between the *colono* and indigenous populations and united them in a community of the dispossessed. This unity took the material form of the *paro*, which jammed the gears of capital accumulation and forced the redirection of oil rents to the region. But those involved in the uprising do not describe it as a bitter struggle for economic justice. Instead, they recall it in terms of "the euphoria of the battles and victories of the people," filled with "moments of great joy" in which "people learned to confront power, to equalize themselves. To speak face-to-face without looking down."[59] Despite the absence of a fantasy frame, and in the face of the state violence unleashed upon it, an insurgent utopia thus possesses an incandescent dimension—"an ecstatic component [that] lives in every revolutionary act."[60]

Besieging the Impossible

The August Uprising brought Ecuador to the brink of economic breakdown and confirmed the exhaustion of the neoliberal project. Meanwhile, Rafael Correa had resigned as minister of economy and finance in the Palacio administration. His departure came just two days after the refusal of the oil companies to attend the meeting with the ABP, which had triggered the uprising. During his brief period in office, Correa had challenged neoliberal orthodoxy, calling for the nationalization of the oil industry and the reversal of IMF reforms. The World Bank had responded by canceling a $100 million loan to the country, which was followed by Correa's forced departure two weeks later.[61] The initial demands of the *paro* had included a call for his immediate reinstatement, on the grounds that he had "valiantly denounced the policy of submission to the interests of the multinationals of President Alfredo Palacio."[62] And at a demonstration outside the Finance Ministry to protest his removal, the crowd had begun to chant, "Correa for president!"[63]

The widespread rejection of neoliberalism, combined with the popular support for Correa, convinced a group of heterodox Ecuadorian economists of the electoral viability of a post-neoliberal project built around the charismatic figure of Correa himself. The group invited Correa to a series of meetings at the house of the ecological economist Alberto Acosta. Huddled around a dining table in a suburban district of Quito, they began to formulate a program to challenge neoliberalism and to launch themselves into power.[64]

These meetings resulted in the publication of a book titled *Besieging the Impossible* (*Asedios a lo imposible*), which served as the "point of departure" for their political project.[65] The book listed the social and economic consequences of Ecuadorian neoliberalism: deindustrialization, the collapse of the internal market, increasing dependency on primary commodity exports, persistent low growth, intensified poverty and inequality, the collapse of public services, a massive increase in the foreign debt burden, profound economic instability, and endemic corruption.[66] Faced with this multidimensional crisis, *Besieging the Impossible* was conceived as a radical call to action, as Acosta later explained: "We were laying siege to a city. That was the idea. The impossible as a city. We were laying siege to the impossible in order to make it possible. . . . The impossible was a free society, a just society, an equal society, an economy that serves humanity and respects nature. We believed that it was possible."[67]

This belief in the possibility of radical social and economic transformation led those around Acosta's table to form a party—Alianza PAIS (Alliance of the Proud and Sovereign Homeland)—and to put Correa forward as a candidate for the presidential elections of November 2006. Correa traveled the length and breadth of the country, campaigning on a post-neoliberal platform based on increased public investment in education and health care and the reassertion of state control over natural resources. This message was conveyed through the twin discourses of "the neoliberal night" and the "dream" of the Citizens' Revolution. The main campaign poster depicted Correa standing in the darkness, with his face turned upward toward the light as if awakening from sleep, accompanied by the slogan: "Your decision is between the dark past and this beautiful democratic revolution."[68] The election manifesto, on the other hand, was presented as "the crystallization of a collective dream."[69] For Acosta, the objective of these combined discourses of dreaming and awakening was clear and unambiguous: "Our idea was to give a positive message. Negative night—positive dream. So that *now we were in the midst of a dream.*"[70]

The campaign was successful, and Correa won the second round of the election in December 2006. In his inaugural speech in January 2007, he repeated the invitation to awaken into a dream, declaring that "the darkest hour is closest to the dawn," and calling on the Ecuadorian people to join him in "constructing the just and sovereign nation that we all dream of."[71] In contrast to Gutiérrez, who had been elected on an anti-neoliberal platform that he had immediately betrayed, Correa quickly implemented several campaign promises, including the drafting of a new constitution. A national referendum for the formation of a constituent assembly was approved in April 2007. In September 2007 Alianza PAIS won a majority in the Constituent Assembly, and Correa then dissolved the conservative Congress, replacing it with the Assembly itself, and giving Alianza PAIS control over the legislature. The party then took the lead in the drafting of the new constitution, which was overwhelmingly approved by a further national referendum in September 2008.

The constitution asserted the rights of nature and was framed in terms of the *Kichwa* principle of *sumak kawsay,* or *buen vivir,* which emphasized harmonious coexistence over economic growth.[72] These concepts, drawn from the indigenous social movements that had played a crucial role in the national struggle against neoliberalism, were combined with an embrace of the Bolivarian Revolution under way in Venezuela. In Correa's words, which again invoked the image of awakening into a dream: "This constitutional revolution . . . marks a before and an after in the long, sad neoliberal night. We have passed from that dreamless night into the shared dream of twenty-first-century socialism."[73]

But like the utopian fantasies of the oil workers, *colonos*, and missionaries through which the initial development of the northern Ecuadorian Amazon had been achieved, this dream did not seek to disrupt the flow of capital. The architects of the Citizens' Revolution were committed to neostructuralist economic theory, which was premised not on dismantling capitalist social relations, but on "the highly seductive notion that international competitiveness, social integration, and political legitimacy can be attained by swimming along, not against, the swift currents unleashed by globalization."[74] The public discourse of Alianza PAIS was dominated by appeals to *buen vivir*, the rights of nature, and twenty-first-century socialism. But these subversive concepts were largely absent from their election manifesto, which announced, "We dream of a competitive nation, in the framework of a systemic competitiveness," and the new constitution committed the Ecuadorian state to pursuing "systemic competitiveness [and a] strategic insertion into international markets."[75] This neostructuralist agenda had provided the unspoken coordinates of the project, ever since the initial meetings at Acosta's house in Quito. As Acosta has since acknowledged, "In the house we didn't debate these things much, because we were in agreement on them."[76]

Notwithstanding its apparently radical aspirations, the Citizens' Revolution would therefore seem to reproduce the tradition of utopian socialism critiqued by Marx and Engels, by promising to resolve the contradictions of capitalist society within the framework of capitalism itself, and by seeking to replace an "upsurge of anonymous utopian energy" with "the harmonious organization of the polity."[77] After all, we should not forget that the "besieging of the impossible" that its architects had sworn to enact had in fact already taken place— not in texts but on the streets, and not in the elite suburbs of Quito but in the impoverished backwaters of the Amazon. Yet these struggles are strangely absent from the pages of *Besieging the Impossible*, despite the fact that the book had been written in the immediate aftermath of the August Uprising of the ABP. In his chapter, for example, Correa argues that "another agenda is possible . . . that gives priority to the poorest and the weakest," while making no mention of the revolt that had just brought the government to its knees.[78] In the discourse of the Citizens' Revolution, the supplications of the poor and weak thus replaced the ecstatic rage of insurrection. What, then, was the "long dark night" from which the people were being called on to awaken? Did its darkness symbolize the despair of a defeated population, or did it throw a cloak over the vitality of an insurgent utopia? Were the people really asleep, or had they already awoken? Did the impassioned calls to "awaken into a dream" herald the collective creation of a radically different future? Or was this dream destined to function as a guardian of sleep?

Fever of Hope

In the northern Amazon, Correa was elected by a landslide. His campaign message to the region had drawn on knowledge acquired during the negotiations he had conducted with the ABP in June 2005 on behalf of the Palacio administration. One member of the ABP recalls that Correa had "managed to sniff out what was happening in the two provinces. He grasped what was in the atmosphere, the level of tension and conflict."[79] His presidential opponent was Álvaro Noboa, a banana tycoon from the coast. Like countless candidates before him, Noboa "just showed up [in the Amazon] to hand out a few gifts: blankets, tools, things like that." But in contrast to the erasure of the ABP from the national discourse of Alianza PAIS, Correa used the accords signed at the conclusion of the August Uprising as the explicit basis for his own detailed proposals for the region. He walked the streets and spoke to the people "in a language that we understood. He spoke of our concerns. He spoke of our problems. He said, 'Bi-Provincial Assembly.' He spoke to who we really were."[80]

Some of the accords had already been implemented by the time of Correa's arrival in the Amazon, and were beginning to bear fruit. But the gains had been partial and uneven, and "the central contradiction continued to sharpen: a ground rich in natural resources and the majority of the population in poverty."[81] There was a desperate desire for radical change, after decades of suffering and years of violent confrontation with the armed forces of a national state from which the region had always been excluded. According to Humberto Piaguaje of the *Secoya*: "When [Correa] arrived, it was like receiving a god who had come to rescue the region."[82] Another member of the ABP recalls that "people wanted a government that could really save the country. Correa grabbed hold of all those hopes at the right moment."[83] In the words of Donald Moncayo, Correa "sowed the fever of hope in the people of Orellana and Sucumbíos."[84]

Once in power, Correa set about implementing a series of reforms demanded by the ABP, including the imposition of a 99 percent windfall tax on foreign oil companies; the cancellation of the free-trade agreement with the United States; the closure of a U.S. military base in the coastal city of Manta; the expulsion of the World Bank and the IMF from the country; and the formulation of a new hydrocarbons law, according to which 87 percent of the profits of oil fields operated by foreign companies would be claimed by the state.[85] This dramatic shift in policy coincided with a continued rise in the oil price, which resulted in a vast increase in state revenues. Much of this newfound wealth was invested in an extensive public works program under the guidance of the newly created National Secretariat of Planning and Development (SENPLADES). This project included a "Special Territorial Plan for the Amazon," which promised to overcome the isolation of the region while meeting the central demands of the ABP Accords in spectacular form.[86] Among the most urgent of these demands was the upgrading of the road network in the region. Correa not only agreed to this demand but supplanted it with a far more ambitious proposal of his own: the construction of an interoceanic corridor, running from Manta on the Pacific coast of Ecuador to the industrial city of Manaus in Brazil and on to the Atlantic port of Belém. During a visit to Coca in June 2007, Correa informed his spellbound audience of this remarkable scheme: "If we achieve this route, the benefits will be enormous. The route will permit us to bypass the Panama Canal . . . and save twenty days of travel [from China] to the Atlantic coast of Brazil. . . . The cargo will enter [the country] at Manta. It will come in trucks to the port of Coca, where it will be shipped on barges down the River Napo until it reaches the River Amazon. This route, Manta-Manaus, will greatly benefit Coca. It will become the most important river port in the whole of South America!"[87]

During the same event, Correa argued, "Instead of little projects here and there, we will dedicate ourselves to macro-projects that have a powerful impact." The ABP Accords addressed education, health care, water, sanitation, and sports facilities, but in the form of the scattered classrooms, water tanks, and volleyball courts long provided by the oil companies. Correa fused these fragmented projects into a promise to build entire towns, with "beautiful houses for everyone, secure urbanizations with decent housing that will massively improve your standards of life!" This vision would later evolve into the planned construction of Millennium Cities throughout the Amazon.

Another of the central demands of the ABP Accords was the establishment of an Amazonian campus of the main state university. The Amazon had no public universities at the time, and the campus would offer the possibility of higher education to families who could not afford to maintain their children in the distant university cities of the highlands and the coast. Again, Correa adopted this demand. But he dramatically enhanced the scale of its utopian vision, promising to construct a world-leading institution specializing in the unparalleled cultural and biological diversity of the region. This university would eventually take the form of Ikiam, the Regional University of the Amazon. In 2007, during a visit to the Amazonian city of Tena in which the campus would be constructed, Correa regaled the delighted crowd with his plans for the university:

> We can now present the concrete projects that we have for the region, which were also campaign promises, like the University of the Amazon. Here we have the biggest and best laboratory in the world, in terms of biodiversity, ethnography, anthropology, and so on. The idea is to create a public university, but to make it international, . . . so that the entire world can come here to study biodiversity and give classes and prepare the youth of the Amazon. . . . With the Amazon in our hearts, this government will repay the historical debt that we have to the region![88]

The modest demands of the ABP were suddenly being realized on a hallucinatory scale. The demand for roads was being met with an interoceanic corridor; the demand for services was being met with the construction of entire cities; and the demand for higher education was being met with a university specializing in biotechnology and staffed with international scientists. This was *the state as dream machine*, funneling up emancipatory energies and expressions of popular discontent and transforming them into extravagant "utopias of spatial form."[89] These utopias were presented not as the outcome of decades of popular struggle, but as manifestations of the magical agency of the Citizens' Revolution, through which "dreams are converted into public works."[90] Ikiam was described as "a dream come true"; Manta-Manaus was "a dream that implied the physical integration of two oceans"; and the Millennium Cities were "a dream . . . that we offer to the Amazonian population."[91]

For a population radicalized by its abandonment, the sudden arrival of this wave of megaprojects was both bewitching and bewildering in the overwhelming scale and immediacy of its symbolic wish fulfillment. As Fernando Coronil has argued in his analysis of petroleum-based development in Venezuela, through the staging of such experiences, the resource-rich state assumes the role of a "magnanimous sorcerer" and "seizes its subjects by inducing a condition or state of being receptive to its illusions."[92] The spatial phantasmagorias of the Citizens' Revolution seized the Amazonian population in precisely this way. As the journalist and activist Milagros Aguirre has observed: "[Correa] arrived in the Amazon with the attitude that 'okay, there was nothing here, and now we are going to bring development, infrastructure, big cities.' . . . It destroyed all forms of social organization. Over the course of many years, through many struggles and *paros*, a very strong, unified, and combative civil society had emerged. And I think that has been dismantled."[93]

"At that point," Donald Moncayo admits, "the doctrine of continued struggle within the ABP was lost."[94] The post-neoliberal state had arrived, laden with all the development projects that their hearts could desire, and the exhausted inhabitants of the northern Amazon had embraced its call to awaken into a dream for what it really was: a seductive invitation to finally get some sleep. As Freud observes, a dream is "a compromise-structure. It has a double function: on the one hand . . . it serves the wish to sleep; on the other hand it allows . . . the satisfaction that is possible in these circumstances, in the form of *a hallucinated fulfilment of a wish.*"[95]

The Savage Road

The Amazon had entered the waking dream of the Citizens' Revolution. But the cutting edge of the oil frontier remained within the space of a more radical awakening. In May 2007 Correa faced the first major *paro* of his administration.[96] It was launched along the Vía Auca—the "Savage Road," which starts on the bank of the Napo opposite Coca and plunges deep into the jungles once dominated by the *Huaorani.* In February 2006 the concession for Blocks 14 and 17 in the remote region of El Pindo had been granted to the Chinese company PetroOriental, which had made a series of pledges to local communities that it was failing to honor. The *paro* shut down the oil blocks and demanded the fulfillment of these obligations.[97] In doing so, it asserted the rights of some of the most marginalized and impoverished citizens of Ecuador against the infractions of a transnational oil company. It was an ideal opportunity for the Citizens' Revolution to demonstrate its commitment to a new oil politics by intervening in defense of the rights of the people and the resources of the nation, led by a president who had sworn to uphold the ABP Accords and to bring justice and development to the Amazon.

Instead, the military broke the blockade with ruthless brutality, attacking demonstrators with nightsticks and rifle butts and injuring over sixty people. Correa referred to the crackdown a few days later, during his weekly address to the nation, which was broadcast on radio stations and television channels across the country. But rather than condemning the excessively repressive actions of the army, he aggressively endorsed them, announcing "the militarization of the oil installations" in defense of "the private goods of the private oil companies," and warning, "We will not permit any more *paros*, any more law of the jungle in the Ecuadorian Amazon."[98]

Incensed by this betrayal, the inhabitants of El Pindo ignored Correa's threat and launched another *paro* six weeks later to protest the continued failure of PetroOriental to meet their demands.[99] This time the military opened fire on the barricades with live rounds, injuring two demonstrators, one of whom was shot in the arm, resulting in paralysis, and the other in the jaw, the bullet entering one side of his face and tearing out his teeth on its way out of the other. Soldiers then invaded the town of Santa Rosa, bombarding it with tear gas, forcing their way into the houses, and driving the inhabitants into the jungle, where they remained for two days and nights, sheltering beneath plastic sheets, fearing for their lives.[100]

Guadalupe Llori, the prefect of Orellana and a militant member of the ABP, responded by accusing Correa of "ordering savage, unjust, and unrestrained repression . . . in defense of the interests of a transnational company that has not complied with the [ABP] Accords."[101] In October 2007 Llori called for a new *paro biprovinicial*. The proposal was blocked by the prefect of Sucumbíos, who was president of the ABP but had allied himself with the Correa regime.[102] But Dayuma, the largest town on the Savage Road, resolved to launch a *paro* alone to demand the paving of the road, which had been part of the ABP Accords. The *paro* began on November 25, 2007, with the seizure of several oil wells and a blockade of the Vía Auca at the entrance to the town. All four pumping stations in the Auca oilfield were shut down, and oil production on the Savage Road ground to a halt.[103]

Correa retaliated by implementing a state of emergency throughout Orellana. On the morning of November 30, five hundred heavily armed soldiers arrived at the barricade blocking the bridge at the entrance of Dayuma. The barricade was unmanned, as a truce had been called the previous evening in preparation for negotiations that were due to begin that day. A representative of the parish council was summoned to the bridge. When he arrived, he was immediately detained. His hands were tied behind his back, and he was thrown into the back of a military truck, where he was beaten and teargassed. At that moment, a dynamite charge was detonated under the bridge. Shots rang out, and a police officer was struck by buckshot in the thigh. No protagonists were ever identified for these mysterious crimes. But the army took them as a signal to invade Dayuma, firing rubber bullets and live rounds, smashing doors and windows, discharging tear gas canisters inside the houses, destroying furniture and possessions, and beating men, women, and children indiscriminately, while military helicopters launched tear gas over the tin rooftops of the shattered town.[104] By midday, the army had reestablished control of the Savage Road, and the oil was flowing once again. The following day, Correa used his weekly television address to the nation to give the official version of events in Dayuma: "[Those involved in the *paros* in the Amazon] are terrorists who use dynamite, rifles, cartridges, shotgun shells, et cetera. They have installed a reign of terror. Other governments have tolerated it, and they think that my government will tolerate it. Don't fool yourselves! *Señores*, the anarchy is finished! The party is over! Law, order, and the interests of all Ecuadorians will prevail over the shameless few!"[105]

Correa paused at this point in his speech to allow the applause to gradually die down. He then turned his attention to Guadalupe Llori, whom he identified as the ringleader of the criminal elements responsible for the violence in Dayuma, a charlatan who masqueraded as "the Mother of Struggle" (*Mama Lucha*), while secretly treating Orellana as her "mafia citadel."[106] Llori was arrested at her home in Coca a week later, in a military operation streamed live on national television, "as if they were pursuing one of the bloodiest terrorists in history."[107] She was held on suspicion of sabotage and terrorism, and Correa predicted, "The magnitude of her network of violence and corruption will gradually reveal itself."[108] No charges were ever brought against her, but a succession of further accusations kept Llori in prison for eleven months and forced her to resign as prefect of Orellana.

By the time of Llori's arrest, the ABP was in disarray. Most of the rebel leaders of the Amazon were already committed supporters of the Citizens' Revolution, and the prefect of Sucumbíos publicly endorsed Llori's imprisonment, on the basis that Correa had pledged to fulfill the ABP Accords.[109] A meeting of Amazonian leaders was convened in the presidential palace in Quito a few days later, at which Correa was presented with the Order of Amazonian Merit on behalf of the Consortium of Local Amazonian Governments. Correa accepted the honor and repeated his message to the region: "The worst way of getting anything from this government is through *paros*."[110]

The crackdown in Dayuma crushed the last remnant of an insurgent utopia and consolidated the hegemony of the Citizens' Revolution. According to one veteran member of the ABP, the repression had been undertaken with the explicit objective of "dismantling the *biprovincial*. And they went in so hard that they managed to achieve it."[111] Another militant has since observed:

Dayuma was part of the *biprovincial*. A bit that got left behind. They tried to reproduce the force of the *biprovincial*, but they couldn't do it. [The government] seized the prefect [of Orellana] and destroyed everything, and that was that. Dayuma was the final niche of confrontation . . . they no longer had the force of both provinces behind them, and they tried to go it alone. They didn't have the support of the masses. The masses were fragmented, divided, confused, distracted. . . . Those were the circumstances in which Dayuma threw itself into battle. And that was the last stand of the *paros*.[112]

But the authoritarian message delivered to the inhabitants of Dayuma was very different from the message conveyed to the nation by the same events. The great majority of the Ecuadorian population knew nothing of this obscure corner of the Amazon. After suffering the hardships of two and a half decades of neoliberalism, they were eager to side with a government that promised them a utopian fantasy of twenty-first-century socialism and *buen vivir*, and that assured them that it would "put an end to the terrorism that was preventing thirteen million Ecuadorians from living off the oil."[113]

This message was reinforced by a film produced by the government and shown at prime time on all national television channels three weeks after the military incursion in Dayuma.[114] It begins with an immense Ecuadorian flag, waving in slow motion against a clear blue sky. The screen fades to black. Gas flares burn in the night. The sound of an explosion. "Dayuma, November 25, province of Orellana." The camera pans a darkened oil platform to the sound of gunfire and further explosions. A stern male voice narrates over menacing music: "Three million dollars a day lost to the sabotage of oil production. Twelve million fewer dollars for public works." Indistinct footage of bleeding soldiers, burned-out vehicles, chaos in the streets. The voiceover blames the violence on "mafias who have enriched themselves on blackmail and chaos." Cut to an "oil worker who fears for his life." His face has been blurred to conceal his identity. He accuses Guadalupe Llori of masterminding the conspiracy. The narrative resumes, over heroic images of gleaming oil infrastructure: "Confronted with this situation, the government had to act in defense of the common good, because for this government, petroleum means the health, education, and well-being of all Ecuadorians." Correa appears in full presidential regalia and declares: "Oil is for the people, for the construction of roads, education, health care. And we cannot allow thirty or forty individuals to blow up our oil wells with dynamite. If I had to [repeat the military operation in Dayuma], with pain in my heart, I would do so. Because I am committed to fulfilling my obligations." Fade to black. The voiceover reads the letters that tap out across the screen: "Dayuma, Orellana. No more violence. This government will not defraud you. The nation now includes everyone." The words "Dayuma, Orellana" disappear into the darkness. Cut to the dawn breaking over the Andes. Like the Ecuadorian people, awakening from the neoliberal night into the dream of the Citizens' Revolution, a man stands silhouetted in the foreground, greeting the rising sun.

3

Amazon Unbound

Only dreamers move mountains.

Molly, in Werner Herzog's Fitzcarraldo

Carlos Fermín had a dream that would not let him sleep. Like the hero of *Fitzcarraldo*, who tried to open a tract of the Peruvian Amazon to rubber exploitation by dragging a steamship over a mountain, Fermín was "planning something geographical."[1] He had spent decades transporting the machinery and materials of the Amazonian oil industry along the intricate network of rivers surrounding the Brazilian jungle city of Manaus. In 2001 he was contracted for the Herculean task of moving a 127-ton generator over 1,500 miles upriver from Manaus to the oil fields of the Ecuadorian Amazon. No one had ever attempted such a feat, and those who knew the Napo—the tributary of the Amazon that Fermín would have to enter in Peru—warned him that its upper reaches could not be navigated by vessels of that size. But Fermín proved them wrong, arriving in Ecuador with his cargo after a grueling, monthlong journey.

On his return to Manaus, Fermín became "preoccupied" with an idea. "I couldn't sleep well," he recalls. "The belief that the river was not navigable was an enormous lie. It was too much for me to bear. God had granted everything I had asked for. Good children, a house, a farm. I had everything. But now there was something in my head that would not leave me in peace." Fermín had realized that the navigability of the Napo opened the possibility of an interoceanic corridor, beginning in Manta on the Pacific coast of Ecuador, crossing the Ecuadorian Andes by road, transferring to river at an Amazonian port on the Napo, continuing to Manaus, and concluding in the Atlantic port of Belém. He was convinced that the corridor would "commercialize the Amazon," which he regarded as "a beautiful world of wealth." For Fermín, the implication was clear and unavoidable: "If you see the light, and your conscience tells you to do something, you must do it. This vision that God has given you is not your own, it is God's, and if you do not follow it, you will not be happy."[2] In 2004 he abandoned his life in Brazil and traveled back upriver to Ecuador, where he settled in Providencia, an isolated indigenous community on a broad curve of the Napo. There he set to work clearing the land and began to search for allies in his quest to make Providencia the Amazonian port of his interoceanic corridor. He called the corridor "Manta-Manaus."

Ten years later, in January 2015, we visited Fermín in Providencia. Outside the dingy oil town of Shushufindi, the rough road was suddenly replaced by a brand-new highway that cut smoothly through twenty-eight miles of jungle. At the end of the highway a sign announced our arrival at the "International Port of Providencia." Twenty-five acres of rain forest had been leveled, and a grid of iron girders had been set into the river in preparation for the construction of the dock. In February 2007 the newly elected president of Ecuador, Rafael Correa, had designated Manta-Manaus as an emblematic project of his administration that would "open a passage from the Pacific Ocean to the Atlantic Ocean."[3] Since then, the state had invested over $1 billion in the infrastructure required for the creation of the interoceanic corridor. Incredibly, it seemed that Fermín's dream had come true. He emerged from the back door of his makeshift home, hastily pulling on a crumpled shirt with his name and "Manta-Manaus" embroidered on the back. We sat down to talk on a ramshackle porch with views across the wide sweep of the river and the vast rain forest beyond. "They used to call me a fat slobbering idiot [*gordo baboso*]! An imbecile!" he told us, laughing. "But now I'm a wise man! 'Watch out for that Brazilian guy,' they say, 'He's a wise man, a genius!'"[4]

This chapter tells the remarkable story of Manta-Manaus. The story reveals the extent to which infrastructural megaprojects are infused with obsessive visions and hubristic ambitions that exceed the instrumental rationalities of capitalist calculability and territorial domination. But it also illustrates the ways in which such dreams become ensnarled in complex and counterintuitive materializations. The chapter traces the knotted plots through which Manta-Manaus was conceived, constructed, and brought to ruin. In doing so, it seeks to disentangle the relationship between the Real of capital, which surges blindly forward in pursuit of its expanded reproduction, and the utopian fantasies with which politicians, planners, entrepreneurs, and chancers all vainly attempt to harness its wild dynamics.

The El Dorado Project

Manta-Manaus is the latest in a long history of similar schemes. Transcontinental missions of various kinds were launched throughout the colonial period, and the rubber boom of the late nineteenth century inspired numerous attempts to open the Amazonian interior to international trade.[5] Then in 1958 the Ecuadorian government proposed the construction of the *Vía Interoceánica*—an "Interoceanic Highway" between the Ecuadorian port of San Lorenzo and the Brazilian port of Belém, a route that would use the Putumayo River, which marks the border between Ecuador and Colombia. A preliminary path was cut through the Ecuadorian jungle to the Putumayo, but the project was suspended following the outbreak of the Colombian civil war in 1964 and was further complicated by long-running hostilities between Ecuador and Peru, through which the corridor would have to pass.[6]

The two nations finally signed a peace treaty in 1998. This historic moment inspired a struggling Ecuadorian businessman named Augusto Celís to resurrect the Vía Interoceánica. Celís's plan would avoid the ongoing conflict in Colombia by cutting out the Putumayo and following an alternative route along the Napo, which was no longer problematic now that Peru and Ecuador were at peace. This was the same path that the conquistadors had taken in their futile hunt for El Dorado back in 1541, and Celís named his plan *Proyecto El Dorado* in honor of their mission. We found him seventeen years later in a crumbling office building in a down-market area of Quito. He was old and sickly, and the walls of his musty office were covered with faded maps of the Amazon, on which the route of his fantasy was etched in red pen. "We weren't looking for El Dorado," he said. "I didn't do this with the aim of making money. I just fell in love with an idea."[7]

Before long, Celís had abandoned his other business plans and was "knocking on every door" to promote his interoceanic corridor. At a trade fair in Manaus he was introduced to Carlos Fermín, who was obsessed with the same vision. Together they created the Corporación Ecuatoriana Amazónica, through which they purchased twenty-two acres of riverside land in Providencia for the construction of their port. They then formed an alliance with the Manta Port Authority (APM), which managed the Manta port on the Pacific coast of Ecuador. The director of the APM at the time was Trajano Andrade, an influential businessman and politician. Fermín recalls striking up a friendship with Andrade and deciding together on the name for their scheme: "You're from Manta, I'm from Manaus. Let's call it Manta-Manaus!"[8]

Andrade invited me to his clifftop mansion outside Manta to discuss his role in the project.[9] Original works by Ecuador's greatest artists adorned the marble reception hall, and the expansive gardens included an infinity pool with a built-in cocktail bar. In 2005, following his meeting with Fermín, Andrade began promoting Manta-Manaus to the Palacio administration. The idea caught the imagination of Rafael Correa, who was minister of economy and finance at the time. As Correa pointed out, the plan was compatible with the Initiative for the Regional Integration of South American Infrastructure (IIRSA), a continental development program launched in 2000 by the Inter-American Development Bank (IDB), which envisioned the potential construction of five interoceanic corridors along the main tributaries of the Amazon, including the route that Andrade was proposing.[10]

As director of the APM, Andrade used the inclusion of Manta-Manaus in the IIRSA to market the Manta port to international investors, promising that the interoceanic corridor would transform Ecuador into "the key node of . . . commercial exchange between the Amazon basin and the Pacific Rim."[11] In September 2006 he secured the concession of the port to the Hong Kong–based Hutchison Port Holdings, the world's leading port operator at the time, in a deal that committed Hutchison to invest $523 million in the port over a thirty-year period. Meanwhile, Correa incorporated Manta-Manaus into his presidential election campaign, in which he promised to complete the corridor by 2011, presenting it as a key component in the radical transformation of the nation from an economically dependent oil state into a technologically advanced competitor in global production networks.[12]

Following his inauguration in January 2007, Correa appointed Andrade as minister of transport and public works and made him responsible for Manta-Manaus. Andrade presented the project to Brazil's

President Lula da Silva at a summit between the two post-neoliberal regimes in April 2007. He argued that Manta-Manaus could provide a direct link between China, which was now Brazil's largest trading partner, and the booming industrial city of Manaus, replacing the congested trade route via the Panama Canal and Belém, and reducing transport times between Chinese factories and Brazilian assembly plants by up to twenty days. The same route, he claimed, would also facilitate the export of soya and other primary commodities from the Brazilian Amazon to the vast emerging markets of East Asia. Lula was convinced, and he approved a $600 million credit line from Brazil's National Development Bank (BNDES) to finance the construction of the corridor. Manta, Lula declared, would become "the gateway between Asia and Brazil."[13]

The IIRSA was subsequently incorporated into the Union of South American Nations (UNASUR). Formed in 2008, UNASUR was the first regional organization to include all twelve South American states, and it was promoted as a model of "post-neoliberal regionalism,"[14] which was not limited to economic exchange but aimed "to construct . . . a space of integration and union in the cultural, social, economic, and political spheres."[15] As such, it was emblematic of the twenty-first-century socialist vision of the *patria grande*—the "great nation" that Venezuela's President Hugo Chávez saw as the ultimate objective of his Bolivarian Revolution against the forces of capitalist imperialism.[16]

But despite being promoted in the revolutionary language of twenty-first-century socialism, the IIRSA was consistent with Correa's less radical commitment to the neostructuralist pursuit of "systemic competitiveness" and "an intelligent insertion into international markets,"[17] to the extent that it was premised on the assumption that "physical infrastructure serves as a platform for growth and competitiveness," which would enable South America to "take advantage of the opportunities offered by globalization."[18] In promoting his vision of infrastructural development, Correa argued that "the attraction of private investment requires good roads, electricity systems, efficient ports and airports, [and] state-of-the-art communications systems. . . . This is precisely what we are doing, and it is called systemic competitiveness."[19] This distinctly capitalistic logic was combined with a message of national salvation through infrastructure development emblazoned on billboards up and down the country: "We have great roads! We have a nation!"

As we have seen, however, the origins of Manta-Manaus lay neither in neostructuralist policy prescriptions, nor in the geopolitical strategies of twenty-first-century socialism, but in the singular obsession of a disheveled Brazilian barge operator, who continued to pursue his vision from a hut in the depths of the jungle. In 2008 the patch of land that Carlos Fermín had purchased in Providencia was selected over Coca as the riverport of Manta-Manaus.[20] The minister who made the decision had been convinced to do so by Fermín himself, whom he recalls as "a visionary who was here in Ecuador without any infrastructure or any support from the state, pushing his dream."[21] Before long, the IIRSA had identified Providencia as one of its "Anchor Projects,"[22] and an American design team was working on an ambitious urban plan for the new port city. By 2010 the Ecuadorian section of Manta-Manaus had expanded to include five hundred miles of new or improved roads; the Manta and Providencia ports; an industrial zone in Manta; a "dry port" in the lowland city of Quevedo; new airports in Manta, the highland city of Latacunga, and the Amazonian city of Tena; and the transformation of the Napo into a "hydrovía"—a modernized waterway navigable by container ships, which would require extensive dredging.[23]

The ecological effects of such major geographical upheavals were questioned by some indigenous social movements and environmental

NGOs.[24] But most of those living along the corridor were enthusiastic about its promise of progress and prosperity. A *colono* who lived near Providencia recalled being "impressed" and "inspired" by a stranger who visited the community with a portable television on which he showed them a video with computerized images of "great ships" arriving at Providencia by river. His aunt awoke him late that night, explaining that she had just had a "spectacular" dream about Manta-Manaus and imploring him to purchase land along the riverbank in preparation for the arrival of the project.[25] The *Secoya*, whose territories were near Providencia, were equally enchanted by the vision of the transcontinental trade route. In contrast to their historical opposition to the oil industry, the president of the *Secoya* announced that they would "take advantage" of Manta-Manaus by converting their territories into African palm plantations and creating export companies to ship the produce to Manaus. The interoceanic corridor, he declared, was "the dream of the *Secoya* nation."[26]

In July 2011, true to his post-election promise, Correa inaugurated Manta-Manaus, embarking on the maiden voyage down the Napo in a barge filled with Ecuadorian products and draped in an enormous national flag.[27] In a triumphant speech delivered on the banks of the Napo a few miles upriver from Providencia, Correa celebrated the progress and potential of the project and emphasized its significance for the Citizens' Revolution: "Today we are taking a firm and irreversible step towards the fulfillment of a dream: Manta-Manaus. This is a great part of the country's future. . . . And we are determined that this dream will be a success. We will overcome all obstacles, and Manta-Manaus will become a powerful hub of national development!"[28] He then boarded the barge and set off downriver. An hour or so later he disembarked in Providencia and allowed the maiden voyage to continue on its way. Reclining on his porch above the Napo in 2015, Fermín recalled how Correa had taken the opportunity to visit him and had "left the press stranded" outside his house for hours while the two of them talked like old friends. Throughout it all, Fermín claimed, Correa had stood by him: "The whole project, President Rafael Correa and Carlos Fermín! . . . No one can take this project away from me! I've never turned away from the decision that I made in 2004. I know it's good, and I know it's the future. It is a reality that is under way, and nobody can stop it!"[29] As we sat with him on his porch that evening, surrounded by the cacophonous jungle and the silent river, it seemed that Fermín really had been granted his extraordinary wish, and that the Amazon really was a place in which the wildest dreams could be materialized in reality.

Lost Highway

The realization of Manta-Manaus demonstrates the constitutive role of utopian fantasy in the capitalist production of space. The project was premised on the reduction of transportation times between East Asian factories and the assembly lines of Manaus, and it was justified in terms of "less time, less cost" in comparison to alternative global trade routes.[30] As such, it embodied what Marx would call "the annihilation of space by time,"[31] through which capital drives toward "the equalization of geographical differences and the shrinking of world space."[32] But this subordination of social space to the abstract logic of capital was infused with seductive images of global integration, continental unity, and geographical freedom, through which capital's furious abolition of spatial limits was dusted with "the glitter of progress, the lure of profit, the promise of circulation, movement and a better life."[33] Without this web of fantasies, and their capacity to inspire the dreams of politicians, entrepreneurs, and indigenous communities, Manta-Manaus would not have come into existence. Such fantasies erase the antagonisms of capitalist development and elide the disruptive agency of the nature they seek to transform.[34] As Marx argued, however, "From the fact that capital posits every . . . limit as a barrier and hence gets *ideally* beyond it, it does not by any means follow that it has *really* overcome it."[35]

Luxuriating in the gardens of his clifftop mansion, Trajano Andrade paused to reflect on the story he had just told about the fate of Manta-Manaus. Along the radiant coastline, beyond miles of golden sand, the port of Manta shimmered in the afternoon heat. "The only thing that has no limits in this world," he concluded at last, "is human stupidity."[36] Carlos Fermín and Rafael Correa both depicted Manta-Manaus as an epic tale of heroic modernization. But by the time Correa launched the project with his bombastic speech on the banks of the Napo in 2011, an avalanche of crises, errors, and absurdities had already condemned it to failure.

The problems began in October 2008, when Correa sent troops to seize the assets of the Brazilian construction company Odebrecht in response to its alleged negligence in the construction of a hydroelectric dam.[37] In doing so, Andrade argued, Correa had "shot himself in the foot" by sending a negative signal to international investors, including Hutchison, the shipping company to which Andrade had granted the concession for the Manta port.[38] The expulsion of Odebrecht coincided with the collapse of Lehman Brothers and the outbreak of the global financial crisis, which resulted in a significant reduction in Pacific Ocean trade. Under these conditions, Hutchison began to scale back its investments in the port of Manta, leading Correa to threaten to cancel their contract in January 2009. Fearing a repeat of the Odebrecht expropriation, and seeing an opportunity to escape a potentially unprofitable venture, Hutchison responded by abandoning the concession.[39] A report in *Business News Americas* concluded, "The concession's failure will prevent Manta from developing into a major international container port and a key player in trade between South America and the Asia-Pacific region," and noted that the failure was "a setback in the development of the Manta-Manaus corridor."[40] Two further bidding processes for the concession of the port failed to receive any concrete offers, and container traffic in and out of Manta collapsed, dropping from 38,749 containers a year in 2005, when Hutchison was bidding for the concession, to just 532 during the whole of 2014.[41]

These circumstances led Andrade and the Manta elite to accuse Hutchison of taking on the concession in order to sabotage the port. At the time, Hutchison was operating the ports at both ends of the Panama Canal, as well as Manzanillo in Mexico, which was the port of embarkation for much of the container traffic that entered the main Ecuadorian port of Guayaquil.[42] From Hutchison's perspective, Manta-Manaus represented a competitive challenge to both the Panama Canal and the Manzanillo-Guayaquil shipping route, while Guayaquil's elite saw Manta as a threat to their commercial dominance.[43] This tangle of competing trade routes and intercapitalist rivalries gave credence to the theory that Hutchison and Guayaquil had conspired to undermine the Manta port in "a minutely detailed and coldly calculated strategy."[44]

Meanwhile, Brazil responded to the expropriation of Odebrecht by canceling the $600 million credit line that Lula had established for the construction of Manta-Manaus and shifting its investment to an alternative interoceanic corridor between Manaus and the port of Paita on the Pacific coast of Peru, which was also part of the IIRSA.[45] The road infrastructure for this corridor was constructed by Odebrecht and was completed in 2015. Paita and a port on the Marañon River were also being upgraded, and the Marañon was being transformed into a *hydrovía* that would connect to the Amazon via the Peruvian jungle city of Iquitos.[46]

For Carlos Fermín, the prospect of another interoceanic project reaching fulfillment before his own was "horrible," and "a catastrophe."[47]

Though he shared the belief that Hutchison and Guayaquil had sabo-taged the concession of Manta, he also criticized the Citizens' Revolu-tion, arguing that "investments have increased in Peru because it hasn't made all the changes that President Correa has made. The union with Chávez, the fights with American and Brazilian companies." This per-spective was echoed in the international business press, which noted that "Correa's nationalist policies . . . have given investors cold feet. Compa-nies once interested in carrying out development initiatives in the coun-try are now looking to Colombia and Peru, where they are finding solid investment guarantees and benefits for private investors."[48] But Correa's partial default on the national debt in 2008, and his renegotiation of foreign oil contracts in 2010, had generated an immense increase in state revenues.[49] This allowed the Ecuadorian government to replace private capital and the BNDES credit line with direct public investment, and by the end of 2014, the majority of the road and airport infrastructure for Manta-Manaus was in place, at a total cost of over $1 billion.[50]

The materialization of Manta-Manaus illustrated the power of oil rents to produce "dazzling development projects that engender collec-tive fantasies of progress."[51] But this phantasmagorical projection was distorted by its backdrop. State representations depicted the road from Manta to Providencia as an electric blue arrow hurtling across the national territory in a clean and rigid line. This arrow, however, took the concrete form of an interminable series of steep and narrow switchbacks bombarded with falling rocks and blocked by landslides, which climbed to an altitude of over 13,000 feet from the Pacific to the Andes, before descending almost all the way back to sea level in the Amazon. When we traveled the road in 2015, the first stretch to Quevedo was narrow and filled with potholes, and the president of the local chamber of commerce had never heard of the "dry port" that was supposed to be located there.[52] Outside the Andean city of Lata-cunga, the highway petered out in a labyrinth of canyons through which dozens of tunnels would have had to be constructed. The belated realization of the scale of this task had led to the abandonment of the project and the rerouting of Manta-Manaus via the decrepit old oil road between Quito and Lago Agrio.[53] This new route bypassed Coca, which had originally been included in Manta-Manaus, and which Correa had promised to transform into "the most important river port in the whole of South America."[54] According to Carlos Fermín, members of the Coca elite had blamed him for the relocation of the port to Providencia, and they had taken their revenge by burning his house to the ground.[55]

Unable to flow freely through this contorted landscape, capital had moved elsewhere. Almost all container traffic now entered Ecuador via Guayaquil and ascended the Andes by a different route, rendering the road from Manta redundant. The airport on the outskirts of Tena had been built to international standards at a cost of $50 million, with the intention of establishing a direct flight to Manaus. But no commercial airline was interested in the route, and the plan had been abandoned. As a representative of the Ministry of Transport and Public Works explained, "We have a lot of problems because the airlines have told us, 'We want to go to Ecuador, but we don't have anything to bring.'"[56] An internal government report listed total metric tons of cargo handled at Tena in 2014 as "0,"[57] and by 2015 the airport was receiving only one passenger flight a day, which arrived from Quito and was being run at a loss by the state airline. The new airport in Latacunga was receiving just two flights a day, while the Manta airport lacked any international cargo traffic. Its only client, a Chilean airline, had been expelled when it was discovered that it had been using the airport not for transporting Ecuadorian exports, but only to fill up on subsidized fuel before continuing to Miami.[58] In the words of a junior minister of planning: "We've invested and invested, but nobody wants to buy. . . . Nothing has come of Manta-Manaus.

None of it is profitable—neither the ports nor the airports nor Manta-Manaus itself."[59]

The difficulties confronting the maritime, terrestrial, and aerial dimensions of the multimodal corridor were further compounded by the challenges of its fluvial section. There was no customs office on the Napo, either at the border with Peru or in Providencia, despite the makeshift sign that Fermín had erected outside his hut, which designated Providencia as an "International Port." In the rare event of cross-border trade, customs officers had to be flown to the Amazon, or the goods had to be transported over the Andes to the customs office in Manta or Guayaquil. Furthermore, there were no fluvial regulations in Ecuadorian law, and river transport companies were obliged to comply with maritime law instead, which included taking out insurance against damaging ocean buoys and undertaking expensive stability tests to prove the safety of their barges on the high seas.[60]

These bureaucratic complications were accompanied by the same lack of commercial demand afflicting other sections of the corridor. A "Commercial Plan" for Manta-Manaus produced in 2011 observed, "Trade between Ecuador and the Brazilian Amazon is almost nonexistent," amounting to $492,000 of Ecuadorian exports to the Brazilian Amazon in 2010, whereas "imports from that region did not exist."[61] One ministerial adviser noted: "In Manaus we have held a few meetings to see what products we can import. Unfortunately, up to now we haven't had a formal interest in exporting things to Ecuador."[62] An American businessman operating in the Amazon observed: "Personally, I don't see how the numbers work. How many kilometers [from Providencia to Manaus]—three thousand? I mean, that's a long way by river! If you could run one product down and come back with other products from Brazil, then, yeah, I could see it. But [otherwise] it's a very expensive method of shipping things. . . . It doesn't seem like it's a viable project. I don't think it pencils out."[63]

An internal government report on Manta-Manaus, produced in 2014, concluded, "The fluvial dimension is totally navigable, *taking into account that we haven't arrived in Manaus as yet*, not for a lack of vessels, or owing to limitations of the river, but rather because there is no demand for our products in Brazil."[64] But though this lack of demand certainly helped explain the ongoing failure to "arrive in Manaus," the greater problem was the fact that the Ecuadorian section of the Napo was *not* navigable by ships large enough to make such a venture profitable for international commerce. This stretch of the river is shallow and meandering, and its course is continually altered by silt washed down from the Andes. A study conducted by the Inter-American Development Bank found that Manta-Manaus would require constant dredging, involving the annual movement of "over 15 million metric tons" of sediment, which would be technically complex, environmentally destructive, and "economically unsustainable."[65]

In 2015, four years after the launch of Manta-Manaus, the only company utilizing the corridor was Amazon Service, which was using only one section of the route. The managing director of Amazon Service, whose cousin was serving as minister of industry and productivity at the time, had received a generous grant from the Ecuadorian Development Bank to construct two gargantuan barges with which to demonstrate the viability of the corridor. Each barge had a capacity of 1,200 tons—three times greater than the largest barges on the river. They were being used to ship cement from the company's port in Providencia to Leticia, on the Colombian border with Brazil (although they were rumored to be smuggling subsidized gasoline and other contraband). Their immense size meant that they had to wait for heavy rains to raise the water level before they could depart and were habitually stranded on sandbanks for days or even weeks on end.[66] Such circumstances are no doubt highly inconvenient for the international cement business. But they would be utterly anathema to the global just-in-time production networks into which Manaus was supposed to be integrated. As Carlos Fermín's son and business partner himself admitted: "The risk is that the captain gets stranded, and the investor would have to run that risk. The containers have to arrive at a given date and a given hour, and if they don't then the entire production line comes to a standstill."[67]

Owners and operators of the local shipping fleet explained that even the smaller barges that worked the Ecuadorian Napo were frequently stranded, flipped over by storm surges, or sunk by hidden tree trunks. And locals who knew the river mocked the idea that it could be navigated by large cargo vessels. One peasant farmer who had lived all his life on the banks of the Napo explained: "Fighting nature is impossible! I don't know what studies and science can hope to achieve. They can clean it up and cut a channel if they like, but this river is a total rebel [*bien bandido*]!"[68] Others agreed, describing the Napo as "very treacherous"[69] and "like a woman. If you don't know her well, you won't get anywhere."[70] The only person who remained convinced of its navigability was Carlos Fermín, whose entire interoceanic fantasy had been founded on this passionate belief, and who dismissed all arguments to the contrary as the devious work of "an ugly black hand."[71]

At the launch of Manta-Manaus, Rafael Correa had channeled the spirit of Simón Bolívar, the great liberator of South America, in a heroic affirmation of the capacity for a united humanity to triumph over nature. Standing on the banks of the Napo, he insisted: "We must all put our backs into it, in order to make this dream succeed. And you know, as Bolívar said, that 'if nature opposes our designs, we will fight against her and we will win.'"[72] But the maiden voyage only served to confirm the project's intrinsic geographical unviability. A member of the presidential entourage reported that the journey downriver was "like riding a bicycle. The slowness of the Napo is enough to drive you insane!"[73] Suddenly a military speedboat came hurtling toward the barge. On board, waving and shouting, was Carlos Fermín. The owner of Amazon Service was standing with Correa at the helm and recalls the scene: "From there he shouted, '¡Presidente!' and [Correa] asked me, 'Who's that madman?' I told him, 'That's the Brazilian guy.' [Then he asked,] 'And what's he doing on a military boat?' And I said, 'I told you he was a charmer.'"[74] When Correa disembarked at Providencia, he did not visit Fermín in his home, leaving everyone else waiting outside for hours, as Fermín had claimed. "Fermín approached him and said, '¡Presidente!' [but Correa] just said, 'How are you?' and shook his hand and moved on."[75]

After Correa had disembarked, the maiden voyage turned the next bend in the river and became stranded on a sandbank. According to a newspaper report, it remained trapped there for five days. In the end it took eighteen days to reach Leticia, at which point the voyage was abandoned; Manaus was still 1,000 miles away.[76] As for Carlos Fermín, his international port had no customs office, his house had been burned down by his business rivals, and Rafael Correa—the man he considered his closest ally—had no idea who he was. A local politician who had dealt with Fermín in the past remarked, "He's all talk, nothing more." She paused to reconsider: "Or maybe he just had a great dream that wasn't realized."[77] Odebrecht's expulsion; Hutchison's departure; capital's indifference; the obstinate bulk of the Andes; the wanton caprices of the Napo . . . Like Fitzcarraldo, who hauled a steamship over a mountain only for the river to carry it back to where he had started, Fermín's dream would appear to be "subservient to a larger destiny over which he has no ultimate control."[78]

The Subtraction Protocol

The fate of Manta-Manaus recalls the words of Ryszard Kapuściński: "Development is a treacherous river, as everyone who plunges into its current knows. . . . The ship looks as if it is still traveling forward, yet . . . the prow has settled on a sandbar."[79] The Bolivarian vision of continental integration had run aground on the sandbanks of the Napo, while the grand plans of the post-neoliberal state had become entangled in geopolitical tensions and intercapitalist competition, confused with the schemes of a silver-tongued dreamer, and bamboozled by market complexities and bureaucratic absurdities. Meanwhile, however, a radical urban design project was seeking to offset the environmental risks associated with Manta-Manaus through the sustainable planning of the port in Providencia. When the Citizens' Revolution came to power in 2007, Santiago del Hierro was studying architecture at Yale. A privileged child of the Ecuadorian elite, del Hierro had been fascinated by the Amazon ever since a journey he had made there several years previously, in which he had retraced the path of the conquistadors from Quito to the coast of Brazil. He therefore followed the progress of Manta-Manaus with great interest. When Providencia was incorporated into the corridor in 2008, he began a research project on the design of the port. His project caught the attention of one of his professors, the critical urbanist Keller Easterling, who regarded the hubristic ambition of Manta-Manaus as "beyond surpassing irony."[80]

At the time, Easterling was developing an approach to architectural activism that she called "the subtraction protocol," which sought to twist the dynamics of large-scale development projects into less pathological configurations.[81] In contrast to architecture's focus on construction as "the customary answer to most problems," the subtraction protocol would operate through the creation of "active forms that gradually ratchet or leverage both clearings and concentrations of development . . . to change not only the shape, but also the organization of space."[82] Activists were encouraged to deploy the same tools used by the "political bullies who play dirty," including "duplicity" and "hoax," on the premise that "it is sneakier when David never bothers to actually kill Goliath, if he can instead use the giant's large size and many multipliers to amplify a change . . . designing a snaking chain of moves to work into and generate leverage against an intractable politics."[83]

Easterling saw Providencia as an opportunity for an intervention of precisely this kind—the creation of an "active form" that could operate within and against the spatial dynamics of Manta-Manaus, in order to transform an environmentally damaging strategy of construction into a sustainable strategy of "subtraction," which would protect instead of deplete the rain forest surrounding the port.[84] Her vision resonated with the work of the South America Project (SAP), a group of architects and planners based at the Harvard Graduate School of Design who feared that the infrastructural projects of the IIRSA would be accompanied by "the entropic, spontaneous colonization of fragile ecologies like the Amazon River Basin."[85] One of the founding members of the SAP was Roger Sherman, director of the CityLab think tank at UCLA. Sherman was working on a book titled *Fast-Forward Urbanism: Rethinking Architecture's Engagement with the City*, which included a chapter by Easterling,[86] and the SAP was assembling "design teams throughout the [Amazon] to investigate low impact alternatives capable of integrating infrastructure with ecology, city and architecture."[87]

Easterling's project was a perfect fit. Providencia was incorporated into the SAP as one of its points of intervention, and Santiago del Hierro joined Sherman in the design team for the new port city. Del Hierro visited Providencia, where he met with Carlos Fermín, who was "very supportive" of the project.[88] Indeed, according to Fermín, Correa had personally informed him of his desire to see Providencia transformed into "a beautiful city" that "preserves nature."[89] Before long, del Hierro had also secured funding for the plan from the local municipal and provincial governments, which were flush with petrodollars and closely allied with the Correa administration.

Through this catalogue of coincidences, the subtraction protocol was woven into Manta-Manaus as another thread in its elaborate tapestry of fantasies. The subversive potential of Easterling's approach, however, was diluted by its synthesis with Sherman's fast-forward urbanism, which endorsed orthodox market mechanisms, based on the conviction that "it is possible for architecture to be both critical *and* commercial, economically driven *and* political."[90] This conviction was evident in Sherman's decision to invite Greg Lindsay to design the economic strategy for Providencia. Lindsay was the coauthor of a brash manifesto of neoliberal urbanism titled *Aerotropolis: The Way We'll Live Next*, which celebrated "the aerotropolis as globalization made flesh" in the form of cities, like Dubai, constructed around airports.[91] According to Lindsay, in an era of "frictionless competition" in which "humans aren't bound by distance, but by time," the proliferation of integrated transport systems implied that "it's possible to imagine a world capital in a place that was once an absolute backwater."[92]

The radical urban transformation of "an absolute backwater" was precisely what the design team had in mind for Providencia. Drafted in 2013, their plan was titled "Divining Providencia: Building a Bio-Cultural Capital for the Amazon." The plan reproduced the strategy of *Aerotropolis*, but with international airspace replaced by the vast fluvial network of the Amazon. Following the principles of the subtraction protocol, "Divining Providencia" was designed to work with and against Manta-Manaus, by hijacking its infrastructure for environmentally sustainable enterprise and reversing its outward-oriented commodity flows into a concentration of commodity production in Providencia itself. Providencia would be transformed from a container port into the "material, scientific, and commercial repository for the biodiversity of the entire basin . . . establishing a synergy between the IIRSA, which will ferry resources there from throughout the Amazon, and the knowledge and artisanal skills of local indigenous peoples."[93] The city would be "a new type of trade zone, one that combines the global presence and exposure of free trade zones with . . . the more buyer-producer model of Fair Trade," and would also become a research center "devoted to the discovery, cataloguing, conservation and commercialization of . . . the entire Amazon basin's biodiversity."[94] Through this combination of culturally sensitive and ecologically sustainable economic activities, Sherman argued, Providencia would become "a kind of cornucopia of the Amazon."[95]

"Divining Providencia" thus deployed Easterling's strategies of subtraction and active form, not in the subversion of the urban status quo, but in the reproduction of the fantasy space of the neoliberal eco-city as "an enclosed, self-contained economic free zone."[96] Meanwhile, the strategy of hoax was being mobilized, not as a means of beating power at its own game, as Easterling had intended, but as a mechanism for displacing peasant farmers from their land and putting them to work in the city. For Sherman, the greatest threat to their plan was posed by the *colonos* who were already opening tracts of land along the new highway to Providencia. According to him, "The point [of the project] is to get all those people off that land," and "the town [itself] is a kind of hoax," functioning to lure the *colonos* into the city, on the promise of employment and the creation of "a large regional market at which what they sell could be loaded onto trucks and sent to Asia. . . . The concept of this giant market is kind of like the holy grail."[97]

The Eco-City That Didn't Exist

We decided to set out in search of this intriguing eco-city, created by some of the most illustrious design schools in the world. But when we arrived in Providencia in 2015, the city was nowhere to be found. From there we traveled to the municipal government offices in the nearby town of Shushufindi to inquire about the progress of the project. A drunken party was in full swing in the main function room. No one seemed to know or care about the "Bio-Cultural Capital of the Amazon." We were redirected to the planning department of the provincial government of Sucumbíos, which was housed in a brand-new black glass building in the center of Lago Agrio, adorned with technicolor murals of indigenous stereotypes. But its representatives were equally nonplussed, and their only suggestion was to ask the municipal government in Shushufindi. At the planning ministry in Quito, the team charged with drawing up the master plan for the Amazon had never heard of Providencia, let alone the experimental eco-city that was supposed to be there.[98] As we have seen, Providencia was not only the fluvial port of Manta-Manaus, but also one of the Anchor Projects of the IIRSA, which was the emblematic development program of UNASUR. But when I asked the Ecuadorian representative of UNASUR about the new port city, I received the same blank stare. "Providencia?" he repeated. "But isn't Providencia in northern Peru?"[99]

Sitting in a sleek restaurant in the most exclusive district of Quito, Santiago del Hierro sought the right words to express his frustration. He had been tasked with the implementation of "Divining Providencia" but had been forced to conclude that the Ecuadorian government "have no fucking idea what they are doing [*no tienen ni puta idea de lo que hacen*]."[100] But del Hierro's superiors were no less ignorant of their own circumstances. Sherman and Easterling had made only fleeting visits to Ecuador, and Lindsay never visited at all. This led to significant confusions. Lindsay claimed that Providencia was located "on the banks of the Amazon at its westernmost navigable point," although the river in question was the Napo, and the point in question was unnavigable; Sherman insisted that Providencia must "harness the shipping trade," even though there was no shipping trade; and Easterling suggested that "a widened river channel would allow the freight to flow all the way to the Pacific," despite the uncontrollable dynamics of the Napo and the unavoidable presence of the Andes.[101]

More fundamentally, the entire design team had failed to appreciate that Manta-Manaus was already an abject failure. "Divining Providencia" was therefore premised on the "sneaky" appropriation of a project that had no effective existence. The biggest hoax of all, in other words, had been played on the hoaxers themselves. By the time they drafted their plan in 2013, the company developing the Manta port had already abandoned its concession; the new highway over the Andes was deserted and disintegrating; and the Ecuadorian section of the Napo had proven to be unviable for vessels of the size required for international commerce. Indeed, ever since the ill-fated maiden voyage that became stranded on a sandbank in 2011, Manta-Manaus had disappeared from the triumphant discourses of the Correa administration, as if in silent acknowledgment of its deserted highways, vacant airports, and unnavigable watercourses.

But amid this impenetrable thicket of commercial failures, material impossibilities, bureaucratic cul-de-sacs, and institutional chaos, the Ministry of Transport and Public Works continued to quietly press ahead with the construction of the port at Providencia and the highway connecting it to the national road network. At the time of the road's completion in 2014, Providencia was an isolated *Kichwa* community of eighty or so people. The arrival of the road triggered a rush of land speculation in the community, and within a year of the road's completion, seven private ports lined the riverbank. This burgeoning entrepreneurial activity might have seemed to spell an upturn in the fortunes of Manta-Manaus. But with the exception of Amazon Service, the shipping company exporting cement to Colombia, the new businesses in Providencia were not concerned with international trade. They were oil companies. One of the private ports had been established by Geolago, a Belorussian company that conducted seismic tests to locate oil reserves in remote territories. Another was operated by Conduto, a Brazilian company that constructed economic infrastructure in Amazonian oil fields. Both companies were involved in the development of Block 43, otherwise known as "ITT" (Ishpingo-Tambococha-Tiputini), a rich and controversial oil field partly located within the Yasuni National Park, which has been identified as the most biodiverse place on Earth. During his first years in office, Correa had promoted the Yasuni-ITT initiative, which sought development funding from industrialized nations in exchange for leaving ITT unexploited. The funding was not forthcoming, however, and in August 2013 Correa announced the abandonment of the initiative and the exploitation of Block 43 by the state oil company Petroamazonas.[102]

By the time the announcement was made, the road to Providencia was almost complete. Block 43 occupies a vast extension of territory adjacent to Peru and is accessible only via the Napo. Providencia was now the nearest point on the Napo accessible by road, and the new highway, which had been designed for the heavy container traffic of Manta-Manaus, was ideal for the transportation of the materials required to construct the infrastructure for Block 43. Conduto and Geolago were not the only companies using Providencia for this end. Amazon Service had also begun using its huge barges to transport gravel to ITT.[103] And even the humble port operated by the local community was being hired out to companies shipping materials to Block 43. As an operator of one of the private ports observed, "Providencia is very much a strategic location for future oil production."[104]

In stark contrast to the harmonious vision of "Divining Providencia," this rapid process of spontaneous urbanization was taking place in the absence of any territorial planning or state regulation. As such, it reproduced the brutal dynamics of unbridled capitalist development that had characterized the region since the discovery of oil, and that the Citizens' Revolution was supposed to have brought under control. In the words of one local politician, companies "come and buy [land], and once they have bought it they do whatever they like."[105] Meanwhile, Providencia remained without piped water or sanitation, despite the fact that the increasingly heavy traffic in and out of its private ports had rendered the river water undrinkable. The privatization of the riverbank had also excluded the community from access to much of the river. Their dugout canoes now picked their way between immense diesel-spilling barges, beneath the towering steel ramparts of the oil ports, buffeted by the waves cast by speed-boats carrying oil executives to and from the airport in Coca.

The accelerating pileup of oil capital had shattered the dreams of market integration and geographical freedom that Manta-Manaus had once inspired in the inhabitants of the region. On the outskirts of Providencia, we spoke to a man who was loading a mule with plantains for sale in the local market. I asked him if he had heard of Manta-Manaus. "Oh, yes," he replied, "I've heard enough about that to send me psychotic! [¡Psicotizado con eso!]. . . . They said it was going to be a good project that would bring benefits for the community. Of course there are benefits, but only for people with lots of money who have come here to take advantage of it. The people from here can't even enter [the port], even though this is our territory." He finished loading the plantains onto his mule and went on his way with a sarcastic shout of defiant ambition: "To Manaus!"[106]

Not everyone, however, was able to laugh at the absurdity of the situation. When we arrived at the home of another peasant farmer, he came to the gate armed with a shotgun. His nerves had been shredded by the oil exploration company that had established its operations on the riverbank adjacent to his land. The company was running a huge generator for twenty-four hours a day, and we had to raise our voices to be heard above its roar. It had also cut an open sewage ditch along the side of his land, and the river breeze now infused his home with the smell of human shit. "We haven't benefited at all from Manta-Manaus," he said. "We just stand here and watch them make their money. And the poor man gets poorer, every day poorer."[107] The indigenous leader who had described Manta-Manaus as "the dream of the *Secoya* nation" explained: "There is no room for the [indigenous] nationalities, or the *colonos*, or anyone; we are just the observers of big deals between big interests. We have nothing. We are in a total desert."[108] In the terse words of another local leader: "They take all the black gold from here and leave us with nothing."[109]

Things were not going to plan for the international coalition of architects and urbanists who had formulated "Divining Providencia." The Real of capital had surged into this remote corner of the Amazon and had obliterated their fantasy of Providencia as "a new model of urbanization: one that is formally unique, socially just, and ecologically progressive . . . leveraging its position in the new export pipeline to find an international market [and] capturing transnational capital flows and recirculating them through the community."[110] Speaking from his plush office in Los Angeles, Roger Sherman shook his head in horror at the news of the proliferating oil ports. "Oh, God," he said, "that's not good. I get this looming sense that I'm going to be, you know, I'm going to realize that I was like Don Quixote, just kind of swinging at, tilting toward windmills."[111]

The Soul of Capital

What could account for the persistence of Manta-Manaus, given the extensive evidence of its material impossibility? In 2006 the IIRSA had commissioned an investigation into the navigability of the Napo and the other rivers of its Amazon Hub, which had concluded that none was appropriate for a multimodal transport corridor.[112] The report questioned the promotion of these transcontinental trade routes, noting the influence of "interest groups with specific objectives and without accurate information about the reality of the Amazon," and warning that the Amazon is "a platform for the generation of myths and false expectations, which if related to specific projects can generate 'white elephants,' resulting in the frustration of the inhabitants of the Amazon when they compare the myths to the realities."[113]

The evident unviability of Manta-Manaus, the transformation of Providencia into an oil port, and the controversy surrounding the exploitation of Block 43 led some to question the motives behind the project. One of the most vocal critics of Manta-Manaus in this regard was Guadalupe Llori, the militant leader of the ABP and prefect of Orellana who had been imprisoned by Correa in 2007 in the aftermath of the military crackdown in Dayuma. Following her release from prison eleven months later, Llori had been reelected as prefect of the province, and she had immediately resumed her confrontation with the Correa administration. For her, the strategy of the government was obvious: "It's a camouflaged way of doing things, in my opinion. They say they are going to make the port for Manta-Manaus, and instead it is serving to develop the oil industry for the exploitation of Yasuni."[114]

Such motives may have existed in the case of Providencia. But they cannot easily account for the concession of the port in Manta, the construction of a highway over the Andes, or the opening of airports across the national territory, all of which were included in Manta-Manaus, and none of which was particularly functional for the oil industry. These actions suggest that the Correa administration was genuinely committed to the success of the interoceanic corridor. From this perspective, the eventual repurposing of Providencia for the expansion of the oil frontier can be explained not as a covert strategy, but as a material expression of the inability "of state policies to determine the modality and course of accumulation within each national space of valorization," and their ultimate subordination to the logic of capital accumulation at the global scale, which operates as "an abstract form of domination."[115] The Ecuadorian Amazon had been historically incorporated into global capitalism on the basis of its oil reserves, and the transformation of Providencia into an oil port was ultimately expressive of the power of capital to dictate the modalities of its own expanded reproduction, regardless of governmental fantasies of logistical integration into global production networks. In this sense, the state can be said to succeed (in its ultimate function of assuring the conditions of capital accumulation) through the very process of its failure (to realize its fantasies).

A similar relationship exists between the Real of capital and the fantasies of capitalists themselves. The owner of a shipping company operating on the Napo had been inspired by the promise of the interoceanic corridor: "I built my barges with that vision, with the vision of Manta-Manaus. That was my illusion."[116] But the failure of the project had forced him into the oil industry. "It isn't what we had planned to do," he said, "but there is no alternative. If you don't invest in the oil business, you can't invest in anything." Another entrepreneur had built a floating hotel to transport tourists to Manaus.[117] But now it was serving the construction workers of ITT and was rumored to be a brothel. And several dredging machines were operating on the Napo. But instead of clearing channels for interoceanic trade, they were digging up sand to make the concrete for Block 43.[118]

Again, these pragmatic responses to economic necessity do not imply that Manta-Manaus was a smokescreen for a conspiratorial agenda to exploit the oil beneath Yasuni. Instead, they illustrate the extent to which, in Marx's words, "value, acting with the force of an elemental natural process, [ultimately] prevails over the foresight and the calculation of the individual capitalist."[119] This would seem to be further illustrated by the case of Carlos Fermín, whose dream now lay in ruins. In 2014 the Ministry of Transport and Public Works expropriated most of his land for the construction of the port. Fermín claimed not to have been compensated, while insisting that this was contrary to Correa's wishes and lamenting the hijacking of Providencia by the oil industry. "It hurts my soul to see this disaster," he said. "No money could make up for their ruining a project that I have struggled so hard to make happen. The president shares my vision. He's going to be upset, and I'm going to be upset. . . . Everyone has come here to speculate, to make money off the government project. [But] I'm not going to sell my soul to the devil. I prefer to be with God and sleep in peace." This conviction had inspired him to create an evangelical church in Providencia, in which he and his son preached "the marvels of the project and the word of God." His family, he claimed, "supports the community here. We are providing medicines, children's clothes, we are feeding the malnourished. Everything I have I try to share with the rest."[120]

This, however, was not how everyone understood Fermín's role in the community. In the words of one inhabitant of Providencia, Fermín "came here promising colleges, a stadium, a sports field, everything. And now [the companies] come and go, and [we] don't even have water, and he denies that he ever [promised] anything of the sort."[121] A local councilor noted that "the companies that arrive [in Providencia] go straight to [Fermín]."[122] This was confirmed by the owner of Amazon Service, who described Fermín as "a snake charmer." According to him, Fermín was using his church to demonstrate his support among the community to incoming businesses. "In the Amazon there is a great fear of the [indigenous] communities," he explained. "Businesses are scared, oil companies are scared. [Fermín] frightens anyone who arrives [in Providencia, saying,] 'If you don't do this or that [for me], I'll throw you to the community, and the community trusts in me.'"[123]

A local trader told us that he would no longer do business with Fermín, who "owes money to everyone,"[124] and the operator of one of the oil ports referred to him in English as "Bullshitter Supreme."[125] A consultant at the Ministry of Transport and Public Works confided that Fermín had been "calling us way too many times," and that the ministry had decided to investigate him.[126] According to her, the investigations had revealed that Fermín was a fugitive who had fled Brazil with "a lot of money" and entered Ecuador via the unmanned border on the Napo, without going through immigration. This was supported by an associate of Fermín, who confirmed that "he kind of left Manaus under strange circumstances. Something went wrong, and he ended up coming here."[127]

Fermín was also said to have acquired his plot in Providencia under murky circumstances. The family of the *Kichwa* man who sold him the land accused Fermín of buying it for a pittance, by getting the man drunk and making extravagant promises that were never kept. We interviewed his family in their hut on the riverbank, which was now surrounded by the private oil ports. The man had since suffered an illness that had left him mute and partially paralyzed. He left the room by pulling himself along the wall by a makeshift wooden rail. It was only then that his daughter told their story, explaining that her father blamed himself for the calamity that had befallen the community as a result of his decision to sell their land, and attributing his sickness to this burden of guilt.[128]

All the indigenous communities along the Napo between Coca and Peru had been organized as *comunas* in the 1970s and 1980s, with the sole exception of Providencia, which was therefore the only place on the river in which land was privately owned and available for purchase. This led to the suspicion that Fermín had selected the site of Providencia out of pure expediency, regardless of its potential as an international container port. One local politician insinuated that the government had been influenced by "someone who infiltrated them and lied about the river—someone interested in their building the port."[129] People with experience of navigating the Napo noted that some of the most problematic sections of the river were located immediately downstream from Providencia, and the owner of Amazon Service described confronting Fermín and telling him, "You and I both know that this port is in the wrong place!"[130] Manta-Manaus had failed. But it had successfully provided the economic infrastructure required for the oil industry. And Providencia was not in the right place for a transcontinental corridor. But it was in the perfect place to exploit the oil fields of the Ecuadorian Amazon. Following the completion of the road to Providencia, and the expropriation of his land for the construction of the official port, Fermín set up a stone-crushing factory and began producing the raw materials required for the oil infrastructure of Block 43.[131] Perhaps, beneath the ruins of his interoceanic fantasy, his real dream had come true.

The truth is indiscernible within such a confabulatory morass of dreams and nightmares. And there is a sense in which this indiscernibility is more significant than the truth itself. The conspiracy theories surrounding the failure of the port of Manta and the construction of the road to Providencia, and the rumor and innuendo swirling around Carlos Fermín, all contributed to the dense entanglement of fantasy and reality through which the spaces of capital are produced, and the accumulation of capital is achieved. As in the case of the state's construction of the road and the port, Fermín's opportunism requires no conspiratorial explanation, and it should come as no surprise. The imperative to accumulate is the drive that animates the fantasies of the capitalist, and these fantasies must ultimately be sacrificed on the altar of accumulation itself. To quote Marx once again: "As capitalist, he is only capital personified. His soul is the soul of capital."[132]

The Gorgeous Road

Over $1 billion was invested in the construction of Manta-Manaus. The aim was to open a multimodal corridor for the accelerated circulation of commodities between East Asia and Brazil, through which Ecuador would replace its dependency on oil exploitation with technologically advanced participation in globalized networks of production and exchange. But the failure to develop the port of Manta, the inadequacy of the road across the Andes, and the unviability of the Napo as a commercial waterway resulted in a stark absence of international commerce passing through the corridor. Meanwhile, Peru was advancing in the construction of its own interoceanic corridor, the Panama Canal was being expanded, and the construction of another interoceanic corridor had been announced in Nicaragua, backed by $50 billion of Chinese capital.[133] Manta-Manaus would therefore seem to constitute a classic case of a failed "spatial fix,"[134] in which overaccumulated petrodollars were speculatively channeled into the production of a new economic space that was rejected by capital. But this is not the whole story. Capital did not simply reject the project but repurposed its infrastructures for the expansion of the oil frontier. Manta-Manaus therefore functioned to reinforce the economic model that it was supposed to be replacing, through the staging of a spatial phantasmagoria that was itself a materialization of massive oil rents.

This chapter has traced the twists of this paradoxical tale, through which I have sought to disentangle the complex relationship between utopian fantasies and the Real of capital in the production of social space. The chapter began by demonstrating the constitutive role of fantasy in framing social reality in ways that both conceal and contribute to the underlying dynamics of capitalist development. A strategy shaped by the drive of capital toward the annihilation of space by time was promoted by the post-neoliberal state as the fulfillment of subaltern desires for inclusion in an imagined world of market integration and geographical freedom. Meanwhile, the same destructive drive was framed by the architects of "Divining Providencia" as a process that could be sneakily inverted into an alternative accumulation strategy, through which the resources of the Amazon would be fashioned into environmentally friendly commodities by the voluntary proletarians of a harmonious eco-city.

These dreams captured the imaginations of politicians, entrepreneurs, and local populations and functioned to "mutually obfuscate . . . the antagonism in question."[135] In practice, however, they were shattered by the materiality of this antagonism, which illustrates the ways through which such fantasies are undermined by the Real they deny. Through the construction of the interoceanic corridor, all the repressed contradictions of uneven geographical development came to reassert themselves in the forms of intercapitalist competition, geopolitical rivalry, and the recalcitrance of nature. Meanwhile, the imperative of endless accumulation drove the expansion of the oil frontier and appropriated the infrastructure of Manta-Manaus, while triggering a chaotic process of accumulation by dispossession that overwhelmed the utopian vision of "Divining Providencia."

But the entanglement of fantasy and the Real is more twisted still. Beyond their dreams of insatiable markets and accelerated modernization, individual capitalists and the capitalist state are ultimately subordinated to the imperative of the expanded reproduction of capital, which is impervious to their intentions. The incorporation of Providencia into the economic infrastructures of the oil industry shattered the fantasies of Manta-Manaus and "Divining Providencia." But it also contributed to the economic growth through which the Citizens' Revolution was politically legitimated, while guaranteeing the solvency of Carlos Fermín and other entrepreneurs who were initially inspired to invest in the interoceanic corridor, but who were eventually obliged to abandon this dream and adapt their investments to the accumulative imperative of the oil boom. The Real of capital thus advances through the creative destruction of its own fantasies, which are both constitutive of the materiality of global capitalism and crushed within the crucible of its implacable dynamics. This, to quote *Fitzcarraldo* once more, is "the reality of dreams."[136]

In telling the tale of Manta-Manaus, I have avoided projecting more coherence onto reality than it possesses, in accordance with the principle of *making sense of the fact that things don't make sense*. Rather than editing out the remarkable catalogue of incongruencies and irrationalities that I encountered in my research, the chapter has lingered over the preposterous plans, extraordinary errors, logistical impossibilities, byzantine conspiracy theories, and intractable bureaucratic labyrinths that constitute the baroque edifice of Manta-Manaus. This overwhelming accumulation of anomalies serves to disrupt the slick self-representations of state and capital. The post-neoliberal state is not a gleaming machine of omniscient planning and omnipotent territorialization, but a muddy field of congealed resource rents, littered with ruined flights of fancy and ridiculous roads to nowhere. And capital does not circulate smoothly through this convoluted institutional and geographical landscape, but blunders blindly forward, staggering from one fuck-up to another and frantically rifling through an interminable repertoire of bad ideas and ham-fisted improvisations.

There is, however, one final twist to this story. We have seen how, through a litany of half-baked schemes, absurd oversights, and drastic miscalculations, Providencia was rapidly and chaotically transformed from an isolated indigenous community into a frontier port of a planetary oil boom, where the unrestrained agglomeration of capital threatened to collapse all social structures into a space of absolute disintegration. But these forces also gave rise to an insurgent utopia.

Providencia was founded by *Kichwa* families, whose forefathers had been brought from the highlands to the Amazon as slaves during the rubber boom and put to work on a nearby hacienda. The hacienda was abandoned in the 1970s, and the families were dismissed and left destitute. They moved upriver to an uninhabited tract of jungle, where they worked to clear the land and establish their community. Unlike other indigenous communities in the area, they did not obtain communal land rights, which facilitated Carlos Fermín's purchase of their land for the construction of his port. Fermín told them about the interoceanic corridor and the riches it would bring. For this tiny isolated community, born of a history of slavery and dispossession and persisting on the most distant margins of state and society, Fermín's vision promised a miraculous transformation. But when the construction of the road was announced, they began to receive warnings of displacement and threats of expropriation. In 2010 they decided to organize to defend themselves against this eventuality. Together they formed an association called *Sumak Ñambi*— "Gorgeous Road"—the name of which reflected the hopes that they still invested in Manta-Manaus.

Sumak Ñambi was established on the principle that no members could sell their land. But as the construction of the road progressed, the pressures of land speculation increased around the port, and in 2012 the community fragmented into two opposing factions, one of which withdrew from the association and began to subdivide their land and sell it off to oil companies and other outside interests. This division was accompanied by further threats of dispossession; the completion of the road; the building of the official port and the multiple private oil ports; the arrival and departure of huge barges shifting materials down to Block 43; and Fermín's construction of a stone-crushing factory in what had been the heart of the community. By March 2015 the few remaining thatched huts of Sumak Ñambi had been engulfed by a churning, roaring vortex of frenzied agglomeration. Confronted with this increasingly desperate situation, the president of Sumak Ñambi, Nelson Castillo, called an assembly. Shouting over the growling engines, blaring reverse sirens, and crashing rockslides of a constant line of trucks emptying gravel onto barges bound for Block 43, Castillo warned of the gravity of their predicament, and he insisted on the urgent need to act: "Look at the machinery they bring here every day, the pollution, the impacts that we suffer without compensation. . . . We are peaceful, gullible people, waiting for the goodwill of someone who might one day decide to help us, when instead we should be demanding our rights. We are going to keep being dispossessed little by little, as is already happening. [But] our organization is based on never having sold a meter of land to anyone. . . . It is time for us to wake up and live in unity!"[137]

Sumak Ñambi decided that the best way to defend their claim to the land would not be to seek to salvage the despoiled fragments of the rural space that remained to them, but rather to assert their right to the city by creating their own urban project on the land they still possessed.[138] Unable to afford an urban planner, they invited a local topographer to draw up a plan in return for a plot of land in the town. The resulting plan located the town in twenty-five acres of rain forest along the riverbank to the east of the official port. Five quadrangular blocks were divided into sixty lots, each of which had space for a house and a large garden. The plan also included a plaza, a cemetery, a soccer pitch, a volleyball court, and a communal meetinghouse.

For an impoverished community faced with imminent dispossession, the realization of such an ambitious vision was seemingly impossible. Not long after Castillo's speech to the assembly, however, a shipping company attempted to buy their remaining riverside land with the aim of opening another private port. Rather than refusing the offer on the basis of the non-alienability of their land, Sumak Ñambi made a counterproposal: in exchange for the lease of a space for the port, the company would cut and surface the roads for their town. Within two months the roads had been sliced through the jungle, and the felled trees provided the wood for the construction of the houses. Every weekend Sumak Ñambi gathered in *minga* (collective community labor), and the town began to take form.

There was nothing overtly utopian about this humble urban project. It reproduced the conventional spatial form of oil towns across the region and was hacked from the jungle with the same ferocity as the private oil ports. It expressed no political ideology and did not aspire to transcend or subtract itself from the dynamics of global capital accumulation. Yet it contained an insurgent utopian kernel—the resolute decision of a historically marginalized community to collectively assert its equal right to the very dream that threatened its destruction. The construction of this simple settlement materialized the presence of those who had been written out of the utopian fantasies of Manta-Manaus and "Divining Providencia." In the words of Alain Badiou: "A change of the world is real when an inexistent of the world starts to exist in the same world with maximum intensity."[139]

The response of the state was swift and uncompromising. As soon as it had been informed of the situation, the municipal government imposed a legal order that halted construction and prevented any further development of the site. The municipality was still financing "Divining Providencia," and Sumak Ñambi's town was being constructed on land that had been designated as a sustainable industrial park for the innovative eco-products of the Amazon. The absurdity of the situation, of course, was that the Napo was not commercially navigable, Providencia had become a de facto oil port, and Manta-Manaus and "Divining Providencia" already lay in ruins. A flourishing insurgent utopia was therefore being extinguished by a utopian fantasy that would never be realized.

The irony ran deeper still. By hijacking the accumulative logic of capital for the financing of an autonomous urban project that subverted the schemes of the state, Sumak Ñambi had come to embody the very principles on which "Divining Providencia" had been based, demonstrating how, in Keller Easterling's own words, "the spectacular failures and powers of infrastructure space [can] inspire nothing less than a different organ of design."[140] Indeed, Sumak Ñambi represented a far more successful actualization of this project than "Divining Providencia" itself, which had been reduced to a parody of precisely the kind of "self-congratulatory or redemptive master-plan" that the subtraction protocol had been designed to undermine.[141] Roger Sherman was now employed by Gensler, the biggest architecture company in the world, which had selected "Divining Providencia" to exhibit at the Venice and Rotterdam biennales of 2016. In a blog on the company website, Sherman described Providencia as "a new port town . . . that is an innovative model of sustainable development. Its design is not just environmentally progressive, but socially and economically as well . . . drawing upon indigenous skills and knowledge [and] raising the standard of living for those peoples in the process."[142] The article went on to explain the layout of the installations at the two biennales. Like the displacement at work in a dream, the fantasy space of "Divining Providencia" was detached from the brutal materiality of Providencia and projected onto the alternative reality of a table in a luxury restaurant:

> At Rotterdam . . . a dining table calls attention to the worldwide consumption of resources, telling through its place settings, plates, glasses and serving dishes how the design [of Providencia] harnesses the shipping trade to instigate local means of production and improve living conditions. Chairs at the table invite spectators . . . to linger and "digest" the project through text, pictures and maps. A tablecloth delineates global trade routes . . . as they pass through the Amazon and Providencia in particular. . . . At Venice, the dining table becomes interactive, comprised of five distinct layers of information

about the project. . . . Each layer is subdivided into a tiled grid of "placemats" available for gallery goers to tear off and take with them as souvenirs of their "visit" to Providencia.[143]

Meanwhile, amid an avalanche of oil infrastructures on the other side of the world, an impoverished indigenous community struggled against its dispossession in the name of this fictitious scheme. In short, "If you're caught in another's dream, you're fucked."[144]

4

Cities of Black Gold

With cities it is as with dreams.

Italo Calvino, Invisible Cities

In a delirious dream about an imaginary socialist revolution, the labor minister might be called Karl Marx. It was therefore entirely appropriate that one of the original architects of the Citizens' Revolution should be a university professor named Carlos Marx Carrasco, who was duly appointed minister of labor of the new revolutionary government. Unsurprisingly, Marx Carrasco felt obliged to live up to his name. In 2014 he published a series of articles in the national press in which he set out a utopian vision for "the original accumulation of twenty-first-century socialism."[1] His vision drew on Karl Marx's theory of primitive accumulation, according to which capitalist social relations are founded on the violent separation of the peasantry from the land, which creates a class of people who are forced to sell their labor power to survive.[2] Marx Carrasco affirmed his namesake's theory. But he claimed that Ecuador was in the process of replacing primitive accumulation with a socialist alternative. In contrast to capitalism, he noted, socialism is a "collective construction" in which "everything that is done has a direct relation to the common good." He went on to argue that "seven years of the Citizens' Revolution have laid the foundations . . . for twenty-first-century socialism." But "just as capitalist production needs its 'original sin'—primitive accumulation—so the development of socialism necessarily requires . . . 'the original accumulation of socialism.'" In contrast to the primitive accumulation of capital, this socialist form of original accumulation would be achieved through "the exploitation of nonrenewable resources" without the dispossession of the peasantry.[3]

Ecuador's principal "nonrenewable resource," of course, was oil. Before the Citizens' Revolution, as we have seen, the exploitation of this resource had provided a textbook case of the dispossession and ecological destruction associated with the primitive accumulation of capital. After coming to power in 2007, Correa had taken advantage of a boom in petroleum prices to renegotiate oil contracts and strengthen the role of the state in the Ecuadorian oil industry. The most significant of these reforms was the 2010 Hydrocarbons Law, which dramatically increased the government's share in oil revenues from 13 to 87 percent, and companies were obliged to comply or face expropriation. Most companies reluctantly agreed to these terms, while the newly formed state oil company, Petroamazonas, took over the abandoned fields of those that did not. These reforms resulted in a significant increase in state revenues, which were channeled into health, education, welfare, and infrastructural programs across the country.[4]

This transformation was embodied in the planned construction of two hundred Millennium Cities throughout the Amazon as iconic spatial symbols of the Citizens' Revolution, in which the marginalized and impoverished indigenous peoples of the region would finally reap the rewards of the oil extracted from their territories. In October 2013, as described in the opening pages of this book, Correa inaugurated the first Millennium City of Playas de Cuyabeno. In his speech, he eulogized the modernity of the city and praised "the great dreamers and promoters of this marvel that today is a reality." Celebrating the transformative powers of oil, Correa acknowledged that "the Amazon was once a land of abandonment and plunder." The "curse of the Amazon," however, had not been the hydrocarbon reserves that it contained but "the corruption of the long, sad neoliberal night. . . . When managed well, our natural resources can be a blessing . . . they can construct the *buen vivir* of all peoples, and here is the proof!" He concluded with a rallying cry for the collective construction of a socialist future: "Extractivism does not condemn us to capitalism. . . . Everything depends on political power. And the Ecuadorian people know that with the Citizens' Revolution the power is finally in their hands! . . . This is the new Amazon! . . . *Hasta la victoria siempre!*"[5]

Correa's words expressed the utopian promise of the original accumulation of twenty-first-century socialism, according to which a new mode of accumulation was destined to replace the violent establishment of capitalist social relations with the rational exploitation and collective appropriation of the natural resources of the Amazon. The first Millennium City stood as a spectacular materialization of this promise and as proof of the post-neoliberal nation that the Citizens' Revolution was bringing into existence. As such, it seemed to continue the modern tradition of the city as the definitive spatial expression of the utopian dream, in which "whole cities are laid out in the mind."[6] This tradition has been celebrated by the utopian Marxist Ernst Bloch, who praised the "daytime wishful dreams" of "castles in the air."[7] But as Freud has pointed out, dreams are very peculiar things, whose interpretation must extend beyond the level of their symbolic wish fulfillment to "elucidate the processes which underlie [their] strangeness and obscurity."[8] The same is true of cities. As Italo Calvino once noted, "Cities, like dreams, are made of desires and fears, even if the thread of their discourse is secret, their rules are absurd, their perspectives deceitful, and everything conceals something else."[9]

Like the interpretation of dreams, the exploration of utopian cities cannot therefore limit itself to the level of their "manifest content"—their overt ideological messages and administrative ambitions. Instead, it must also delve into their "latent content"—a deeper layer of desires, conflicts, and antagonisms that give rise to utopian fantasies, and which such fantasies are structured to conceal.[10] This chapter approaches the Millennium Cities in these terms. It begins at the level of their official discourse before descending through the collapsing layers of a utopian dream, in which each apparently solid foundation is revealed as another fantasy.

Resources That Build Happiness

The 2010 Hydrocarbons Law stipulated that 12 percent of the royalties of every barrel of oil extracted from the Amazon would be reinvested in the region. In 2011 a public company called Ecuador Estratégico (Strategic Ecuador) was created to administer these funds. Between 2011 and 2014, Ecuador Estratégico invested over $850 million in development projects, including schools, roads, houses, clinics, water systems, telephone lines, and sewage treatment centers throughout the Amazon. These projects were promoted in leaflets, magazines, videos, television advertisements, and information stands, and on billboards scattered along roadsides across the region. Every element of this publicity campaign featured a stylized image of an "e"-shaped oil spigot spurting a rainbow-colored flower, together with the company slogans: "Resources that build happiness" and "Dreams are transformed into reality with the Citizens' Revolution."[11]

These images and slogans conveyed the phantasmagorical power of modern infrastructures on the peripheries of global capitalism, where they are the conduits not only of material flows, but also of "the aestheticized dreams of tomorrow's utopia."[12] This dimension was further evoked in a free magazine called *Estratégico*, which focused on a different development sector in each of its monthly issues, treating its themes not only in terms of their material benefits, but also as the fulfillment of utopian dreams. The first issue led with the following editorial message: "It might seem easy to enumerate the achievements of our enterprise—easy in terms of kilometers of road, of number of schools constructed, of functioning health centers, of housing projects, of water and sanitation systems, of computer centers, of electricity projects, etc. But what we are doing goes beyond this. It is invaluable, because [it] has changed lives, has created opportunities, and, above all else, has made it possible to realize an Ecuador that once was only a dream."[13] Each issue of *Estratégico* included a "Literary Pause," in which the infrastructure of the month was romanticized in a poem. The first issue featured a poem that represented roads as sentient beings who protect those who travel on them: "And without us knowing they care for us / And in a way they have their own life."[14] Another issue, on communications infrastructure, was titled "Connecting Dreams" and opened with a poem by Walt Whitman, which included the line "Never stop dreaming, because in a dream, man is free."[15]

The utopian promise of these spatial phantasmagorias was entangled with the fetish quality of the oil that sprang from the ground beneath them, which seemed to transform into money in midair before falling back to earth in the shape of the infrastructures themselves. In the pages of *Estratégico*, oil was personified and endowed with agency in the form of a drilling rig with waving arms and a smiling face, which announced the latest infrastructure projects beneath the slogan "Oil constructs and connects."[16] Billboards declared that "oil improves your community" and "oil propels *buen vivir*." And Correa repeatedly invoked the magical powers of oil in his inauguration of infrastructural projects throughout the Amazon, announcing, "Today, oil is a blessing for Amazonian communities: it is oil revenues that allow us to free these historically forgotten communities from poverty."[17]

In October 2010 Correa drew the first barrel of oil from the Paña-cocha field, which was the first extraction project to be undertaken by the new state company, Petroamazonas.[18] This was a highly significant moment in the construction of the new oil politics. The inauguration took place in the midst of the renegotiation of foreign oil contracts, and Pañacocha was located in a region of the Amazon that had previously been part of Block 15, the concession for which had been held by the American company Occidental before its expulsion in 2006 in the aftermath of the August Uprising of the ABP.[19] The opening of the well therefore embodied the reassertion of sovereign control over the natural resources on which the legitimacy of the Citizens' Revolution depended.

Dressed in the hard hat and blue denim of an Ecuadorian oil worker, Correa declared that the field would provide $650 million of annual income for the Ecuadorian state, and he triumphantly announced: "We are not just inaugurating an oil field. We are inaugurating a new petroleum era!"[20] He then presented the local communities of Pañacocha and Playas de Cuyabeno with an enormous symbolic check for $21.2 million, which would be dedicated to their development.[21] The check seemed to demonstrate his commitment to the original accumulation of twenty-first-century socialism. In his words, it confirmed that "those who used to be in the last place, the most forgotten, are now in the first place of the entire country, because this is the source of the natural resources that have maintained all Ecuadorians for so many years. Congratulations!"[22] He shook hands with the leaders of the two communities, and the ceremony moved toward its conclusion, although we will have cause to return to it before the end of the chapter.

Soon after the ceremony, it was announced that the check would be invested in the transformation of Pañacocha and Playas de Cuyabeno into the first two Millennium Cities.[23] Ecuador Estratégico was formed a year later, and the Millennium Cities became its most iconic project, in which all the infrastructures romanticized in the pages of *Estratégico* were assembled in a single place, replete with "basic services, streetlights, sidewalks, curbs, green spaces, wireless telephones, computer centers, and even Millennium Schools."[24] In the Millennium City, a multiplicity of infrastructural enchantments and petroleum fetishes were concentrated in the ultimate utopian form of the modern city itself.

A Star Fallen from the Sky

The inauguration of the first Millennium City in 2013 coincided with the launch of a new National Development Plan. The plan outlined "the socialism of *buen vivir*," in which the original accumulation of twenty-first-century socialism would be combined with a radical transformation of everyday life:

> The socialism of *buen vivir* questions the hegemonic accumulation regime, which is to say, the neoliberal form of producing, growing, and distributing, and proposes a transition to a society in which life itself is the supreme good. . . . This is the utopia that guides our path. . . . It is based on an emancipatory transformation of existing social relations, which aims to rebalance social rhythms, abolish the gendered division of labor, and reduce the pressures of work in favor of other dimensions of social existence: creative luxury, art, eroticism, democratic participation, festive celebration, care for people and nature, and participation in community activities.[25]

The Millennium Cities represented an ideal opportunity to implement this "emancipatory transformation" in the production of a new urban form. But the first Millennium City of Playas de Cuyabeno bore no resemblance to the radical vision of ludic collectivism contained in the National Development Plan. Instead, it took the form of a conservative fantasy of twentieth-century American suburbia, magically transposed into an isolated corner of the Amazon. Neat rows of identical white houses were evenly spaced along straight streets and centered on the local police station and the community soccer pitch. There were green lawns and picnic tables, and a little red fire hydrant stood on every corner. The state newspaper described Playas de Cuyabeno as "a modern indigenous community" comprising "71 houses, a Millennium School, a market, two laboratories (one for computing and the other for science), a health center, an administrative area, sports fields, and viewpoints."[26] Each house was valued at $60,000 and equipped with water, electricity, sanitation, an electric cooker, pots, pans, a refrigerator, beds, modern furnishings, a telephone, and a computer with an internet connection.[27]

Despite its incongruity with the radical utopian vision of the National Development Plan, the mainstream modernity of the Millennium City resonated with Correa's understanding of economic development. As we have seen, notwithstanding his occasional invocations of socialism, Correa was a neostructuralist economist who believed that "economic policy should explicitly integrate . . . human and social capital."[28] From this perspective, as an earlier plan had made clear, the task of urban policy was to "guarantee equal access to infrastructure, public services, and knowledge. . . . Through this process, urban centers can be integrated on an improved social basis into the processes of the globalization of capital."[29]

During one of his first visits to the Amazon as president of Ecuador, Correa had drawn attention to the stark contrast between the modern luxuries enjoyed by oil company managers in their heavily guarded compounds and the poverty and abandonment of the communities beyond their walls. As a local representative of Ecuador Estratégico recalls,

Correa insisted that "the communities must be equal [to the oil camps]. They must have electricity, running water, sports facilities. . . . The Millennium Cities emerged from this. If an oil engineer eats well, rests well, enjoys himself, has water, electricity, a soccer pitch, a nice place to hang out, then the population should have the same."[30]

The Millennium Cities were therefore an embodiment not of the socialism of *buen vivir*, but of Correa's own modernizing utopia. As such, they reproduced what James C. Scott has described as the "high modernist ideology" of twentieth-century urbanism, which "envisioned a sweeping, rational engineering of all aspects of social life in order to improve the human condition."[31] This ideology was evident in Correa's celebration of the Millennium Cities. In a televised address to the nation in 2014, for example, Correa emphasized the modernity that the first two Millennium Cities had delivered to the indigenous communities in the region of the Pañacocha oil fields: "The 'before and after' is spectacular! From communities that lived by fishing on the riverbanks in conditions of subsistence to tremendous upper-class communities [*tremendas comunidades peluconsisimas*]! Now we have communities with Millennium Schools, police stations, health centers, a house for every family, connectivity, telecommunications. . . . All thanks to the fact that their territories have a strategic oil project. Now oil is no longer a curse! [Now] these resources are a blessing!"[32]

As Holston argues in his analysis of the utopian city of Brasília, the staging of this "utopian difference" between "an imagined and desired future" and "the negation of existing conditions" is central to the aesthetic of the developmental state.[33] But Correa's modernizing commitment to the liberation of indigenous communities from the supposed backwardness of subsistence and tradition was challenged by critics who drew attention to the disciplinary regulations imposed in the Millennium Cities, where houses were allocated only to married couples, dogs and chickens could not be kept, food crops could not be grown, the exterior of the houses could not be modified, and *chicha*—the local *Kichwa* drink—could not be brewed. From this perspective, the Millennium Cities constituted "a civilizing model for the Amazon" that had been designed as "concentration camps for indigenous and peasant populations stripped of their lands, with the aim of controlling and disciplining them."[34] This "accelerated modernity," it was argued, "equates the mode of life to be abandoned with poverty and marginalization, when in fact it implies greater autonomy, a better use of local resources, and alternative civilizational values appropriate to a jungle community."[35]

Despite these criticisms, however, Correa's "high modernist ideology" would appear to have infused the dreams of the inhabitants of the Millennium Cities themselves. At the inauguration of the first Millennium City of Playas de Cuyabeno, the state newspaper quoted one grateful woman as saying, "Now that I have a dignified dwelling it feels as if I'm dreaming,"[36] and another exclaimed: "I feel like I'm in one of those big hotels. This is my American dream!"[37] Meanwhile, in the second Millennium City of Pañacocha, one elderly man said he was living in "paradise";[38] another recited a poem he had written, which depicted the city as "A star fallen from the sky / On the banks of the River Napo."[39]

At the inauguration of Playas de Cuyabeno, Correa seized on this enthusiasm to launch a passionate defense of his vision of modernity as the collective construction of a utopian future:

> Misery is not part of culture, it is a consequence of injustice ... and it must be overcome as quickly as possible. .... Families without houses, without water, without sanitation, without electricity, without technology, without adequate schools, without health centers. This is how our ancestral peoples live, and this is what certain confused people call "culture" or

"tradition." We have to break with . . . the belief that misery is normal, part of folklore, part of identity, part of culture, especially of our ancestral peoples. . . . We are constructing the nation of tomorrow, and we must not reject the future for the sake of those who want to return us to the past![40]

But beneath the sound and fury something else was going on. Despite their bitterly opposed positions regarding the relative merits of Western modernity and indigenous lifeworlds, Correa and his critics shared a common understanding of the Millennium Cities as a meticulous developmental project devoted to radical modernization. And *this is precisely what the Millennium Cities were not.*

Surreal Existing Socialism

"To dare to live a dream is to live a fantasy of the impossible." These words were emblazoned on the wall of the Millennium School in Playas de Cuyabeno, which included "classrooms and laboratories for information technology, languages, physics, chemistry, and natural sciences, as well as a library, sports grounds, and other infrastructures."[41] The words were supposed to encourage students to follow their dreams. But seen after weeks spent wandering the surreal streets of the Millennium Cities, they struck me as a satirical commentary on the cities themselves. We visited Playas de Cuyabeno in July 2015, less than two years after its inauguration. By this time the Millennium School was barely functioning. The internet connection had been lost, and the computer laboratories were untouched. The school had twelve teachers to cover eighteen positions, and classes were being taught by the secretary, the librarian, the security guard, and the caretaker. The situation was the same in the second Millennium City of Pañacocha, which we visited in June 2015, less than eighteen months after its launch. In this case, the security guard was teaching fourth grade, the operator of the school canoe was covering literature classes, and the librarian was teaching chemistry, despite having no knowledge of the subject.

The other modern institutions of the Millennium Cities were in similar states of dysfunction and disrepair. The health clinic in Pañacocha was providing only first aid, and anyone requiring further treatment was forced to travel five hours upriver to the city of Coca. In Playas de Cuyabeno the clinic had been closed indefinitely. The doctor had left two months previously and had not been replaced. The police stations had no cells for holding prisoners and no launches to transfer detainees elsewhere. Stripped of any substantive authority, the police were incapable of enforcing the draconian regulations of the Millennium Cities: people kept dogs and raised chickens, *chicha* was widely prepared and openly consumed, and haphazard structures were being erected in the spaces around the houses. The policemen languished in their empty offices or pedaled morosely around the Millennium Cities on bicycles mounted with little blue and red lights.

The wide streets and raised sidewalks of the Millennium Cities would seem to be designed for motor vehicles. But there were no cars. Indeed, there was no road access to either city, and the streets simply ran to the edge of town before stopping short at the verge of the jungle. In both cities, the telephone and internet systems had failed, and irregularities in the electricity supply had destroyed cookers and refrigerators. The houses had been constructed with cheap plaster walls designed to resemble concrete, which were already starting to deteriorate. Playas de Cuyabeno had been built on an exposed riverbank that was rapidly washing away. Flood barriers had been installed but were already collapsing back into the churning water. In Pañacocha the park benches along the riverside had been built with their backs to the river. No one ever sat on those benches. And no one in either city had any idea what the ornamental fire hydrants were supposed to be for.[42]

At the launch of the second Millennium City of Pañacocha in January 2014, Correa had assured the inhabitants, "There will undoubtedly be an economic boom, because the whole world would love to live in a community like this!"[43] But this boom had not been forthcoming. Jobs and agricultural projects had been promised but had not materialized. And although water and electricity were being provided free of charge, inhabitants had been informed that service charges would soon be introduced. Faced with a lack of monetary income, combined with the threat of charges that they could ill afford, many people had begun to abandon the cities and return to the jungle. One inhabitant of Pañacocha described the everyday experience of this perplexing reality: "They say the houses are pretty, so our situation has improved. But they aren't worth anything to us, because we're just sitting here. What are we supposed to do? There's no work. [They told us] everything was going to improve; that we would all have work; that education, health, our lives were going to get better. But things have gotten worse and now we don't know how we are going to pay [the bills]. People are asking, 'What we are doing here?' The houses are being abandoned."[44]

By the time we arrived in Pañacocha, many of the houses stood empty, and the city was falling apart. A member of the local council explained: "The government came and completed the project and that was that. Now they've just left us here."[45] Vivid green slime stretched down the interior walls of the vacant government offices. Grass was growing through the streets, the market was deserted, the public toilets were broken, and the playing field was a thick mass of vegetation crawling with venomous snakes. One of the two water pumps had broken five months previously, and water was available for only three hours a day. The drainage system was frequently blocked, causing roads to flood and mosquitoes to breed in stagnant pools. The sewage system had also broken, and a stream of effluent filled the road beside the Millennium School.

The depth of dysfunction was even greater in Tereré, which had been constructed several miles upriver to house members of the *comuna* of Pañacocha whose land was located a long distance from the Millennium City and who had not wanted to move there. Tereré was a single overgrown street, one end jutting into the rainforest, and the other petering out near the riverbank before reaching a port that had been promised but never built. There were fifteen houses, but only one was occupied. There was no electricity, and yet each house had been equipped with the refrigerator and computer that were standard issue for the Millennium City. There was no running water or sewage system either, and after heavy rain the shit would rise out of the toilet bowls.

Measured against the utopian discourse with which Correa had launched the Millennium Cities, their farcical reality confronted their inhabitants with "utopia as it were backward, or from the other side of the mirror, [an] incomprehensible area of radically other space."[46] A man who had abandoned Playas de Cuyabeno and returned to his land on the other side of the river observed: "All of this has made us feel that it is like a screen, and in the end [the government] has forgotten about us. At first it was beautiful but now it is falling apart."[47] This sentiment was shared by an inhabitant of Pañacocha: "They come and say 'Wonderful! What lovely houses! How *bonito*.' But all the same it is just an appearance and now the facade is being destroyed."[48]

I shared their sense of disorientation. The Millennium Cities did not constitute a genuinely modernizing project in the positive sense evoked by Correa's utopian vision, or in the pejorative sense deployed by their critics. Transubstantiated from oil revenues into mirages of modern urbanism springing miraculously into existence in the midst of the Amazon rain forest, they were cities without work, filled with roads without cars, schools without teachers, clinics without doctors, police stations without cells, computers without internet, and little red fire hydrants with no discernible function whatsoever. As such, they recalled the Potemkin villages of eighteenth-century Russia—fake villages constructed to give the fleeting impression of a flourishing economy to passing dignitaries. And just as Prince Grigory Potemkin had created his "miniature utopia" on the banks of the Dnieper River to deceive Catherine the Great,[49] so Ecuador Estratégico had collaborated with Petroamazonas in the staging of the Millennium Cities on the banks of the Napo and the Aguarico, while ensuring that Correa's experience of their modernity was meticulously controlled. Both Millennium Cities were inhabited before their official inauguration, and many of their failings were apparent by the time of Correa's arrival. At Playas de Cuyabeno, for example, residents had already complained about the absence of lighting on the dock and the unreliability of the internet in the school. On the morning of the inauguration, the lighting was installed, but it was removed again as soon as Correa had departed; the school internet began to work just before his arrival but collapsed again soon afterward.[50]

In January 2014 the inhabitants of Pañacocha arrived at its inauguration with placards detailing the extent of the problems in the Millennium City. But the placards were confiscated by security, and the demonstrators were prevented from communicating with Correa. Before the president's arrival, Pañacocha swarmed with Petroamazonas workers, and "even the bosses . . . came to clean and sort things out."[51] One inhabitant recalls Correa being led to a house in which the telephone connection had been prepared in advance: "The president arrives, makes a call, sees that the internet works, and there you have it! And afterward there was nothing. It all went."[52]

Correa was suitably impressed by his experience, after which he gave an impassioned speech announcing: "We will continue to sow the Amazon with Millennium Communities! Just as Pañacocha has been transformed, just as Playas de Cuyabeno has been transformed, so we will radically transform the reality of our Amazon!"[53] But storm clouds were gathering, and the managers of Petroamazonas were concerned that heavy rains would delay the departure of the presidential helicopter and reveal the drainage problems in the city. As soon as his speech was over, Correa was whisked away. The situation was summed up by one inhabitant: "They didn't even let the poor guy walk the streets. The Petroamazonas people were stuck to him like glue to make sure he didn't wander off anywhere. They had selected a specific house for him to visit, and that was it. They led him around like he was blind. . . . He went to the field and gave his speech, and he thinks that everything has been sorted out and that everyone is happy."[54]

Like the hero of Peter Weir's *The Truman Show*, who is unaware that his small-town American existence is an elaborately staged fake, Correa strolled through these simulations of American suburbia, delighted by the modernity of his surroundings and apparently unaware that their success was being staged for his benefit. But what had been the point of the Millennium Cities in the first place? Why invest vast resources in the construction of entire towns, and then just walk away and let them rot? One night, on the way from the port of Pañacocha to the house where we were staying, I paused for a moment in the middle of the city. The night was unusually clear and still. The smoke rising from the gas flare of a distant oil field was a shifting mass illuminated by hidden flames. A streetlight flickered fitfully. Toads croaked in the undergrowth of the abandoned soccer pitch. The road was still flooded from the afternoon rain. The sense of senselessness was overwhelming. Was the city a pure fetish? A hollow shell collapsing in on itself? A material residue of the Real of capital, whose spectral presence could be glimpsed in the glow thrown on that cloud?

Jungle Gasoline

The petroleum from the Pañacocha oil field is piped under the Napo to the processing center in Edén. Swinging in his hammock, an inhabitant of Edén gazed across the river at the shimmering mirage of the Millennium City. He could not understand why the *comuna* of Pañacocha had been chosen to receive it. After all, as he pointed out, Pañacocha had just one oil well nearby, whereas "Edén has one hundred and fifty. But since they started drilling they've never given us anything."[55] The president of the parish council of Cuyabeno similarly noted that "for the other communities of the parish it's unjust, because they've spent millions of dollars [on Playas de Cuyabeno] while the other communities have received nothing."[56] When I asked the inhabitants of Pañacocha why they had been chosen to receive a Millennium City, they seemed equally nonplussed. "We haven't got a clue," one old man replied.[57] "I don't know why they gave it to us," another said with a shrug. "No other president has ever given me as much as a bottle of water."[58]

One afternoon in the restaurant at the port of Pañacocha, we found ourselves sitting alongside a member of the local parish council who had stopped for lunch on his way upriver. I mentioned the fact that no one seemed to know why the Millennium City was there. His reply took us by surprise. "They wash their hands of it and say that the houses were a gift from God," he said. "But that's not the case. Those houses are the outcome of a long blockade on the Aguarico, where the communities of Playas and Pañacocha were united."[59] He listed the key figures in the struggle, and over the following days a hidden history began to emerge. We then traveled to Playas de Cuyabeno to continue our investigations. The president of the local *comuna* had played a central role in the struggle and granted us permission to review its archives. We borrowed his keys and let ourselves into a gloomy office with a broken air-conditioning unit chugging pointlessly in the corner. Sifting through piles of moldy documents, we unearthed the secret origin of the Millennium Cities.

The history of Pañacocha and Playas de Cuyabeno is marked by successive waves of dispossession. The first inhabitants arrived in the region from downriver in the late nineteenth and early twentieth centuries, fleeing enslavement by Peruvian rubber barons. Others moved to the area to escape the 1941 war between Ecuador and Peru. Some were displaced by the armed conflict in Colombia and others abandoned oil-polluted lands in other parts of the Amazon. Like many *comunas* in the region, Pañacocha and Playas de Cuyabeno were both formed in the 1970s to defend their territorial claims in the context of the encroachments of oil companies and mestizo colonizers. The Pañacocha oil field was opened in 1972 by the American corporation Grace Oil and Minerals, which drilled exploratory wells throughout the territory.[60] Inhabitants of the Millennium Cities recall being fascinated by the oil. People painted their houses with it, and children would open the spigots and bathe in the crude. The company left the field unexploited, but oil and formation waters continued to leak into the ecosystem, poisoning water sources for decades afterward.

In 1985 Occidental was granted the concession for Block 15, which at that time contained the Pañacocha field (which was subsequently incorporated into Block 12). But Occidental did not exploit that field either. Following the company's expulsion from the country in 2006, Block 15 was opened to bidding once again. At this point the communities of the region began to receive visits from the state oil company, Petroecuador—soon to be replaced by Petroamazonas—which was campaigning to acquire the concession.[61] But this was not the only company seeking to garner their support. In 2005, at the height of the mobilizations of the ABP against transnational oil companies, an influential *Kichwa* leader named Rafael Alvarado created an indigenous oil company called Sacha Petrol—or "Jungle Gasoline" (*Sacha* means "jungle" in *Kichwa*). Unlike previous indigenous movements, which had opposed the exploitation of oil in their territories, Sacha Petrol proposed to take control of the natural resources of the Amazon and put them to use for the benefit of the indigenous population.

It incorporated six indigenous nationalities—the *Kichwa*, *Cofán*, *Siona*, *Secoya*, *Shuar*, and *Zápara*—and had the support of the principal Amazonian indigenous association—the CONFENIAE, as well as the Interprovincial Federation of Kichwa Communes and Communities of the Ecuadorian Amazon (FICCKAE).[62]

In 2006, when Block 15 became available, Sacha Petrol launched a concerted campaign to acquire the concession, proposing a division of revenues for the exploitation of Block 15 in which the state would receive 56 percent, the partner company 21 percent, and Sacha Petrol 23 percent. Alvarado and other representatives of the company began traveling the rivers of the northern Ecuadorian Amazon, offering bonds to the indigenous population with the promise of distributing dividends on future oil profits, while pledging to use the majority of their revenues to implement development programs throughout the region.[63] At the same time, they encouraged the *comunas* to oppose the proposal of Petroecuador. In Alvarado's words, Petroecuador "wanted everything for themselves, nothing for the *indígenas*. Just little gifts, but little gifts are worthless. Forty years of oil exploitation in Ecuador and the *indígenas* are poorer than ever."[64]

As part of their campaign, Alvarado and his team visited the *comunas* of Playas de Cuyabeno and Pañacocha, and the nearby *comuna* of Pukapeña, to explore the possibility of reopening the Pañacocha oil field. He recalls encouraging them to "join our indigenous company and participate in the oil wealth; otherwise, we all know that you will be poor for the rest of your lives." All three *comunas* responded by rejecting the overtures of Petroecuador and endorsing Sacha Petrol's proposal to collectively exploit the Pañacocha field. In a letter sent to Correa in February 2007, immediately following his inauguration, the leaders of these *comunas* denounced the fact that "far from the paradise promised by the oil companies, the provinces of the northern Ecuadorian Amazon are the most deprived and excluded regions of the country, and the territories that we inhabit have been irreparably damaged in social and environmental terms." They hailed Correa's electoral victory, announcing, "We can finally say that the nation is in the hands of Ecuadorians," while reminding him that "the *indios* of the northern Amazon are also Ecuadorians." The letter declared that the *comunas* "roundly oppose" the presence of Petroecuador in their territories and demanded that the government grant the concession of the Pañacocha field to Sacha Petrol instead. It concluded with a single phrase in capital letters: "This is justice."[65]

This message was reiterated two months later in a letter from members of the parish council of Cuyabeno to the president of Petroecuador, which warned him that they would not permit "any operations related to oil exploitation in the areas of Cuyabeno and Pañacocha on behalf of Petroecuador and its affiliates."[66] Over the following months Sacha Petrol rapidly gained support not only from the *comunas* surrounding the Pañacocha field, but also from indigenous people throughout the Ecuadorian Amazon. At the annual meeting of the Parliament of the Indigenous Amazon, the CONFENIAE resolved to support Sacha Petrol's plan for "the development and exploitation of the Pañacocha oil field . . . in the territories of the communities of Playas de Cuyabeno, Pañacocha, and Pukapeña."[67] As many as 18,000 *indígenas* submitted applications for a Sacha Petrol bond, and people would spend all night sleeping in the doorway of the FICCKAE offices in Coca to present their details.[68]

The growing strength of Sacha Petrol confronted the Citizens' Revolution with the contradiction between its "logic of fantasy" and its "logic of production."[69] In ideological terms, although Sacha Petrol was a profit-oriented enterprise, its vision of the collective appropriation of the natural resources of the Amazon for the benefit of its indigenous population embodied the utopian promise of the original accumulation of twenty-first-century socialism promoted by the Correa administration.

But in material terms, Sacha Petrol threatened the state control of the oil rents on which the Citizens' Revolution depended. This threat continued to grow. On October 3, 2007, the dissident prefect of Orellana, Guadeloupe Llori, officially endorsed Sacha Petrol's claim to Block 15.[70] On the same day, the three *comunas* and their respective parish councils issued a joint statement declaring that Sacha Petrol would become "the door through which the indigenous population of the Amazon will seize control of our own destiny."[71]

The very next day, however, the government announced that the concession had been granted to Petroecuador, and that plans were under way for the state company to initiate operations in the Pañacocha field.[72] A few weeks later Sacha Petrol also lost its most influential political supporter when Llori was imprisoned, following the military crackdown against the *paro* in Dayuma. Meanwhile, Petroecuador intensified its campaign in the Pañacocha field. The president of Playas de Cuyabeno at the time claims he was offered $20,000 to withdraw from Sacha Petrol,[73] and an indigenous leader from Pañacocha recalls that representatives of Petroecuador began visiting her "day and night," pleading with her to abandon the indigenous oil company and promising development projects for the community.[74]

These activities were denounced by the presidents of Pañacocha, Pukapeña, and Playas de Cuyabeno in a letter sent to the minister of the Amazon in March 2008, in which they observed that Sacha Petrol had evidently "perturbed the mafias . . . who consider themselves to be owners of our oil, and who believe that, as *indios*, we do not have the right to struggle for a better future for our children." Adopting an increasingly confrontational discourse, they insisted that "the necessary first step in the transformation of our country is the recuperation of the sovereign development of the natural resources of our ancestral peoples, not the ceding of the small part that still remains to us." This, they noted, had been "the central proposal of the electoral campaign of our President Rafael Correa," but it was now apparent that "the snobs [*pelucones*] continue to run the show." The letter concluded by announcing their intention to extend membership of Sacha Petrol to all the indigenous nationalities of Ecuador, as well as mestizo peasants and "our Afro-Ecuadorian brothers," united in "a struggle of the dispossessed and displaced . . . that will revolutionize Ecuador and Latin America."[75]

Sacha Petrol was now articulating a truly radical version of "the original accumulation of twenty-first-century socialism" and was placing this politics in direct confrontation with the Citizens' Revolution. These tensions exploded on September 3, 2008, when members of the *comuna* of Playas de Cuyabeno suddenly saw three barges approaching from downriver with a military escort, laden with machinery for the exploitation of the Pañacocha field. The oil company that they had banned from their territory was arriving uninvited, to extract the resources that they were determined to appropriate for themselves. One of the *comuneros* recalls the moment: "We saw the barges coming and we said, 'No! Not a chance!' . . . We immediately organized ourselves, grabbed our canoes, [and intercepted the barges.] The soldiers launched tear gas. . . . We were armed with spears and when we saw them firing at us we threw [our spears at them]."[76] The *comuneros* succeeded in detaining the barges at the curve of the river where the Millennium City now stands. The next day two more barges arrived and were also detained. Meanwhile, the *comuneros* set up camp on a broad sandbar in the middle of the river, from which Playas de Cuyabeno (Beaches of Cuyabeno) takes its name. In the evenings they visited their lands to gather food before returning to the beach to maintain their vigil.

Military reinforcements arrived a few days later, and the barges began to advance upriver once again. By this time, however, members of the *comuna* of Pañacocha had arrived in support of the blockade.

According to their testimonies, the *comuneros* boarded the barges and engaged the soldiers in hand-to-hand combat. They seized control of one barge, while five of them were detained by the military on another. By nightfall the stolen barge had been returned in exchange for the detainees, and the standoff resumed. Over the next few days, sacks of rice and other supplies were sent in support from communities upriver, and representatives of other indigenous nationalities arrived to join the struggle, including the *Shuar*, the *Siona*, and the *Cofán*.

The blockade at Playas de Cuyabeno had now become the first major *paralización* to have occurred in the Amazon since the military repression of the *paro* in Dayuma. On October 1, 2008, twenty-seven days after the initial confrontation, hundreds of heavily armed soldiers were flown in by helicopter to the site of the blockade. The *comuneros* responded by arming themselves with the chemical pumps used to spray their crops, which they filled with hot chili sauce to spray in the eyes of the soldiers. When battle commenced, however, the soldiers began firing live rounds, while tear gas canisters were launched from helicopters circling overhead, in a repetition of the tactics deployed during the crackdown in Dayuma. The man who had seized control of the barge during the previous confrontation recalls that this time, "We fled in fear. They were firing at our canoes from a great distance."[77] Footage shot from one of the military helicopters shows six canoes speeding away from three barges filled with soldiers and advancing ponderously upriver with a cargo of trucks, portacabins, gas tanks, and machinery, accompanied by a boatload of soldiers moving stealthily through the undergrowth along the riverbank. One of the inhabitants of Playas de Cuyabeno received a bullet wound that left him partially blind. According to one of the leaders of the *paro*, an elderly woman who inhaled tear gas during the confrontation died as a result of respiratory problems a few weeks later.[78]

The blockade was soon broken, and the barges continued upriver. The *comuneros* reassembled their forces, however, and gave chase. By the time they caught up with their adversaries, the barges were already moored at the site of the first oil well, and trees were being felled for the construction of the platform. The *comuneros* halted the operations and demanded dialogue. Two weeks later, an assembly was held in Playas de Cuyabeno, attended by government ministers under military guard and by representatives of the indigenous peoples of the region armed with spears.[79] This was the first of a series of negotiations over the following months, which concluded with the leaders of Pañacocha and Playas de Cuyabeno agreeing to abandon their autonomous oil company and accept the exploitation of the Pañacocha oil field by Petroamazonas. They did so in return for a comprehensive development project—which eventually took the form of the Millennium Cities.

And so we return to the moment described at the start of this chapter, when Correa inaugurated the Pañacocha oil field in October 2010, announcing the beginning of "a new oil era" and presenting a huge symbolic check for $21.2 million to the leaders of Pañacocha and Playas de Cuyabeno. Like the inauguration of the Millennium Cities themselves, the event had been carefully staged by Petroamazonas. Following the presentation of the check, one of the leaders of the blockade was instructed to deliver a prepared speech. He recalls, "I had to say to the government, for one thing, 'Thank you,' and the other was to ask them for forgiveness."[80] After the speech, he was told to walk alongside Correa to the pumping house from which the first barrel of "the new oil era" would be extracted. Standing in front of the gleaming machinery, they pushed the button together.

The *paro* at Playas de Cuyabeno exposed the contradiction at the heart of the Citizens' Revolution, between a logic of fantasy based on a socialist form of original accumulation and a logic of production based on hydrocarbon exploitation and its associated processes of accumulation by dispossession. As such, it constituted what Žižek would describe as a rare "moment of openness . . . when the very structuring principle of society is called into question. . . . The moment of crisis overcome by the act of founding 'a new harmony.'"[81] The delivery of the check and the opening of the oil well, accompanied by a public apology for the *paro* on the part of the *comuneros* and the declaration of a new oil era by the president of the republic, were the acts through which this "new harmony" was established. From this moment onward, the *paro* was erased from history. No mention was made of it by Correa during the inauguration of Pañacocha or Playas de Cuyabeno. No reference can be found to it in the countless official declarations and newspaper reports concerning the Millennium Cities. And their inhabitants would discuss the cities without referring to the violent struggles and utopian dreams through which they had been gained, and which now lay buried beneath them.

The parish councilor had finished his lunch, and his boat was ready. "People say that the Millennium City was a gift from the president," he said as he was leaving, "[but] all the advances of the *pueblo* have been achieved through struggle, nothing has arrived like just 'Here, this is for you.' Everything has been obtained though violent conflict [*golpes de lucha*]."[82] He jumped aboard the motorboat and sped out across the river, cutting a wide arc beyond the sandbanks, away from the set on which a fantasy had been staged, and beneath which a violence had vanished.

The Dreams of a Dog

This chapter has interpreted the utopian city as a dream—first by exploring the *manifest content* expressed in the revolutionary discourses and modernizing infrastructures of the Millennium Cities, and then by deciphering the *latent content* concealed within them: the

CITIES OF BLACK GOLD

struggle for the creation of an indigenous oil company and the violent repression of that prohibited desire. At this point, as Freud noted of his method of dream interpretation, "we are naturally impelled to return to the individual dream problems, in order to see whether the riddles and contradictions which seemed to elude us when we had only the manifest content to work upon may not now be satisfactorily solved."[83]

At the level of their manifest content, the Millennium Cities appeared as the materialization of the original accumulation of twenty-first-century socialism, through which a new society would be founded on the appropriation of nature without the dispossession of the peasantry. Amazonian oil rents were magically transformed into a surreal pastiche of small-town USA, as the paradoxical fulfillment of this promise of a socialist modernity. This vision proved remarkably successful in gaining acceptance for the expansion of the oil frontier from communities long committed to its rejection. The president of a community downriver from Playas de Cuyabeno told us its residents had always opposed the oil industry, but "having seen the benefits of an oil company exploiting your lands, a strong group [within the community] is now convinced that having a Millennium City would be the best thing in the world."[84] The *Huaorani* demanded a Millennium City in exchange for the exploitation of the oil beneath the Yasuni National Park.[85] And the *Cofán*, who had steadfastly resisted oil extraction for decades, also agreed to the opening of new wells on their land in return for a Millennium City.[86] The Millennium Cities were even incorporated into the shamanic practices of the region. In 2013 the death of a member of a *Zápara* community opposing oil exploitation was widely attributed to a shamanic curse that had been placed on him by other community members who were determined to sign an oil contract in the hope of receiving a Millennium City.[87] And the shaman of Playas de Cuyabeno reportedly promised to provide another community with a Millennium City like his own, in return for their shaman's lifting a curse on his community, which had been blamed for the deaths of several children.[88]

These tales further illustrate the apparently occult power of petroleum to transform social reality. The source of this magic lies not in the inherent properties of oil itself, but in its status as a bearer of ground rent. According to Marx, as we have seen, value is socially necessary labor time, and capital accumulation is based on the extraction of surplus value through the exploitation of living labor in commodity production. This implies that, despite constituting an immense store of use values for incorporation into the production process, nature is not productive of value.[89] Nevertheless, the global scale of the accumulation process allows national states in resource-rich regions of the world to participate in the accumulation process through the appropriation of ground rent, as a claim on a fraction of global surplus value, which they receive in exchange for granting capital access to the nonreproducible resources under their monopoly control.[90] In such circumstances, nature appears to embody value, leading to what Marx described as the ascription of "magic powers to the soil."[91] As a bearer of ground rent, oil is infused with this seemingly magical power.

During an oil boom like the one that was under way when Correa came to power, the governments of oil-rich states like Ecuador are transformed into "the visible embodiments of the invisible powers of oil money, powerful magicians who pull social reality . . . out of a hat."[92] But such magic has its limits. In contrast to the discourse of the original accumulation of twenty-first-century socialism, the Citizens' Revolution was based on a limited redistribution of hydrocarbon rents, as opposed to a radical transformation of capitalist social relations. This rent-based form of capital accumulation required the production of nature as a stock of resources available for exploitation, which necessitated the dispossession of the populations in whose territories these resources were located, including the future inhabitants of the first two Millennium Cities. Far from embodying a socialist form of original accumulation, the Millennium Cities were therefore monuments to the primitive accumulation of capital that the Citizens' Revolution was supposed to have transcended.

The crushing of the *paro* in Playas de Cuyabeno was only one moment in a broader process of dispossession. As already discussed, the 2010 Hydrocarbons Law dedicated 12 percent of royalties from each barrel of oil extracted from the Amazon to social expenditures in the region. These royalties, however, were not removed from corporate profits or from the budgets of more privileged regions but were taken from the pockets of Amazonian oil workers, who had been entitled to 15 percent of the royalties from local wells as one of the key concessions gained by the August Uprising of 2005. This 15 percent had been reduced to 3 percent by the new Hydrocarbons Law, and the remaining 12 percent was designated for expenditure by the local governments of the region. In 2011, however, these resources were redirected to the central government through the creation of Ecuador Estratégico. Enrique Morales, a leading figure in the ABP, described this maneuver:

> All that money that, according to Correa, was supposed to be destined for the decentralized governments and for community development—the [central] government cheated us out of it. They lied to us, and that money went instead to a company created by the government itself, called Ecuador Estratégico, which very strategically robbed us of all our money! With those resources Ecuador Estratégico created Millennium Schools, Millennium Cities. They distributed the funds all over the country and they never provided any account of

their activities. . . . All that money disappeared. It vanished. And that led to a further debilitation of the ABP.[93]

The objective of Ecuador Estratégico, however, was not only to appropriate the resources gained through the struggles of the ABP, but also to invest those resources in infrastructural projects that would preempt a resurgence of resistance provoked by the dispossession implicit in the expansion of the oil frontier. An executive manager of Ecuador Estratégico explained, "We have to break the historical relation of begging, blackmailing, blockading."[94] Within this logic, the function of the Millennium Cities was to create "a simple vision of what could be done with strategic resources . . . to make people desire to live near a strategic project. That is our vision of the future."[95]

Beneath the slogans of "resources building happiness" and "converting dreams into reality," Ecuador Estratégico was therefore dedicated to the co-optation of the subaltern social forces that might otherwise threaten the state's capacity to appropriate the rents on which the Correa regime depended. Sacha Petrol, by contrast, had developed an increasingly radical vision for the collective appropriation and egalitarian distribution of social wealth, which seemed to genuinely embody the original accumulation of twenty-first-century socialism. As one indigenous leader recalls, Sacha Petrol "had a very social vision. The capital would help our people with health care, education, culture. It was not just about the ambition to make money."[96] This utopian vision, however, was inconsistent with the accumulative logic of the Citizens' Revolution, which responded by repressing it and displacing its emancipatory dimension into the distorted form of the Millennium Cities.

Once its latent content has been taken into account, the Millennium City is thus revealed not as the fulfillment of the manifest wishes of the post-neoliberal state, but as what Freud would call "*the (disguised) fulfilment of a (suppressed, repressed) wish*"[97]—the forbidden desire of its inhabitants for autonomous collective control of the resources beneath their feet. This ambivalence was inscribed into the everyday lives of the inhabitants of this urban dream. One afternoon we visited Doña Rosa, one of the leaders of the blockade at Playas de Cuyabeno. She proudly recounted the history of Sacha Petrol, the *paro*, and the negotiations, before listing the multiple failings and absurdities of the Millennium Cities and insisting that "things would have been much better" if Sacha Petrol had succeeded, "because it would have benefited not only my community but many more as well." Then she paused, and in the brief silence I looked around the room. Her Millennium House was immaculate. The computer and refrigerator had been given pride of place, and she was sitting on the sofa, watching an American talk show on TV. The sound was turned down low, but in the quiet of the room I could hear snatches of a debate about seances and Ouija boards. Outside, the Millennium City was bathed in sunshine. "I am content," Doña Rosa said at last, "as you can see . . ."[98]

For Doña Rosa, the modernity of the Millennium City was both a source of material comfort and a symbol of political defeat. This was modernity as "the 'shadow' cast over bourgeois society by the failure of revolution, at once a compensatory substitute and the ineliminable trace of vanquished hopes."[99] And yet the object of these hopes turned out to have even less substance than the Millennium Cities themselves. After completing our research in Pañacocha and Playas de Cuyabeno, we went in search of Rafael Alvarado, the founder of Sacha Petrol, the indigenous oil company on which these hopes had once been pinned. In Coca we were directed to the offices of the FICCKAE, the *Kichwa* federation of which he had been president, and which had endorsed the company. Night had fallen by the time we arrived. The offices were in the corner of a dank internal courtyard cluttered with burned-out hard drives, battered filing cabinets, and broken toilet bowls. Everything was in darkness except for one room, lit by a single bulb, where several *Kichwa* men were talking quietly. We asked for Rafael Alvarado. No one responded at first. Then a man sitting behind a desk on the far side of the room shouted across at us: "We don't want to hear about Rafael Alvarado! He has been expelled from the organization and we have cut all contacts with him!" Others muttered about "corruption," and "luxury offices in Quito." According to them, Alvarado had defrauded the FICCKAE by secretly taking out a loan against its property and failing to repay it. As a consequence of this, the organization was now on the verge of homelessness and bankruptcy.

The next day we headed to the *comuna* of San Pedro, on the outskirts of Coca, where we had been told that we might find Alvarado. We drove through flooded slums, past the neon signs of brothels scattered among the heavily guarded premises of foreign oil companies. San Pedro was just a handful of huts at the end of a rough road. Alvarado, it turned out, had moved to Quito. We followed him there and managed to arrange a meeting. The offices in which he rented a desk were not so luxurious after all, and Alvarado was nowhere to be seen. While we waited in the foyer, one of his associates offered us the opportunity to join a pyramid scheme for a new medicine that cured cancer and most other illnesses and guaranteed a life expectancy of over one hundred years. He hastily excused himself when a young indigenous woman arrived, carrying her newborn child. She had learned about the scheme on the street outside and was eager to sign up.

Alvarado was over three hours late and abruptly announced that he had little time to talk. Dressed in a shiny gray suit, he ushered us into a dingy meeting room. Sacha Petrol would have rescued the Amazon from poverty, he explained. But Petroamazonas had "talked nonsense" that had "defamed" him, telling people that "'Rafael Alvarado is a liar, a criminal," and convincing them to abandon his company and "continue on the path of poverty, which is exactly what they have done. But in my case God has given me the necessary strength." His voice began to rise at this point, and he seemed to have forgotten his other, more pressing engagements: "Because I pray to the Father, to Jesus! To my Lord: 'Give me strength!' And I will be victorious. I have other alliances, allies with whom I will build a beautiful business!" The unfortunate saga of Sacha Petrol had been consigned to the past, and Alvarado was eager to tell us about his new scheme, a cacao project, which already had 3,300 indigenous members, and which would benefit over 90,000 impoverished families in the Amazon: "Not for Rafael Alvarado, but for the people! This is the righteous path!"[100]

Back in Coca, we spoke to Valerio Grefa, an elderly *Kichwa* leader who had served as president of the FICCKAE on four occasions. According to him, Alvarado had financed Sacha Petrol with the funds stolen from the FICCKAE, while masquerading as the cousin of Lucio Gutiérrez, the ex-president of Ecuador, in a far-fetched and fruitless attempt to gain ministerial support for his project. But the local indigenous population had proven more receptive to his scheme: "They handed over their details with absolute faith that it was a serious business. Of course, if I offer you a company [and tell you] that it is going to be our company, a company of the people, you will be enthusiastic. You will get in up to your nose, your eyes, until you are in over your head."[101]

We also visited the president of Pukapeña, one of the three *comunas* that, along with Pañacocha and Playas de Cuyabeno, had campaigned on behalf of Sacha Petrol. Sitting in his house on a ridge above the Aguarico, the president described his excitement when Alvarado had first told him about the project. "The idea was fantastic!" he recalled. "I told him we would be delighted to be involved."

The *comuneros* of Pukapeña joined the company as shareholders, but over time he began to sense that "it smelled like a con job." He asked to see the company statutes and proof of Alvarado's claims of ministerial support. At this point, Alvarado allegedly "became aggressive and offensive" and refused to provide the information. Pukapeña then withdrew from the project. This was shortly before the blockade on the Aguarico, on the basis of which the other two *comunas* negotiated the Millennium Cities. Ultimately, he claimed, the presidents of these *comunas* had also realized that Sacha Petrol was a scam. He recalled meeting with the president of Playas de Cuyabeno, who told him: "You were right to abandon [the company]. There's nothing there. It has all been false, a lie."[102]

Valerio Grefa concurred with this assessment. Sacha Petrol, he concluded, had been "an immense dream without any basis whatsoever. People dream, and dreaming is all well and good. But these things must be based in reality, not in the dreams of a dog."[103] Such baseless dreams, however, cannot be quite so comprehensively dismissed. After all, as this chapter has demonstrated, they can result in the production of entire cities. The *comunas* of Pañacocha and Playas de Cuyabeno had been so profoundly deceived by Sacha Petrol that they had gone into battle against the Ecuadorian military to avenge the defeat of their nonexistent enterprise. Their commitment to this "dream of a dog" was powerful enough to force the Millennium Cities into material existence as an elaborate compensatory substitute for their vain and vanquished hopes. But these cities were themselves a lie, a sham, a superficial and duplicitous facade. One simulation of an emancipatory modernity had been exchanged for another, and the entire fantastical assemblage had functioned only to reproduce the social relations from which both utopias had promised an escape.

If there is a truly utopian moment within this miasma of illusions, then it exists in the awakening that fleetingly emerged between these two fantasies—after the dream of the indigenous oil company had been dashed, and before the dream of the Millennium Cities had been negotiated. In Playas de Cuyabeno, one of the leaders of the blockade showed us his mobile phone footage of the standoff on the sandbank. Instead of the tense scenes of militant mobilization that we had expected to see, the flickering screen showed glimpses of people laughing, drinking *chicha*, playing soccer on the beach, and frolicking in the sand. The barges were moored against the riverbank beneath the setting sun. No one worked during this period, and it is remembered as a time of joy and unity as well as struggle. In these fragmented images, perhaps, we can discern the outline of an insurgent utopia embodying the subaltern desire for freedom from toil, the solidarity of a pitched battle against impossible odds, and the collective decision to act when confronted with no other choice. It is in such rare moments of radical awakening, when our illusions have been shattered, and before we can be seduced by another fantasy, that an insurgent utopia has the potential to emerge. As Mladen Dolar has noted of the moment between the dreams of sleep and those of waking life: "There is this encounter in the gap between two fantasies. . . . It embodies the break between two worlds. And in that break, something comes up for a moment that doesn't belong to either. . . . How to make it endure? How to hold on to something utterly vanishing? [What is required is] a persistent attempt to show fidelity to what emerges between two dreams."[104]

5

The Mirage Laboratory

I must dream on in order not to perish; just as the
sleep-walker must dream on in order not to tumble down.

Friedrich Nietzsche, The Gay Science

An enormous abstract condor of concrete, glass, and steel soared
above the humble dwellings on a highway leaving Quito. This was
the headquarters of UNASUR, the pioneering institution of post-
neoliberal regionalism. Constructed by the Citizens' Revolution at a
cost of over $50 million, the building symbolized the liberation of
South America from the eagle of U.S. empire. In July 2015 the headquarters hosted an international conference on sustainable development organized by the Correa administration. One of the keynote
speakers was René Ramírez Gallegos, a young economist who was
among the most radical and creative intellectuals of the Citizens' Revolution. Correa had run for office in 2006 promising to transcend the
"irresponsible and pitiless exploitation of nature" characteristic of
neoliberalism,[1] and the new constitution of 2008 had become the first
in the world to enshrine the rights of nature. As the head of the newly
created National Secretariat of Planning and Development (SENP-
LADES), Ramírez had sought to operationalize this agenda under the
rubric of "biosocialism," which aimed to replace Ecuador's dependence on the "finite resources" of Amazonian oil reserves with a sus-

tainable development model based on the collective ownership of the "infinite resources" of knowledge and biodiversity.[2]

Among the myriad utopian visions of the Citizens' Revolution, biosocialism stood out as the most complete utopia in the classical sense of the term, understood as "the detailed schematization of an alternative society—the ready-made representation of a no place that is generated as if directly willed from the brain of the author."[3] It was also the most uncompromising in its formulation of an explicitly anticapitalist project. According to Ramírez, biosocialism was based on a combination of "innovative concrete proposals" and "great ethical, theoretical, and utopian orientations," and it sought not to "take better advantage of capitalism but to transform it. This is the great historical challenge that must be confronted by the intellectual and political left. . . . To change the structural roots of the problem, the capitalist mode of accumulation and distribution."[4]

This radical vision had been materialized in the form of Ikiam, the Regional University of the Amazon, which was inaugurated in October 2014. At Ikiam—which means "jungle" in the language of the *Shuar* indigenous nationality—an interdisciplinary team of international scientists would research the biodiversity of the region, exploring the industrial and pharmaceutical applications of its flora and fauna, while training a future generation of Amazonian scientists to work in Ecuador's nascent biotechnology industry. The main campus was located on the boundary of the 230,000-acre Colonso-Chalupas Biological Reserve, which Correa described as a "living laboratory for the study of biodiversity, which we believe will be the great resource of the twenty-first century."[5]

Ikiam was a focus of attention for CENEDET, the research institute that I was working for at the time, which was affiliated with SENPLADES. Ramírez had been instrumental in the establishment of CENEDET, having invited David Harvey to create the institute in

2013. I had been assigned to assess Ikiam on behalf of CENEDET, and my first task was to attend the conference at the UNASUR headquarters, where I hoped to hear Ramírez speak. Before I came to Ecuador, my research had focused on the development projects of Jeffrey Sachs, the pioneer of the "shock therapy" reforms first implemented in Bolivia in 1985 and subsequently repeated around the world.[6] In the late 1990s, Sachs had advised Ecuador's President Jamil Mahuad on the imposition of a brutal program of privatization and austerity. The outcome had been a profound economic crisis, which resulted in Mahuad's removal from office by an indigenous uprising. Sachs's neoliberal shock therapy, it was fair to say, was the absolute antithesis of Ramírez's biosocialist utopia.

A red carpet extended from the main entrance of the abstract condor, in preparation for the arrival of the presidential motorcade. I entered through a different door and passed into a dark and cavernous atrium. As I descended the sleek escalator toward the central chamber, a group of dignitaries was gathering for a photo shoot. There was René Ramírez, the very image of a utopian socialist, dressed in the muted black attire of a Parisian intellectual, with long black hair, bright red shoes, and thick-rimmed spectacles. A man in a business suit was reaching out to shake his hand. I stared in astonishment as the escalator drew me down toward them. There could be no doubt about it. The man shaking hands with René Ramírez was none other than Jeffrey Sachs!

As I stood marveling at this impossible scene, a collective intake of breath signaled the arrival of the president. Gliding down from the atrium, Correa glad-handed among the crowd before embracing Sachs like an old friend. Once again, as on so many occasions during my research on the Citizens' Revolution, I experienced what Todorov would call "the contradiction between two worlds, that of the real and that of the fantastic."[7] From this moment onward, my research on

Ikiam was concerned less with my designated task of assessing the strengths and challenges of the project, than with my struggle to make sense of the senselessness of this initial experience. As Jameson has observed, "The basic story which the dialectic has to tell is that of the dialectical reversal, that paradoxical turning around of a phenomenon into its opposite."[8] This chapter tells the story of Ikiam as a metamorphosis of this kind, in which, through a labyrinthine entanglement of fantastical schemes and material dynamics, a utopian project was gradually transformed into a monstrous reproduction of the thing it was attempting to replace.

Visions of Biopolis

René Ramírez begins one of his essays with a cryptic epigraph adapted from the fifty-fourth aphorism of Nietzsche's *The Gay Science*, in which Nietzsche describes the experience of having "suddenly awoke in the midst of [a] dream, but merely to the consciousness that I just dream, and that I must dream on in order not to perish; just as the sleep-walker must dream on in order not to tumble down." From this image of a dream within a dream, Ramírez distills his epigraph: "To 'continue to dream, aware that I am dreaming' [*Para 'continuar soñando sabiendo que estoy soñando'*]."[9] The message can be read as an affirmation of his commitment to utopian thought. As Correa wrote in the prologue to one of Ramírez's many books: "[René Ramírez] is conscious of the necessity of boarding the train of history, of doing so while holding on to the hope of transformation without ceasing to closely examine reality . . . and of dreaming socially, with the objective of scrupulously realizing our vision of *buen vivir*."[10]

Ramírez had been Correa's student in the late 1990s, when Correa was teaching economics at the University of San Francisco in Quito. Correa had been impressed by Ramírez's ability and conviction, and in 2005 he invited Ramírez to join his ministerial team, following his appointment as minister of economy and finance in the Palacio administration. At the time, however, Ramírez was in the Netherlands, studying for a master's degree in development economics. He returned to Ecuador a year later and joined the group of economists that was gathering at the home of Alberto Acosta to plot the Citizens' Revolution.[11] Following Correa's election, Ramírez entered the government as one of a cohort of "young post-neoliberal experts" who now occupied the "commanding heights of the state apparatus."[12] In contrast to the neoliberal technocrats who had dominated previous administrations, Ramírez and his cohort were drawn from academia rather than finance, grounded in heterodox economics and postcolonial theory instead of econometrics, and "committed to the construction of a utopian society."[13]

In 2008 Ramírez was appointed secretary of SENPLADES and tasked with the implementation of a development strategy consistent with the new constitution, which stated that "nature, or *Pachamama*, . . . has the right to integral respect for its existence, and for the maintenance and regeneration of its life cycles, structures, functions, and processes."[14] It was in this context that Ramírez set out his vision for biosocialism as "the materialization and radicalization of . . . the Citizens' Revolution."[15] Biosocialism would replace the anthropocentrism of Western modernity with "biocentrism."[16] In contrast to the instrumentalization of nature characteristic of "the productivism that has dominated capitalism," biosocialism would privilege "the intrinsic value of nature" and "the ethico-moral value of life itself."[17]

Ramírez's appointment as secretary of SENPLADES confronted him with the immediate necessity of translating his ambitious vision into concrete policy proposals. After all, as he noted, while the constitution may have established the "principles, objectives, and goals" of biosocialism, it had little to say on "the factors of accumulation for the construction of a different type of economy."[18] He was clear that "the new social pact that has been signed by Ecuadorian society cannot coexist with an economic strategy of primary resource exportation. . . . Ecuador must overcome its role as a provider of primary goods that degrade nature."[19] But he was equally aware that this injunction posed the urgent question of how to construct a new economic model, given that "if an economy that seeks to be anti- (or even post-) capitalist does not improve the material conditions . . . of the population's social life and does not allow for overcoming poverty, not only is it politically unviable, but it is also ethically undesirable, no matter what 'non-capitalist accumulation' it presupposes."[20]

Ramírez responded to this formidable challenge by proposing "a new bio-strategy of accumulation" based on a transition from the "finite resources" of oil and other primary commodities to the "infinite resources" of "bioknowledge," understood as the application of scientific knowledge to the immeasurable biodiversity of the Ecuadorian Amazon in the production of collectively owned public goods.[21] This project was complicated by the dearth of research facilities in the country, which Ramírez attributed to the decadence and complacency of a society immersed in oil wealth: "We have been exploiting petroleum for 40 years, and we do not have even one center for scientific research. . . . This is the stupidity of abundance."[22] The Citizens' Revolution, however, would "sow the oil and harvest a productive matrix for the knowledge society" by using the revenues of the oil boom to construct the missing research centers.[23] In Ramírez's words: "It is no longer enough to expound theoretical sophisms. [We] must construct paradises of bioknowledge open to *buen vivir*."[24]

In 2011 Ramírez was tasked with overseeing this process as secretary of another newly created department, the National Secretariat of Science, Technology, and Higher Education (SENESCYT). The flagship projects of biosocialism were unveiled the following year, when SENESCYT created Yachay, a knowledge city in the highlands devoted to the development of technological industries, and Ikiam, the Regional University of the Amazon, which was "dedicated to the generation of bioknowledge" and located next to the newly created Colonso-Chalupas Biological Reserve.[25] In recognition of the principle of biocentrism, the architectural competition for the design of Ikiam was titled "Wild Architecture." The winners of the first round included laboratories constructed in the shape of leaves and "bridges that change direction organically, evoking the structures of trees."[26] The selected design was equally experimental, based on the vernacular architecture of the *Huaorani* and conceived as "a hybrid that reinterprets . . . the millennial knowledge of this incredible culture."[27]

Ikiam and Yachay constituted the initial phase of Ramírez's vision for the construction of "Biopolis . . . a society whose greatest wealth lies in life and whose capacity to reproduce itself comes from intangible knowledge."[28] In setting out this strategy, Ramírez was aware of parallels with the neoliberal knowledge economy, which was likewise premised on the fusion of academia and industry in the production of biotechnological innovations and other "immaterial" goods. Since the 1980s, university research in Europe and the United States had been increasingly incorporated into processes of capital accumulation through the development of a "triple-helix" of integrated relations among academia, industry, and government. The biotechnology sector had been a central driver of this process, through which capital asserted increasing influence over academic research agendas, and departments were financed and judged in terms of the quantity of capital accessed and the number of patents acquired.[29]

As Ramírez himself acknowledged, "Bioknowledge . . . is the mainstream of capitalism at the present time," and "in the advanced capitalist countries, innovation goes hand in hand with the accumulation requirements of the great transnational companies. Universities and scientists become embroiled in this dynamic and . . . world commerce ends up dictating what must be researched and produced."[30] He was confident, however, that Ecuador could "break with the tragedy of the anti-commons" and construct "another type of bioknowledge, that we might call 'bioknowledge for *buen vivir*,'" based on the principle that "knowledge is naturally a public good . . . an infinite resource that can be freely and easily distributed" if separated from the privatizing and profit-oriented logic of capitalism.[31] According to Ramírez, this project had the potential to achieve the ultimate dialectical inversion envisioned by Marx: "In this new framework, the benefits of science are accumulated not privately, but rather socially and publicly. This could perhaps confirm Marx's thesis that scientific and technological development, even as they permit capital to reproduce itself more effectively, might also exacerbate the social contradictions that drive capitalism toward its own abolition."[32]

Ramírez was adamant that biosocialism would not only transcend the neoliberal knowledge economy but also overcome "the colonial perspective" of "the dominant concept of development."[33] The concept of a "living laboratory" through which Ikiam was promoted by the Correa administration echoed the colonial vision of "the Amazon as an enormous, unsullied laboratory for the scientific . . . classification of nature,"[34] which had inspired numerous expeditions based on the conviction that "if forest and river could produce poison for arrows, latex that bounced, fish with electricity, intoxicants, and insecticides, and if they enabled the Indians to lead lives of indolence, the area plainly had more to reveal than could be seen upon its surface."[35] Despite these colonial resonances, however, Ramírez insisted that Ikiam was crucial to the decolonization of the Ecuadorian economy:

> If we continue in a productive matrix based on primary exports and technological imports, it will be impossible to construct a different social order. . . . Ikiam is fundamental in this

regard. . . . The new era will be based on information related to life-forms and biodiversity, and if we don't have the knowledge required to contest the commodification of life-forms, then we will not be part of this new era. That is why we must find out what exists in the living laboratory of the Amazon. Everyone loves to tell us how biodiverse we are. . . . They come from the universities of the North to steal the biodiversity of the South. They commit biopiracy, generate products, and then sell them back to us. . . . We must overcome this neo-dependency, which not only occurs in the case of industrial products but is also a cognitive and technological dependency.[36]

The Paradise of Bioknowledge

In December 2012 fifty-six international academics from the natural and social sciences were invited to a four-day workshop in the Amazonian town of Misahualli, on the banks of the upper Napo, near the site of Ikiam. The event had been organized by the Ecuadorian government to discuss "the academic proposal for the establishment of the University of Ikiam, its guiding principles, management policies, research strategies, [and] interaction with Ecuador's National Development Strategy."[37] The opening address was delivered by Guillaume Long, the minister of knowledge and human talent, and a close ally of René Ramírez in the Correa administration. Long announced that Ikiam had "political will [and] a lot of capital" behind it, including "the support of the president" and "$207 million for each of the next four years." Plans were moving forward very quickly, he explained, with the objective of launching the university and delivering the first classes in under two years' time, in October 2014. He concluded by describing Ikiam as "a fantastic dream," and he was followed by a junior minister who spoke of "this dream . . . of knowledge as an infinite source of wealth for our people." The governor of the province then delivered a speech in which he identified Ikiam as "the icon of the Citizens' Revolution" and implored all present to ensure that "the final product is made of gold, so that Ikiam can really become the university that we all dream of."

The stage was set for Ramírez to outline his vision of biosocialism. But instead it was announced that "René Ramírez sends his greetings and apologizes for not being able to be here." In his place, the opening session was introduced by three representatives of the Massachusetts Institute of Technology (MIT), who delivered a paper titled "Presentation of the MIT Report: A Proposal for the Establishment of the University of the Amazon in Ecuador." The essence of the proposal was set out by the senior industrial liaison officer of the Office of Corporate Relations:

> We see some specific ways of involving industry right from the beginning: Invite key industry leaders to act as advisors to the rector and the leadership, and participate in the formulation of the strategy for the university; involve companies in curriculum development and course work, inviting them perhaps to co-develop class projects for students [and] invite companies to participate in the planning of university research efforts in which the companies will be happy to collaborate both intellectually and importantly financially. . . . Here is a quote from a recent World Bank policy research working paper: "Besides teaching and research, universities are increasingly expected to make a direct contribution to economic development and the wellbeing of society. This new role requires universities not only to produce but also to commercialize knowledge. That is, to use research results to create intellectual property and to create new processes in products tradable in the market."

This was not a biosocialist strategy for the overthrow of neocolonial capitalism. On the contrary, it was a simulacrum of the MIT's own model of corporate neoliberalism, in which every element of teaching and research would be subordinated to the interests of transnational capital, and the value of knowledge was to be measured strictly in terms of its commodification. This fantastic inversion of Ramírez's vision permeated the entire workshop. In contrast to the decolonial discourse of biosocialism, the whole event was conducted in English, and no members of local communities or representatives of indigenous nationalities were invited. Of the fifty-six academics in attendance, forty-seven were from universities of the Global North, and many were involved in corporate biotechnology. The MIT proposal met with general approval, and discourses of entrepreneurialism, commercialization, and public-private partnerships were reproduced ad infinitum across the various panels and plenary sessions. Biosocialism, by contrast, was not mentioned once, and post-neoliberalism was raised on only a single occasion, when a Venezuelan anthropologist pointed out, "There is something very important here, which is that these plans to make this type of university are based in the Citizens' Revolution, [which] proposes a post-neoliberal regime [that calls for] a more egalitarian and democratic concept of knowledge." The response of the MIT's senior industrial liaison officer was once of blank incomprehension: "I didn't understand what you were referring to. Excuse me, could you please say it in some other way, or say it more clearly, please?"

Despite appearing to be diametrically opposed to biosocialism, the MIT proposal became the model on which Ikiam was constructed. Within a year of its launch in October 2014, the university had assembled a multidisciplinary team of international academics devoted to the cataloguing of the biodiversity of the Ecuadorian Amazon, the isolation of potentially marketable active agents, and their patenting and commercialization.[38] In the words of one scientist, the overarching objective was "to exploit the megadiversity of the Amazon. What we want, essentially, is to study a plant, learn how it is used in the [indigenous] community, test its active ingredient and isolate this type of drug in distinct cellular models."[39] The resulting products would be marketed by the Center for Entrepreneurship, which was devoted to "the commercialization of patents. Each time a researcher has found a new method of extracting a component, we [will] start the process of getting a patent. . . . We are looking toward the U.S. [to learn] how you can live from your patents as a university."[40]

In fact, this strategy was not quite as distant from biosocialism as it seemed to be. From the outset, the explicitly anticapitalist discourse of biosocialism had been underpinned by an implicit commitment to neostructuralism, which was the unspoken ideological consensus that united Correa, Ramírez, and the entire team of economists who had formulated the manifesto of the Citizens' Revolution. As we have seen, in contrast to the "spurious competitiveness" of Latin American neoliberalism, which was based on cheap labor and natural resource exploitation, neostructuralism advocated a state-led shift to "systemic competitiveness" based on technological innovations, productivity gains, and "an intelligent insertion into international markets."[41] Central to this strategy was the promotion of "knowledge-intensive sectors," which would drive "the transformation of the productive matrix."[42]

Eager to formulate a viable accumulation strategy, Ramírez had seized on this ready-made policy framework while repackaging the shift from spurious to systemic competitiveness in the more "biocentric" terminology of a transition "from finite to infinite resources." In practical policy terms, biosocialism therefore came to be formulated as a neostructuralist strategy for the "transformation of the productive matrix" from primary commodity production to "technology, innovation, and knowledge," premised on the principle that "science and education . . . contribute to competitiveness" and based on the development of "higher-performance crops, . . . the genetic modification of organisms," and the deployment of "biological and genetic information [in the] diversification of national exports, [including] bio-prospection, bio-production, and bio-commerce."[43]

This transition from finite resources to infinite resources did not entail a transcendence of capitalist social relations. On the contrary, it implied a leap from the formal to the real subsumption of nature to capital, "replacing a logic of extraction with one . . . in which industrial and natural processes become integrated in the pursuit of increased productivity and profitability."[44] This paradoxical transformation of biosocialism into a strategy for the intensified subordination of nature to capital was consistent with a broader drift to the right within the Correa administration. Beneath his revolutionary rhetoric, Correa had consistently sought to maintain a balance in his cabinet between two core groups, which came to be known internally as the "Leftists" and the "Pragmatists." The Leftists included the economists who had first gathered around Acosta's dining table to plot the Citizens' Revolution, while the Pragmatists included figures who had served in previous neoliberal regimes and who maintained close connections with key capitalist interests.[45] According to one of Ramírez's advisers, it was Correa himself who was "the great mediator of these two tendencies within the government. Correa is the great strategist, the one who understands the economic complexity of being inserted into a global capitalism."[46] While Leftists like Ramírez and Guillaume Long operated the ideological machinery of the planning and education ministries, the Pragmatists controlled the key economic ministries of trade and production. Over time, the Pragmatists had grown in strength and influence, whereas the Leftists were increasingly reduced to providing ideological cover for this shift with concepts like biosocialism. As Alberto Acosta—one of the original Leftists—reflected in retrospect: "We debated ideology. They concentrated on power."[47]

This drift to the right, and the relative weakness of Ramírez and his fellow Leftists in the cabinet, also helps explain the perplexing encounter among Ramírez, Correa, and Jeffrey Sachs with which this chapter began. In April 2014 Correa had embarked on a tour of some of the most prestigious universities in the United States, with the aim of generating collaborations between those schools and Ikiam and Yachay.[48] In a speech delivered at Yale, the Ecuadorian president distanced himself from biosocialism by embracing a version of technological utopianism that explicitly rejected Marxist principles: "I firmly believe in the transformative power of science and technology. . . . I have always considered that any attempt to reduce . . . the advance of human societies to simplistic laws like dialectical materialism is condemned to failure. And I am convinced that scientific and technological advances can generate greater well-being and be greater engines of social change than class struggle."[49]

The tour had been organized by the Ecuadorian ambassador to the United States, Nathalie Cely Suárez. Cely was a neoliberal economist who had studied under Sachs at Harvard and had served in the Mahuad administration that Sachs advised on its disastrous shock therapy program, before being appointed as one of the Pragmatists in Correa's first cabinet. Sachs, meanwhile, had shifted his focus to neoliberal environmentalism, and he was now heading the Sustainable Development Solutions Network (SDSN)—a United Nations initiative based at the Earth Institute at Columbia University, which was directed by Sachs and financed by a host of multinational corporations.[50] As part of Correa's tour of the United States, Cely had organized a meeting with Sachs, after which Correa had praised Sachs during his weekly television address, describing the Earth Institute as "one of the most powerful institutes [in the world] in terms of environmental questions" and insisting that it "could assist us academically, for example, in Ikiam. . . . Just imagine having an extension of the Earth Institute in Ikiam!"[51]

Soon after their meeting, Ikiam was incorporated into the "Amazonian Hub" of the SDSN, and a new "Andean Hub" was created, which was headquartered in Yachay and launched at the conference at which I had witnessed the surreal encounter between Sachs and Ramírez.[52] Like the Ikiam workshop three years previously, the conference made no reference to biosocialism. Instead, it featured a presentation on corporate social responsibility by a representative of Coca-Cola and a speech by the director of the Center for Sustainable Global Enterprise, who invited the audience to see "poverty, ecosystem degradation and climate change [as] new business opportunities."[53] Nathalie Cely, who had recently returned to the Correa cabinet as minister of production, employment, and competitiveness, presented an overtly neoliberal program of "incentives and regulations that . . . motivate efficient entrepreneurial operations," and the conference concluded with Sachs's pledging to contribute to Ecuador's "transformation . . . toward a knowledge-based economy of infinite resources."[54] Meanwhile, the visionary progenitor of biosocialism was reduced to a shadowy figure standing awkwardly at the edge of the conference hall. Unlike the other presentations, his speech was not posted on the government website, and when he reached across the red carpet to shake Sachs's hand, the expression on Sachs's face betrayed a telling fact: Jeffrey Sachs had no idea who René Ramírez was.

Build the Fucking Thing Now

From its origins as a radical biosocialist utopia, Ikiam had been rapidly transformed into a potential site for the real subsumption of nature to capital. The realization of this potential, however, would require extensive planning and preparation. In 2012, just as plans were getting under way for the construction of Ikiam, Correa invited the eminent climate scientist Arturo Villavicencio to take up the prestigious position of rector of Ikiam's sister project, Yachay, which was already under construction in the Andean highlands. Like Ikiam, Yachay had been conceived as a central component of biosocialism. But it had taken the equally antithetical form of a neoliberal knowledge city, which offered foreign investors a "competitive environment," based on "the best incentives in the region," including "credit for investment . . . reduction of taxes for company investors" and "a customs destination with unique financial, tax, and commerce alternatives," such as a reduction in corporate income tax and tax exemptions on the importation of capital goods and raw materials.[55]

Villavicencio declined Correa's offer. His refusal, however, was not due to the neoliberal nature of Yachay, or its betrayal of the principles of biosocialism, which he dismissed as "just an ideology that creates huge expectations."[56] Instead, it was due to what he perceived as the reckless haste with which the project was being implemented. Correa had been impressed by a visit to South Korea in 2010, and he told Villavicencio that he wanted Ikiam and Yachay to be modeled on the South Korean knowledge city. Villavicencio explained that this was an unrealistic objective, given that South Korea's successful transition to a knowledge economy had been the outcome of a decades-long process of industrial development and was driven by Korean-based multinational corporations, whereas Ecuador lacked the industry, capital, and personnel required for such a project. According to Villavicencio, however, Correa had angrily dismissed his argument, insisting on the necessity of "thinking big, leaping forward. . . . I was surprised by the vehemence of his commitment to rapid change. . . . He didn't understand that you can't simply jump over these processes."[57]

Correa's belief in the possibility of radical and immediate trans-formation, and the pressure to demonstrate concrete results, had caused Yachay and Ikiam to be implemented in the absence of a clearly defined plan for the transition to infinite resources. As Villavi-cencio observed: "The government has the idea of abandoning nonre-newables and leaping forward. But where to? And suddenly they have the idea of the great wealth of biodiversity, as the new goose that lays golden eggs. . . . Our scientists are [supposedly] going to investigate . . . the wealth of this biodiversity and discover some miraculous medicine that will permit an extraordinary leap forward. It seems naive to me."[58]

Villavicencio was blacklisted by Correa following their dispute and went on to publish a critique of biosocialism in 2014, in which he noted that "there is still no official document that coherently defines the objectives, strategies, and priorities in the fields of science and technology."[59] This was acknowledged by Carlos Ávila, the rector of Ikiam, when interviewed in 2015: "We are attempting to create an economy of science, technology, and innovation without having a solid basis in planning. . . . We are trying to solve structural problems without being clear what those problems are."[60] Ramírez, he said, had never met with him to discuss these matters, despite the fact that Ávila had been involved in Ikiam since its inception. Ávila and others described Ramírez as a reclusive intellectual, an insomniac who was constantly ensconced in his office, and who inhabited an isolated realm of high theory while delegating the prosaic trivialities and petty corruptions of everyday policy implementation to an extensive team of technocrats and fixers. In response to Correa's insistence on emulat-ing the South Korean knowledge economy, for example, Ramírez had dispatched his advisers to contract a South Korean consultancy for the spatial planning of Yachay and Ikiam. The $9.7 million contract was reportedly negotiated in some of the most exclusive brothels of Quito and resulted in unworkable plans that were ultimately abandoned.[61]

This elusiveness may account for the absence of Ramírez from the workshop at which the team from MIT had set out their proposal for Ikiam. The participants in the event had initially celebrated the pioneering vision of a state-of-the-art biotechnology university in the heart of the Amazon rain forest. A specialist in Earth systems heralded the "remarkable" prospect of "a campus integrated with the forest environment . . . a living laboratory . . . located in one of the last frontiers of the world." A professor of biological sciences exclaimed that "this is the most biodiverse place on Earth and it is mind-blowing how many species can coexist!" And a professor of biotechnology described the region as "a gold mine to discover . . . secondary metabolites, gene discovery, you name it."[62]

But over the course of the workshop these experts began to realize that there was no strategy for Ikiam beyond the generic neoliberal outline sketched by the team from MIT. Midway through the second day, a professor of Earth sciences intervened to raise an awkward question: "It is not very clear to me regarding what is expected of us. I feel like we can just throw ideas. . . . What is the purpose of us gathered here around this table?" No answer was forthcoming, and as the event progressed, the same question was posed with increasing frequency and frustration. On the morning of the third day, a professor of neuroscience interrupted a discussion on the structure of the university to observe: "Two days ago there were three schools, yesterday we talked about engineering as a possibility, and now we are talking about three or four additional faculties. There is a lack of clarity." A professor of urban planning similarly noted: "It seems to me that one needs to go back and ask oneself: What is this all about? What should our fundamental objectives be?" And a professor of physics exclaimed, "It is frustrating to think about exactly what we are trying to do here."

Eventually a professor of environmental science turned to the rector, Carlos Ávila, who was chairing the discussion, and posed the question directly: "What is the purpose of this university? I think that as experienced professors, we do not have an answer to this. . . . We need to learn to walk before we can run." In the absence of meticulous planning, as many of the participants repeatedly pointed out, Ikiam was in danger of becoming an "elite oasis in the jungle"—an enclave of privileged scientists, which would exclude the impoverished communities of the region while unleashing an avalanche of urbanization, deforestation, and other "cascading consequences in which there may be no visible intersection at all between the action and the consequence." In the words of one participant, "One of the dilemmas, and almost a contradiction, is that we are taking this bubble of excellency and we are inserting it in the Amazon, a very poor region." Another warned that "we might be running the risk of a new form of colonization." And a third noted, "The location of the university is very special, but we cannot escape the reality of the region, the country, and the world," before wearily concluding, "I do not know why we are here."

By the morning of the fourth day, the relationship between organizers and participants was on the verge of breaking down completely. Ávila began by announcing that the theme of the day would be "the organization track for Ikiam." A Stanford professor responded with withering brevity: "What does it mean?" Ávila replied with a barrage of rudimentary questions about the establishment of an academic institution: "Do we need a core of applied sciences? . . . Do you think Ikiam should have an academic year? . . . What would be the structure that you recommend for Ikiam? Do we need young professors? . . . How do the materials work? How do the human sciences work?" When he paused for breath, the director of the Center of Tropical Agriculture at a German university curtly informed him, "It is essential that Ikiam get itself a strategy. . . . It is difficult for us to say what you should do because it is up to the university to decide a focus area." By now it was evident to all in attendance that they had not been invited to the Amazon to fine-tune the final stages of a world-leading research institution, but rather to offer any clues they might have about how to build a university from scratch. As the event drew toward its conclusion, the assembled experts began to insist that the planned launch of the university in October 2014 would have to be postponed. A professor of Earth sciences from Imperial College London remonstrated: "There are no universities, neither in Europe nor in the United States, that do things so quickly. So, very well, if you manage it, perfect. But we will see that there will be many problems along the road."

The organizers of the workshop, however, responded that Ikiam had to be launched by the deadline of October 2014, regardless of the feasibility of doing so, because "those decisions are going to be taken from the point of view of politicians and statesmen." That point of view, as one of the architects of Ikiam later explained in English, was that "there is no time! *Build the fucking thing now!*"[63] The intense pressure to complete Ikiam was driven partly by the need to demonstrate success ahead of the presidential elections of 2017. But it was also symptomatic of the peculiar temporality of "the time of oil"[64]—the sudden explosion and unpredictable longevity of the oil boom that had made Ikiam possible, and on which the transformation of the productive matrix depended. The deadline was imposed. The warnings went unheeded. And all the worst predictions came to pass.

What You Do Is a Piece of Shit

Ikiam was launched, as stipulated, in October 2014. The contract with the South Korean consultancy for the design of the main campus had fallen through, and the Ecuadorian architectural firm that had

been brought in to replace it had yet to complete its plans. The entire
university was therefore temporarily housed in the administrative
buildings, a set of prefabricated office blocks that had not been included in the architectural design. Far from the bioengineered ecoto-
pia envisioned by the architects, the makeshift campus was described
by a member of a local indigenous community as "a chicken coop."[65]
Staff complained that its white surfaces attracted swarms of insects
from the surrounding forests, and the smooth walkways were treacherous in the frequent rainstorms, which had resulted in several injuries. Before the inauguration, a cellular structure had been stretched
between the office roofs, in a futile attempt to conceal the humility of
the campus beneath a vague symbolic reference to biotechnology. A
section of the structure collapsed during the event, destroying a concrete wall, the wreckage of which had been covered in a banner pro-
claiming, "Biodiversity Is Our Future."[66]

The campus had been promoted by Correa as the fulfillment of a
key demand of the ABP Accords: the construction of a public university accessible to the students of the region.[67] But the MIT proposal
conceived of Ikiam as an "elite university" capable of competing in
the global biotechnology sector, and the university was accordingly
demanding the very highest grades of its prospective students—grades
that local students were unlikely to attain. As one of the Ikiam workshop participants had pointed out in response to the MIT proposal:
"If you go to a school in [the Amazon], there may be a room called a
laboratory, it may have a skeleton hanging in the corner, but it has no
equipment, and there is no real science going on in that school. So
there is a very big problem in producing students to enter [Ikiam]." In
practice, only eight of the first three hundred students to enroll in
Ikiam were from the Amazon. Most students were members of
wealthy white and mestizo families from the highlands and the coast,
in contrast to the cleaning and maintenance staff, who were drawn

from the local *Kichwa* population. A planner at the municipal council explained that the inhabitants of the region had "mistakenly imagined that the university was for local people, but it wasn't like that. It's an elite university for privileged groups."[68] In the words of the headmaster of a local college: "They treat us like strangers. It's as if students from [the Amazon] are not Ecuadorians."[69]

The exclusion of the local population extended beyond the campus to encompass the "living laboratory" of the Colonso-Chalupas Biological Reserve. Correa had created this immense reserve by executive decree following a visit to the construction site of Ikiam in 2013, when he scaled a nearby hilltop and declared the protection of all the forests around him with a regal wave of his hand.[70] The Ministry of the Environment had imposed the decree by banning local communities from entering the reserve without permission, while simultaneously making it available "as an open field of investigation" for the researchers of Ikiam.[71] One member of a community on the boundary of the reserve observed: "They go to the jungle, do their research, but the community cannot [enter the reserve]. In my parents' time the forest was free, it belonged to the community."[72]

The Ikiam campus was initially planned for construction on the site of an abandoned airfield in the nearby city of Tena, which had been replaced by the new international airport that formed part of the Manta-Manaus transport corridor. When the architectural team first visited the site, however, they were driven past the airfield and onto a newly constructed highway leading deep into the jungle, illuminated by a parade of streetlights with Ikiam flags and images of Correa fluttering from the lampposts. Correa, it transpired, had been captivated by the fantasy of Ikiam as "a capsule in the jungle" and had overridden the original plans, insisting that the campus must be located in the middle of the rain forest.[73] A member of the architectural team recalls their arrival at the site: "I was completely shocked. I was crying at the end of it. I was, like, 'Oh, my God, what did I get into? This completely goes against everything I believe in. Why did they choose this site?' . . . It's creating a new pole of development where we need it the least—more entropic urbanization of the Amazon, more deforestation, greater growth of the agricultural frontier."[74]

In the absence of a territorial plan for Ikiam, the new highway rapidly became the site of a chaotic process of unregulated urbanization. Luxury residences and ostentatious vacation homes had been hastily constructed for international scientists and the Quito elite, and they dwarfed the wooden shacks and concrete huts of preexisting communities that continued to subsist without water or sanitation. Displaced from the land along the highway, many local peasants had been forced farther into the jungle or onto the roadsides of other agrarian frontiers, clearing the land that they needed to survive and exacerbating broader processes of regional deforestation.

On the approach to Ikiam the highway curved across a bridge, and a fleeting glimpse could be caught of a solitary street of cramped concrete houses implanted in the jungle a few hundred yards downriver. The houses had been constructed at the same time as Ikiam. Within a year their roofs were leaking and mold was growing on the interior walls. They were inhabited by members of a *Kichwa* community who had been located on the path of the highway. The construction company had given them fifteen days' notice before destroying their crops, their fruit trees, and their houses and had eventually rehoused them here, after they had lived for over a year in makeshift shelters constructed from the remains of their demolished homes. One man said that the government had treated them "like dogs" and made the motion of kicking an unwanted animal out of the way.[75]

Biosocialism was committed to "overcoming the structural racism of the colonial state."[76] In Ikiam, however, just as the post-neoliberal dimension of biosocialism had been transformed into a reproduction of the neoliberal norm, so this decolonial project had been twisted into a reproduction of the colonial practice of dispossessing indigenous communities and excluding them from a privileged space constructed on their territories and dominated by a foreign white elite. In the words of one of the architects: "My problem with Ikiam . . . is that the idea is all the way up here in terms of the concept"—she pointed toward the ceiling—"But the *how*, the *making*, the actual reification of that concept is very poor."[77] One of her colleagues was more concise. Imagining that René Ramírez was in the room, he turned to address him: "What you say is fantastic, and what you do is a piece of shit! [*¡Lo que digas es fantástico, y lo que hagas es una cagada!*]"[78]

Pulling Our Hair from Our Heads

As Ikiam was inaugurated in October 2014, the time of oil struck for the Citizens' Revolution. The long boom of the past decade had finally reached its peak a few months previously, and now the international oil price began to slide. At first it could be dismissed as a blip, then interpreted as a minor adjustment, but by the end of the year the price was in freefall, and in 2015 it collapsed completely, plunging from $112 a barrel in June 2014 to just $27 a barrel in January 2016.[79]

When we arrived at Ikiam in November 2015, the effect of the oil crash was already starkly evident. The university budget had been repeatedly cut over the course of the year, from a commitment to invest $207 million at the start of 2015 to an estimated expenditure of only $16 million by the end.[80] All infrastructural developments had been suspended, just as the construction of the laboratories was getting under way. Without such facilities, it was impossible to isolate active molecules or identify genetic codes, and the research team had been reduced to producing inventories of plant and animal species with potentially marketable properties. Despite Correa's increasing eagerness to forge links with Ecuadorian capital, these inventories were unlikely to be developed by nationally based industries, for the simple reason that no such industries existed. As the CEO of a small tech start-up explained, there was still no national plan for the biotechnology sector and "no commercial structure to exploit the biodiversity," and Ecuador's oligopolistic bourgeoisie was more concerned with "drowning" potential competition than with investing in national development.[81] Indeed, as the rector of Ikiam ruefully observed, although Ecuador aspired to be a world leader in the highly competitive biotechnology sector, the reality was that "we don't even have the capacity to produce our own toilet paper."[82] He pointed gloomily down an overgrown path that led to the site of the abandoned laboratories. We followed it and found that the initial structures had already been engulfed in suffocating foliage. Vines unfurled across the mossy floors, and the doorposts protruded like the rotting hull of an abandoned ship.

In the absence of laboratories in which to research and develop their discoveries, and without a national biotechnology sector to bring these products to market, Ikiam would be obliged to export the genetic wealth of the Amazon for development by foreign research institutes and corporations. In the words of one member of the research team: "If we don't invest properly, if we cannot advance beyond producing an inventory, . . . then that inventory will go [abroad], because it's a very competitive area."[83] An economist working on the transformation of the productive matrix made a similar point: "You need an industrial base in your country that can use all this knowledge that you are generating . . . otherwise it will just fly to other countries. In the end you are just making cheaper research for other people elsewhere, who are going to exploit all these results."[84]

The oil crisis was thus adding a further twist to the transformation of biosocialism into its opposite. As we have seen, biosocialism had initially mutated into a strategy for the real subsumption of nature to capital through the patenting of genetic sequences and the development of biotechnological commodities. But it was now threatening to merely reproduce the formal subsumption of nature on which Ecuadorian capital accumulation had traditionally been based, by extracting primary resources in the form of flora and fauna samples and exporting them for their incorporation into processes of real subsumption under way elsewhere. Furthermore, this process of formal subsumption was premised on the appropriation of indigenous knowledge. As one scientist candidly explained, in the absence of laboratories, Ikiam was entirely dependent on the knowledge of indigenous shamans and herbalists, and the anthropologists and ethnobotanists on the research team had already constructed "an extensive database, because they've developed contacts with the communities, they've inventoried certain species, . . . and [now] they need to pursue international collaborations for their development."[85]

Early one morning we visited the leaders of the *Kichwa* community of Atacapi, which was located across the river from the university campus. By the time we arrived, the social scientists of Ikiam had already assembled the women of the community in the local volleyball court and were encouraging them to collaborate on a project on their family *chakras* (agricultural plots); Ikiam was offering nutritional advice in return for information about their plants and "ancestral knowledge." When I asked the president of the community about the project, he laughed and spat on the dirt floor:

> We're too smart to let them make us dance in our own *chakras*! . . . I've participated in [the university's] investigations and I've noticed that all their research concerns the natural, biological aspects of our plants. They are compiling information on the ways in which our elderly people use medicinal plants. Their research is not going to benefit us. They

are obliging us to get all the information from our grandparents on the medicinal uses of all the plants that exist. They are going to process it at the scientific level, and our knowledge that has been generated for generations is going to be useless to us. How are we going to benefit from it? . . . It's like they are pulling our hair from our heads one hair at a time, and one day we will end up bald, and will have nothing left to comb![86]

In a speech promoting Ikiam in 2014, Correa had condemned the practice of biopiracy, referring to the case of an analgesic extracted from a species of frog endemic to the Ecuadorian Amazon, the utility of which "was discovered thanks only to the collective ancestral knowledge of our *pueblos*, but was extracted by foreign scientists and exploited by international pharmaceutical corporations without any benefit for our country."[87] But Ikiam itself was now in danger of reproducing the very same practice. This danger had been repeatedly identified by the participants at the initial planning workshop back in 2012. One had explicitly warned of "the possibility of biopiracy by international researchers coming to the place." Another had emphasized that "patents, bio-commerce, biotechnology, products of innovation, have to be realized and executed with legal agreements, clear, concrete, and concise from the beginning." And a third had suggested that "we are talking about biodiversity . . . biotechnology, bio, bio, bio many things. . . . It sounds like an ethical problem. Maybe we need, like, an ethical committee, a council?"

No such legal agreement or ethical committee had been put in place. Most of the scientists at Ikiam seemed unconcerned by this scenario. But an American anthropologist named Maggie Cavendish told me that she was "really afraid of what I'm seeing happening in Ikiam right now."[88] Cavendish had spent her entire career working with indigenous communities in the Ecuadorian Amazon and had recently joined the team at Ikiam. She confirmed that indigenous knowledge and biological samples were being acquired in the absence of any regulatory framework, and the researchers "aren't even paying people, or are paying below the minimum wage, which isn't even legal, okay? And they're working for a government institution." On her insistence, Ikiam had invited representatives of the indigenous nationalities of the region to a two-day workshop to be held later that month, with the aim of producing a "Code of Ethics" to govern the conditions under which research would be conducted. This had not made her popular among her fellow staff. "The Ikiam people are mad at me!" she said. "And they [are] really mad about this conference. . . . They came to me and said, 'Maggie, you cannot do this, [the indigenous population are] going to get ideas.' And I said, '¡Ojalá que sí!' [I hope they do!] That is precisely why we are doing the workshop!"

The objective of the workshop was to discuss and revise a document drafted by Cavendish and circulated before the event, which was "intended to serve as a basic ethical framework for Ikiam researchers."[89] From the perspective of biosocialism, a framework of this kind would necessarily oppose the commodification of knowledge. In the words of René Ramírez, "It is impossible to create a new social order with a unit . . . as dehumanizing as money."[90] But like the MIT proposal presented at the initial planning workshop, Cavendish's document made no reference to biosocialism, and it was likewise framed in the language of neoliberal common sense: "In the case of research that includes potential commercial applications—the creation of commercial products or processes that could result in commercial patents or production—the researcher must negotiate with the individual or community, before the research begins, as to who has intellectual property rights to the information and how the community or individual will be compensated for providing this knowledge."[91]

From Cavendish's point of view, the casting of the Code of Ethics in commercial terms was not an ideological project but a pragmatic strategy in defense of indigenous rights and livelihoods, given that the researchers at Ikiam "are making so much more money than these people and are so selfish about paying them," while the indigenous communities "need to commercialize this stuff because they can't live traditionally anymore, and they have to find . . . other ways of living."[92] This perspective was shared by the majority of the indigenous representatives in attendance, most of whom were eager to begin negotiations. This was no coincidence, as Cavendish had carefully selected the invitees from among her own trusted network of indigenous collaborators. No one from Atacapi or any of the other communities in the immediate vicinity of Ikiam had been invited, and members of radical indigenous social movements had been deliberately excluded, as Cavendish explained:

> We've got a lot of the [indigenous] *politicos* mad at us! Because . . . we decided that we wanted . . . really pragmatic advice. We wanted people—"Okay, you've worked with an anthropologist, you've worked with a linguist. What do you think it's worth? What do you think they should pay you?" We wanted that kind of pragmatic stuff that you can't get from people who haven't done it. We also wanted people that weren't radically political. We didn't want a bunch of political speeches about "You're exploiting us." So we invited people who we know are thoughtful, that we know can see both sides of the situation.[93]

This strategy, however, was not entirely successful. In addition to her personally selected invitees, Cavendish had been obliged to invite an indigenous delegation from the Department of Ancestral Knowledge of SENESCYT—the secretariat headed by René Ramírez and responsible for Ikiam. Midway through the morning of the first day of the workshop, a member of the delegation intervened to remind Cavendish and the rest of the participants that "in Ecuador traditional knowledge is constitutionally recognized as a collective right. Traditional knowledge does not belong to the individual but to the community."[94] The privatization of such knowledge, as he pointed out, threatened to violate Article 322 of the 2008 constitution, which prohibited "all forms of the appropriation of collective knowledge."[95]

Maggie Cavendish was taken aback by this unexpected intervention, and by the audible murmur of agreement that slowly spread around the room. "I also have plenty of traditional knowledge," she responded testily. "The knowledge that I teach is the traditional knowledge of Europe." Was the representative of the Department of Ancestral Knowledge really suggesting that "Europeans can have individual rights [to their knowledge] but *indígenas* cannot?" Was "traditional knowledge really so different from [the knowledge of] Western culture?" The man from SENESCYT replied that it was indeed different, as "Western knowledge might be individual, but indigenous knowledge is collective for many reasons. It is knowledge rooted in its surroundings, in the existence of the community, mediated by a cultural relation." Cavendish interrupted to sarcastically observe that "all cultures have a 'cultural relation.'" Another member of SENESCYT asked Cavendish to "let him finish what he was saying," but she was herself interrupted by a biologist based at Ikiam: "So, mathematics was invented by the Greeks. That isn't traditional knowledge anymore. It's universal, and if the Greeks started claiming that we have to ask their permission to use it, then we would all be in trouble!"

This remark was met with a bemused silence from all in attendance, and Cavendish took the opportunity to briskly announce, "We can move on to another theme," before introducing the main business of the day. "I'm going to pass a sheet around," she explained to the indigenous representatives, adding that the sheet contained a list of services to which they would assign prospective prices. "Then the professors over here will make a counteroffer," she continued. "They will send [the sheet back] to you, and you can make another offer. This is something we can all negotiate, don't you agree?" The man from SENESCYT, however, did not agree:

> Our *compañeros* have set us the task of coming up with numbers. The question is "How much is indigenous knowledge worth?" It's a good question. The criteria on which we are valuing traditional knowledge have not been defined. What we are doing is negotiating, commercializing, sitting down at the table, and suggesting numbers. I'm not sure that this is the right road to go down. The criteria for calculating the benefits of traditional knowledge, given that it is collective, should be based on other considerations. I'm not sure it can be done in percentages as we are doing here. I don't think so.

One of Maggie Cavendish's indigenous assistants intervened at this point to reassert the official line: "Well, I *do* think so. . . . It's not perfect, but it allows us to deepen our analysis to arrive at a real valuation." Cavendish had been holding her hand up in frustration throughout the latest intervention of the man from SENESCYT, while rolling her eyes at her fellow researchers and indigenous invitees. Now she doggedly returned to the negotiation of prices. Crucially, the prices to be calculated were not related to the property rights governing the active ingredients of the flora and fauna of region, or the indigenous knowledge of these ingredients, but comprised a pay scale for the provision of specific services to researchers by members of the indigenous communities of the region, measured in labor time. Hourly and daily rates were discussed for a predetermined list of services that included manual labor such as trail cutting as well as the communication of specialist knowledge. By shifting the debate from property rights to wage labor, the delicate question of the ownership of the knowledge itself was subtly avoided.

At this point, the workshop broke into groups to discuss prices for each of the listed services. Maggie Cavendish collected their lists at the end of the day and compiled them overnight. The second day was due to begin with a presentation by the Department of Ancestral Knowledge on intellectual property rights. Cavendish, however, was determined to finalize the price negotiations before the man from SENESCYT could confuse matters again. She altered the timetable accordingly, and the day now began with her rattling through a list of price differentials for a bewildering variety of services before arriving at an apparently arbitrary decision on the final price of each, as if performing a Dadaist commentary on the mundane nonsensicality of everyday price formation:

> The price to stay in someone's home with food: there are prices 40–30–20–25—I think we will settle on 28 dollars. . . . Without food the price was 20–10–5–13: 10 dollars when a person brings their own food. . . . Expert [knowledge]—the price is 20–12–50–20—at the end of the day, that's more or less 20 [dollars]. . . . Organizers making contacts, programming interviews, all that stuff . . . by month 1,000–500–600–1,000. That's 766 [dollars]. Guide—that's someone who finds plants or whatever—300–380–340–325. I pay 300 [dollars] and that's fine. . . . Is there anything else you people want to mention?

Having established her list of prices, Cavendish must have felt that she could finally relax. But just as the belated session on intellectual property rights was getting under way, Franklin Sharupi, a prominent *Shuar* member of the CONAIE and a bodyguard to the militant indigenous leader Salvador Quishpe, burst into the workshop unannounced, armed with a ten-foot-long ceremonial spear. He immediately intervened in the debate: "We are First Nations [*Naciones Originarias*], and what is ours is collective property, not individual commerce! You say that it must have commercial applications, but I reject your system and your Westernization [*occidentalización*]! We have never seen our science as commerce. It is a form of cultural life." He went on to criticize the exclusion of indigenous political organizations from the event and warned: "We cannot be [treated as] objects of investigation! We are subjects! . . . The results [of these investigations] must be for the benefit of our cultures, and we have to be very clear about the political dimension [of Ikiam]."

The Ikiam researchers were in a state of shock. Sharupi's comments were similar in substance to those made by the man from SENESCYT the previous day. But now they were being uttered by a furious *Shuar* warrior brandishing an enormous spear. This time, Maggie Cavendish was not rolling her eyes in contempt. Instead, she mumbled apologetically that "Carlos [Ávila, the rector of Ikiam] says that there must be some form of recognition for you because you have discovered the plants, but it's very complex . . ." Other members of the research team gradually regained their composure, however, and insisted that Ikiam had the right to assert full ownership of any patents obtained through their research. According to one biologist, "The patent [will be] for the application, not the plant," and "The innovation [will have] nothing to do with traditional uses." During the closing session, Cavendish's indigenous allies also rallied around her, attacking the "indigenous bureaucracy" of the CONAIE, emphasizing that "this is a meeting of experts," and concluding that "the important thing is to move forward [in our negotiations with Ikiam].

If we don't do it, then no one else will do it for us, and Ikiam will go ahead without us." Even the man from SENESCYT ended up abandoning the radical stance that he had previously adopted and defending the commodification of knowledge against the representative of the CONAIE. "The world functions as it does, and not as we would wish," he concluded with a shrug. "What can we do in the face of this system?"

In his reflections on the construction of biosocialism, René Ramírez had warned that without a genuine "connection with the collective," Ikiam and Yachay would "merely reproduce a socially exclusionary and unjust system."[96] Rather than pioneering a new form of collective engagement, however, the Code of Ethics workshop embodied the depoliticized governance of neoliberal environmentalism, in which a naturalized market logic structures the predetermined coordinates of debate, "'irresponsible' partners are excluded," and antagonisms are disavowed by "displacing conflict and disagreement onto the terrain of consensually manageable problems, expert knowledge, and interest intermediation."[97] In the words of Franklin Sharupi, the representative of the CONAIE who had gate-crashed the event: "Everything is done in form, but not in substance. . . . They just call upon specific people to act as 'consultants,' take us to a white elephant [that is, the Ikiam campus], shut us in a room and tell us: 'Everything has already been decided, sit down, we need you to fill in these forms.' We are just informants. Almost as if we were objects. As soon as the academics have gotten what they need, as soon as they have achieved their objective, they say: 'Thank you very much,' and that's that."[98]

The objective to be achieved in this case was to set the terms and conditions under which knowledge as a collective use value would be extracted and transformed into a scarce resource under private monopoly control. This was not the meticulous scheming of a team of market fundamentalists. Rather, it was an illustration of the phantas-matic power of neoliberal common sense, even in the context of a post-neoliberal project. The participants in the workshop were un-consciously involved in the social construction of a commodity, and the complexity of the event demonstrated the extent to which the commodification of the commons is "a contingent and sometimes rudderless task for those who must make markets work on the ground."[99] But the outcome was the same. Far from engineering a transition from finite resources to infinite resources, Ikiam was at-tempting the precise opposite: the transformation of the infinite re-source of knowledge into a finite resource delimited by the commodity form.

The Limits of Infinity

According to the doctrine of biosocialism, the transition from fi-nite resources to infinite resources was not just a question of develop-ing the Ecuadorian biotechnology sector, but also demanded a simultaneous reduction in the exploitation of hydrocarbons and other "primary resources that degrade nature."[100] This would not be an easy task, as René Ramírez acknowledged: "If we are to maintain this tran-scendent objective, . . . we must bind our hands to the mast of the nonexploitation of oil, in order to avoid the temptation of being se-duced by the song of the sirens—the revenues of exploitation."[101] But despite this cautionary appeal to Homeric metaphor, the MIT pro-posal for Ikiam included two secondary campuses devoted to oil and mining, which were located in the petroleum-producing region of the northern Amazon and the mineral-rich region to the south. In the words of a professor of geophysics from MIT: "Petroleum, mining, and the conservation of the biosphere: I think those are the topics that should be deemed fundamental to be taught at Ikiam."

The seemingly paradoxical inclusion of extractive industries in Ikiam was entirely consistent with the material trajectory of Ecuadorian capital accumulation. Although Ramírez was still diligently composing his radical excursuses on biosocialism within the confines of his office, the rest of the government had long since abandoned its initial opposition to the oil and mining sectors and was engaged in the aggressive expansion of the primary resource frontier. During a televised address to the nation in October 2015, Correa warned that the siren song to be resisted was not the temptation of extractivism, as Ramírez had suggested, but that of its rejection: "We must be intelligent. We must act with reason and with passion [*con razón y corazón*], with conscience, efficiency, and justice, *compañeros*. We must not allow ourselves to be dragged away by the siren song of the same irresponsible people as always: 'No to mining, no to oil, and let's all starve to death.' . . . Enough of these inconsistencies! We must take advantage of our natural resources in a responsible manner, in order to confront the principal challenge facing our country: the necessity of overcoming poverty as rapidly as possible."[102]

Over the course of the Correa administration, the legitimacy of the government had become increasingly reliant on high levels of public investment, which remained heavily dependent on oil revenues. Furthermore, following the exclusion of Ecuador from international credit markets in 2008, after it had partially defaulted on its debts, Correa had signed several "loan-for-oil" contracts with China, and the repayment schedule provided additional urgency to the expansion of oil production. From 2009 onward, the government had opened a series of bidding rounds for new oil blocks throughout the northern Amazon, while signing contracts with foreign multinationals for the joint exploitation of Ecuador's mature reserves.[103] In 2009 Correa also issued a new mining law, which reversed his initial moratorium on mining activities and opened the sector to transnational capital. The law allowed companies to undertake mineral prospection in indigenous territories and made it possible for public consultations to be held after concessions had already been granted, while stipulating that any obstruction of mining activities by popular resistance could be met with the use of force.[104]

The secondary campuses were conceived in the context of this newfound commitment to the formal subsumption of nature to capital. In November 2015, in the depths of the oil crisis, we left the main campus and set out in search of them. We began by heading north, into the region of oil production, toward the campus that was focused on the oil industry. The road followed the contours of the Andean foothills for several hours before cutting out across the lowlands through what had once been jungle, past overgrown cattle pastures and orderly African palm plantations, through improvised towns of putrefying gray-green concrete and blue-mirrored windows, beneath decrepit drilling towers and grimy vultures spiraling through the black smoke flares of low-grade crude.

In the nondescript town of El Eno, an immense billboard welcomed us to the campus with an image of a luxuriant pink flower blooming in the depths of the jungle, beside the Ikiam slogan: "Biodiversity Is Our Future." The image was streaked with long lines of thick brown mold. Behind the billboard, a rusted oil pipeline snaked across a grubby river. We inquired about the campus in a restaurant on the roadside and were put in touch with a man known as Don Pazmiño, who had sold the government the land for its construction. We drove through a grid of fields chopped out of the jungle, to the end of a rough track, where we were met by Don Pazmiño himself, dressed in the rubber boots, ragged trousers, and string vest of the *colono*. From there, he led us into the forest, cutting a path with his machete. We stopped in a small clearing. "Well," he said after a pause, "Here we are!"[105] We were standing in the middle of the campus. But the campus was not there.

Back in El Eno, the president of the parish council described Ikiam as "a marvelous dream."[106] The creation of a university campus in the region had been welcomed as the fulfillment of a central demand of the ABP Accords. But construction had been repeatedly postponed, and ten days before our arrival the cancellation of the campus had been quietly announced, as one of the austerity measures imposed in response to the oil crisis. Despite the collapse of the oil price, however, new wells continued to be drilled in the mature fields of the region, and the expansion of the oil frontier proceeded apace, including the concession of oil blocks to foreign companies such as Belorusneft of Belarus, SINOPEC of China, and Schlumberger of France.[107] Many of the new wells were located along the Vía Guanta, one of the first oil roads to have been cut through the region and the site of some of the strongest *paros* in the era of the ABP. The gravel road left the highway a few miles beyond the site of the nonexistent campus. We passed a military base that had been installed at the time of the *paros* to protect the oil infrastructures and break up the blockades. Soon we came to a checkpoint operated by Petroamazonas. The security guards saw our government plates, checked our passports, and waved us through.

A tangled mass of dilapidated pipelines stretched along the roadside, through which ten thousand barrels of oil were extracted every day. Each turn in the road revealed another platform—a fenced-off slab of concrete with a line of oil pumps at one end and a blackened gas flare at the other. Most platforms were under armed guard, and private security patrolled the road. There were fields between the platforms, and the pipelines stretched across the front yards of wooden shacks. The oil flowing through them still contained the heat of the Earth, and families had spread their laundry out on them to dry. There was no sign of the Citizens' Revolution here. The houses had no running water and no sewage system. The clinic lacked basic medicines, and the school lacked drinking water.

The president of the local *comuna* lived beside one of the platforms, beneath the constant glow of the gas flare. She showed us where a cracked pipeline had drained into the land behind her house. "The whole stream was completely black," she said, "Two cows were covered in it. They drank the water and died."[108] Farther down the road the wind picked up and the air was suddenly filled with floating seeds. A rainstorm followed and washed them out of the sky, while the flames of the gas flares sputtered in the downpour. In the stillness after the rain, I became aware of an almost imperceptible seething: the rush of warm crude sliding through corroded pipelines.

From there we headed south, toward the campus in the mining zone. We drove for two days, into the mountainous southern Amazon, densely forested and unmarked by the oil industry. Outside the town of El Pangui, our arrival at the Ikiam campus was announced by another billboard, featuring an enormous green insect and a different slogan: "Development and Harmonious Coexistence." We followed the sign off the highway, but the road soon petered out in a maze of dirt tracks. We continued on foot, along a trail through fields of maize, where we met a laborer who agreed to take us to the site of the campus. He led us through a forest to a clearing, which had been squatted by a destitute *Shuar* family who gathered anxiously in the doorway of their hut, fearing that we were about to evict them. Once again, the campus was not there.

As in the case of El Eno, the campus in El Pangui had been canceled just before our arrival, as a consequence of the oil crisis.[109] By this time, however, it had served its ideological purpose. El Pangui had been a center of resistance to the Ecuadorian mining industry, owing to its proximity to the site of El Mirador—an open-pit copper, gold, and silver mine located in the nearby Condor Mountains. In 2000 the mining concession for the region had been acquired by EcuaCorriente (ECSA), which was owned by a Canadian consortium.

Fierce local resistance had prevented the company from advancing in the development of El Mirador, and in 2006 a series of violent confrontations had resulted in the indefinite suspension of operations. During his election campaign of the same year, Correa had visited the region and had pledged to oppose large-scale mining in the area. In 2009, however, the investor-friendly terms of the new mining law, and the increasing strength of China-Ecuador relations resulting from the loans-for-oil program, combined to create the conditions for the purchase of ECSA by a Chinese consortium. In March 2012 the Ecuadorian government had signed a $1.4 billion contract with ECSA for the exploitation of El Mirador. The mine would be 1.5 miles wide and 2,100 feet deep, and would involve the removal of 590 million tons of rock and the construction of roads, camps, and a tailings reservoir for the storage of millions of liters of toxic sludge.[110]

The signing of the contract marked the inauguration of large-scale mining in Ecuador. The CONAIE responded by organizing a march that began from the site of the mine and concluded in Quito, demanding the renewal of the moratorium on mining and the observance of the rights of nature enshrined in the 2008 constitution.[111] The new contract also threatened to rekindle the resistance of the local population because of the perceived social and ecological effects of the mine and its location on *Shuar* territory and the land of *Kichwa* and mestizo peasants. As part of the contract, however, the Correa administration had secured the forward payment of $100 million of "anticipated royalties," the majority of which would be invested in a series of public works in El Pangui and the surrounding area, including roads, a hospital, and three Millennium Schools. The construction of the Ikiam campus in El Pangui was announced to coincide with this package of infrastructure projects, and a Millennium School now stood opposite the sign for Ikiam on the highway.[112] During the inauguration of the school, Correa emphatically declared: "[Mining] will transform El Pangui . . . and the entire southern Amazon! The immense majority of the *pueblos indígenas*, just like any other sector of humanity, want roads, energy, communications, they want health, they want education, they want modernity!"[113]

But as we turned onto the dirt road to El Mirador, the symbols of modernity that lined the highway dissolved into a different scene. Hillsides were being torn down to widen the road, and a constant stream of dump trucks thundered past us in a cloud of red dust. The river was being dredged for sand, and a gravel factory stood beside a newly constructed brothel on the riverbank. Just upstream from here we arrived at the humble wooden home of the *Shuar* antimining activist José Tendetza, which lay at the bottom of a narrow gorge. We clambered down from the road and picked our way across the boggy ground. Tendetza's brother was waiting outside the house, with a machete in his hand. He was frank in his assessment of the Citizens' Revolution:

> We have nothing. In what way have they helped us? . . . They
> created a constitution that speaks of justice and the rights of
> nature, but what is it worth if they don't respect the law them
> selves? [Correa] calls this "*buen vivir.*" You, as educated peo
> ple, what do you make of it? I see it as absurd. . . . This isn't
> *buen vivir*, it's abuse. As a *Shuar*, I see it this way. It cannot be
> just, what they are doing to us. [But] the people applaud.
> Like kittens licking the plate of the government: "Long
> live the government that brings us development!" . . . It's
> laughable.[114]

José Tendetza had been one of the most prominent figures in the opposition to El Mirador. On November 28, 2014, he had boarded a bus to a nearby town for a meeting of the resistance movement, in preparation for a UN environmental summit to be held in Lima the following week, at which he would present the case against ECSA. He did not arrive at the meeting. Four days later his family learned that his body had been pulled from the Zamora River by police and hastily buried in a grave marked "No Name," after an autopsy had attributed the cause of death to drowning. His body was exhumed, and a second autopsy determined that he had in fact been tortured and strangled before being thrown into the river with his hands tied behind his back.[115]

A few miles farther up the road, we rounded a curve in the valley and the mine came into view. Deep red gouges had been cut into the lower slopes of an emerald green mountain filled with copper and gold. Along the road and high on the hillsides, dozens of identical signs had been erected reading, "Private Property." Crossing the river, we drove out across a long, broad plain that had been stripped of trees in preparation for the construction of the tailings reservoir. This had been the site of the community of San Marcos, formed by *Kichwa* and mestizo peasants who had been forced to abandon the southern high-lands during the drought of the 1960s, descending from the moun-tains for days along the riverbank, their food and possessions loaded onto mules. Like the *colonos* of the northern Amazon, they had opened a path through countless miles of jungle, clearing land with shovels and machetes and constructing their homes, a church, and a school.[116]

San Marcos was an obstacle to the mining project that ECSA and the government portrayed not as a long-established community, but as a group of opportunistic squatters who had invaded the land illegally in order to extort resettlement fees from the company.[117] On May 12, 2014, two busloads of masked police and private security forces arrived in San Marcos without warning and sealed off the area, while ECSA personnel used excavators to demolish the church and the school before tearing holes out of the earth and burying the rubble to erase all traces of these symbols of a collective historical existence. As in the case of Sumak Ñambi in Providencia, the community responded to this harbinger of its imminent displacement by creating an association called the Community of Social Action of Condor-Mirador (CASCOMI) to defend their right to the land. They began to reconstruct the church and the school and to build additional houses for friends and family members who wanted to join the struggle as a collective material assertion of their right to exist, which one inhabitant described as "a strategy of resistance by creating presence."[118] Like the urban project of Sumak Ñambi, this precarious space embodied the spirit of an insurgent utopia, created in a moment of urgent confrontation with the violence of capital. Signs began to appear on the site of the tailings pond, written in both Spanish and Chinese, which read: "Collective property of CASCOMI: Any person or company that enters or damages this property will be subject to legal action or submitted to indigenous justice."[119] In the words of one member of CASCOMI, "We were in the process of reclaiming the entire area."[120]

On September 20, 2015, before dawn, private security personnel marched into San Marcos, supported by two hundred heavily armed police officers. They moved from house to house, giving the occupants five minutes to gather their possessions before demolishing their homes. Then they erected barbed-wire fences and "private property" signs. When we arrived in December 2015, only a few scattered homes remained in the valley and on the mountainside. A few days later these homes were also destroyed in dawn raids backed by government security forces. As one member of CASCOMI exclaimed: "We have no legal or juridical support. Everything is in favor of the state and the Chinese company. They can dispossess communities, kill people, destroy the environment, whatever. The only things that interests the government is the money from the mine."[121] The same process was explained by a representative of ECSA in matter-of-fact terms: "The problem with the communities is that they think the copper belongs to them. . . . It's a confusion of theirs. [But] the state acted . . . and since then most of them have come to see things our way. . . . Correa stands firm. Where other governments wouldn't get involved [in confronting resistance], he sends in the security forces."[122]

On the highway back to Quito, I noticed that the billboard for Ikiam had disappeared.

Science Fiction

This chapter has traced the convoluted process through which a utopian fantasy was transformed into its opposite. Biosocialism began as the most radical dimension of the Citizens' Revolution, which envisioned the transition from a capitalist economy based on the finite resources of primary commodity extraction to a post-capitalist economy based on the infinite resources of knowledge and biodiversity. This project was materialized in the form of a pioneering Amazonian university, which would break with the colonial legacy of biopiracy to become a sovereign center of biotechnology, bringing international scientists and indigenous nationalities together in the collective transformation of the productive matrix. But biosocialism had to urgently prove its worth as an accumulation strategy. This led to the adoption of neo-structuralist policy prescriptions, which framed the transformation of the productive matrix in terms much closer to the cognitive capitalism of neoliberal knowledge economies than the collectivist vision of biosocialism, while Ikiam ended up being inspired by South Korean knowledge cities and designed by corporate relations strategists from MIT.

Biosocialism was thus transformed into a neoliberal strategy for the real subsumption of nature to capital. But this was only the first of its involutions. The constant pressures of accumulation and the febrile atmosphere of the oil boom compelled the hasty implementation of

Ikiam, which came to assume the colonial spatial form of an elite enclave that excluded the indigenous population while unleashing a wave
of gentrification and dispossession across the surrounding landscape.
Soon after its inauguration, however, the collapse of the oil price
stripped Ikiam of the resources required to fully realize even this per-
verse distortion of its original project. In the absence of research laboratories, the university was reduced to appropriating indigenous
knowledge of the flora and fauna of the region with the aim of exporting samples to foreign facilities. This process threatened to reproduce
the neoliberal commodification of the commons and the neocolonial
practice of biopiracy by establishing local biodiversity as a new frontier
of primary commodity extraction.

A disavowed strategy for the real subsumption of nature to capital
was thus transformed into an inadvertent reproduction of the logic of
formal subsumption that biosocialism had been designed to transcend. But this proved ineffectual as an accumulation strategy, and
the Correa administration became increasingly committed to the expanded reproduction of the oil and mineral frontiers—a commitment embodied in two secondary campuses devoted to these themes.
As the oil crisis began to bite, however, these campuses were abandoned, and their corresponding resource frontiers were forced open
to foreign capital with increasing ferocity, producing spaces of environmental degradation and violent dispossession that completed the
transformation of biosocialism into its opposite.

The contours of this story have been shaped by the dynamics of
global capital accumulation, which impose severe constraints on any
accumulation strategy that seeks to escape from the formal subsumption of nature to capital, to the extent that the expansion of the primary resource frontier in resource-rich regions of the world is a
necessary condition for processes of real subsumption under way in
the global centers of surplus value production. But as we also saw in

the case of Manta-Manaus, these dynamics should not be thought of as mechanistic forces automatically carving the world into the image of capital. Instead, they frequently play out in the form of fantastical visions, farcical encounters, hasty decisions, and stupid mistakes. This chapter has traced these trivialities and contingencies through a labyrinth of obscure tracts, pointless meetings, dead ends, and dirty secrets in an attempt to capture the quotidian absurdities of the dialectical process.

Ikiam was ultimately revealed as a living laboratory without laboratories, a mirage laboratory produced by a laboratory of mirages. Perhaps unsurprisingly, this proved to be my final assignment for CENEDET. In 2013, as already discussed, René Ramírez had played a central role in the establishment of CENEDET in the Ecuadorian state. From that point onward, however, he had maintained his distance. Meanwhile, his wife had been appointed acting rector of the university with which CENEDET was affiliated. By the time of her appointment, CENEDET had begun to disseminate our research findings on the flagship development projects of the Citizens' Revolution. At this point it became clear that we had been employed to contribute to the ideological tapestry of the Citizens' Revolution, and not to explore the uncomfortable truths that it concealed. A dean of the university described a meeting at which Ramírez's wife had hurled a pamphlet of our papers across the desk in fury, shouting that the university could not be associated with such controversial material. Our research on Ikiam was the final straw. In December 2015 we had traveled to the southern Amazon to investigate the campus there. As we have seen, the campus turned out not to exist, and we were instead confronted with a wave of violent displacements conducted by the government in defense of foreign mining interests. While in the field, I received a telephone call informing me of my immediate dismissal, and CENEDET was shut down at the end of the year.[123]

By the time I was fired, however, CENEDET had already contributed to the organization of an international conference at a think tank composed of advisers to René Ramírez, of which Ramírez himself was president. We presented our research on Ikiam, the failure of biosocialism, and the violent expansion of the primary resource frontier.[124] Ramírez's advisers were aghast, and a Twitter feed that had been set up to provide updates on the conference ceased to function for the duration of our talk. The following day, Ramírez arrived to deliver the keynote address. He set out his vision of biosocialism, insisting that "these things don't just spring from the head of René Ramírez," while his advisers shifted uncomfortably in their seats.[125]

Ramírez left the conference immediately after his speech. With nothing left to lose at this point, and given that he was evidently unaware of our research, I rushed into the atrium, pushed my way through the gaggle of secretaries, advisers, and bodyguards that surrounded him, and requested an interview. He agreed, and a few days later I was ushered into the palatial office of a high-ranking minister whose wife had just fired me, and whose doctrine I had just deconstructed on the stage of his own think tank. Was it possible that he had no idea about any of this? Could he be oblivious to the utter failure of biosocialism and ignorant of the dispossession and destruction under way behind its facade? Were power and ideology so profoundly entangled with one another that capitalist social relations could be reinforced by someone committed to changing the world in the opposite direction and convinced that he was doing so? Ramírez had been delayed, but he was sure to arrive soon. I was shown to my seat and asked to wait. As I looked around me, I recalled his version of Nietzsche's aphorism: "To continue to dream, aware that I am dreaming." His office had high ceilings, bare white walls, and expansive views of verdant gardens. After the door had closed, it was completely silent.

CONCLUSION
Avalanche of Infamies

The imminent awakening is poised, like the
wooden horse of the Greeks, in the Troy of dreams.

Walter Benjamin, The Arcades Project

Ever since Correa had come to power in 2007, the slogan had been the same: "Dreams are transformed into reality with the Citizens' Revolution." But ten years later, in the runup to the presidential election of 2017, a new message appeared on the billboards: the transformation was complete, and Ecuador was now living "the revolution of dreams come true [*Ecuador vive la revolución de los sueños cumplidos*]." Of all the regions of Ecuador, it was the Amazon that was said to have gained most from the Citizens' Revolution. As the election approached, the government produced a promotional video celebrating its achievements in the region. Set to stirring music, and accompanied by aerial footage of sparkling clinics, schools, highways, bridges, and Millennium Cities, the narrator proclaims that "the communities living alongside oil and mining projects could previously only dream of these things. . . . Now it is no longer a sacrifice to live in the Amazon. Now it is an honor, a pleasure, a source of pride." An elderly *Shuar* man thanks "President Rafael Correa for realizing our dream," followed by a message from Correa to the people of the region: "A new nation of joy, hope, unity, and revolution receives you in an immense embrace. Ecuador has been transformed. We have regained our nation, and we will have our nation forever." The video ends with the slogan: "Land of dreams come true."[1]

The Correa regime had indeed transformed the Ecuadorian Amazon, from the stark abandonment of the neoliberal night into a reality structured by the fantasies of the post-neoliberal state. But the dream of the Citizens' Revolution had taken a far stranger form than such images and slogans would suggest. Each of the iconic Amazonian megaprojects explored in this book—Manta-Manaus, Ikiam, and the Millennium Cities—repeated a common pattern, in which promethean efforts to wrench the nation free from natural resource dependency ended up reinforcing the economic model they had sought to escape. Rather than integrating Ecuador into smooth logistical networks of globalized production, the infrastructure of Manta-Manaus was appropriated by the oil industry; far from constituting a socialist form of original accumulation, the Millennium Cities served only to legitimate the primitive accumulation of capital; and instead of catalyzing a transition from the finite resources of hydrocarbon reserves to the infinite resources of biodiversity and scientific knowledge, Ikiam was reduced to transforming the infinite resources of the intellectual and ecological commons into the finite resources of privately owned commodities. In each case, a utopian dream was transformed into a satirical self-parody, a progressive vision was inverted into a circular journey to nowhere, and a grand ambition was swept away by forces beyond its control.

Standing outside his thatched hut in the village of Atacapi, with the white walls of Ikiam shining through the trees across the river, a *Kichwa* leader reflected on this perplexing situation: "The Amazon used to be a myth. They called us *indios*, savages. For the rest of the country the Amazon did not exist. So, on one hand Rafael Correa has done well to place the Amazon on the same level as the other regions

of Ecuador. . . . But on the other hand, what does it really amount to?
. . . *White elephants and serpents of steel*, as we call the pipes that take
the oil from the Amazon and send it to other countries. Those serpents that give our wealth to others."[2]

Like a surrealist dreamscape strewn with impossible objects, this
image vividly captured the fantastical materiality of the "land of
dreams come true," in which the elephantine utopias of the Citizens'
Revolution had become hopelessly entangled in the serpentine dynamics of the Real of capital—as lithe as snakes and as hard as steel.
The failure of the Correa regime to break out of its subordinate position within these dynamics was evident in the official statistics. The
transformation of the productive matrix away from primary resource
exploitation should have been reflected in an increase of industrial
goods as a proportion of Ecuadorian exports over the course of the
Citizens' Revolution. Instead, this percentage decreased, falling from
26 percent in 2007 to 23 percent in 2016, while overall manufacturing
activity declined as a percentage of Ecuadorian GDP, falling from
14 percent in 2007 to 12 percent in 2015.[3] The constricting grip of the
serpents of steel was further demonstrated by the economic effect of
the end of the oil boom. From 2007 to the beginning of the oil crash
in 2014, the economy had grown at an annual average of 4.3 percent.
But by September 2015 Ecuador was in recession, and in the depths of
the oil crisis in 2016, the economy contracted by a further 1.5 percent,
while state oil revenues reportedly fell to zero.[4]

In June 2016 I returned to the megaprojects discussed in this
book. In the continued absence of petrodollars, they had all been put
on hold or else abandoned entirely. The first two Millennium Cities
continued their decline, and only one more was being built, of the
two hundred that had originally been planned. The construction
of the container port at Providencia had been postponed. The
half-completed site was overgrown with weeds, while the eco-city of

"Divining Providencia" still existed only in the fantasies of Ivy League design schools. From there I traveled to the main campus of Ikiam, which remained without laboratories, and on to the international airport on the outskirts of Tena, which had been a key component of Manta-Manaus. I descended a desolate highway, crossed a vacant parking lot, and entered the departure lounge. The airport was fully equipped with check-in desks, security systems, restaurants, and souvenir shops. A cleaning woman was polishing the gleaming floors. But no one else was there. The state airline could no longer afford to run empty planes from Quito at a constant loss, and the airport had received its last flight in December 2015. I walked through the unmanned security system and out onto the airstrip. Wandering across that vast deserted runway, under the immense Amazonian sky, I was captured once again by an overwhelming sense of inhabiting a reality in which things do not make sense, and "the fantastic becomes the rule, not the exception . . . a generalized fantastic which swallows up the entire world."[5]

As the oil rents receded from the stage set of the Citizens' Revolution, it was increasingly revealed as a theater of the absurd. Reports began appearing in the national press, in which one megaproject after another was exposed as an abject failure. In January 2016 a leading national newspaper published a cartoon depicting four white elephants, one of which was branded with the name "Tena Airport." The other three were named "Yachay"—the knowledge city in the highlands, in which over $1 billion had been invested with negligible results; "UNASUR"—the condor-shaped headquarters of post-neoliberal regionalism; and "The Refinery of the Pacific"—a vast oil refinery planned for construction on the coast near Manta, which had been abandoned after an expenditure of $1.2 billion on the clearance of the site.[6] The following Saturday, Correa used his weekly television broadcast to respond to the cartoon:

What are they calling a white elephant? UNASUR? Ridiculous! Take note, okay? They are going to be ridiculed by history! Yachay? . . . Yachay is the most important project in the history of this country! They are trying to rob us of our joy, our hope. . . . The Refinery of the Pacific as a white elephant? It hasn't even begun yet! And finally, Tena Airport. [The state airline] has suspended its flights. But . . . its usage will increase with the development of Ikiam, which is another of our emblematic universities. Ikiam—a collective dream! The university with the biggest and best natural laboratory on the planet—our Amazonian jungle! But how can we expect these poor, mediocre pamphleteers to understand? Their only concern is to spread hatred and confusion and to rob us of our happiness![7]

The irony, of course, was that the "collective dream" of Ikiam, to which Correa was appealing in order to demonstrate that Tena Airport was not a white elephant, was itself a white elephant. Yet over the following months, Correa continued to stubbornly dismiss all reports of project failure. He repeatedly rejected criticisms of Yachay, for example, claiming that it would be among the one hundred highest-ranked universities in the world by 2035[8] and applauding a speech in which a Yachay student declared: "We are the constructors of the country of knowledge. There are no white elephants here."[9] On another occasion, he turned his attention to Manta-Manaus:

A minister told me in a meeting the other day: "President, the media are saying that [Manta-Manaus] is not a viable project." So now they think they're more intelligent than the president? . . . Do you know why we haven't exported anything to Manaus? . . . The problem isn't the navigability of the rivers, due to natural factors. The problem isn't the lack of infrastructure or the absence of roads. The [only] problem is that we don't yet have official permission to navigate the rivers of Brazil. . . . This is one of the most important projects in the whole of Latin America! . . . It's going to replace the Panama Canal![10]

In fact, as we have seen, the problem was precisely that the Napo was *not* navigable by vessels of the size required to make the route commercially viable, and the road and port infrastructure *were* inadequate for an interoceanic corridor. The unfortunate minister was only trying to inform Correa of a fact of which everyone else was by then painfully aware: Manta-Manaus was *not* a viable project, and it was certainly *not* going to replace the Panama Canal.

Here, as on many other occasions reported in this book, Correa seems to have been alone in his ignorance of the shortcomings of the projects he was celebrating. Often, as in the inauguration of the Millennium Cities, his experience of the apparent success of these projects was meticulously organized by those around him in advance. As one local politician observed: "It's a joke. . . . What does the president do? He inaugurates something and thinks that everything is fine, but there are things that escape his notice. If only he could see the sad reality. But anyone who said anything would be punished for it, so they keep him in the dark."[11] This sentiment was expressed on countless occasions over the course of my research. Time and again, people would describe the failures of one utopian scheme or another, before insisting that "if the president only knew what was really happening, then everything would be different." But according to a minister who had attended the inauguration of one of the Millennium Cities, Correa was perfectly aware that the project was a disaster. He pretended to be convinced by the staging of its success, delivered his triumphant speech, and waved happily from the departing helicopter before slumping back in his seat and clutching his head in despair.[12]

If this is the case, then Correa was deliberately allowing the wool to be pulled over his eyes, and he was passionately defending projects that he knew to have failed. But why would he choose to play the fool? Perhaps he had realized that an ideology can function without anyone believing in it, so long as this belief is collectively attributed to *someone else* and embodied in what Žižek has described as "the ritualistic staging of a theatrical spectacle in the truth of which no one [actually] believes."[13] Through his tireless performance of the "subject supposed to believe,"[14] in endless public appearances and the weekly ritual of his national television address, Correa convinced his audience *to believe that he believed* in the success of the Citizens' Revolution. The collective belief of the nation thus continued to be embodied in the persistent theatrical staging of presidential conviction, even as its individual citizens abandoned all faith in the project. As Žižek has observed of similar rituals in other nominally socialist regimes, this was "not a simple subjective semblance (nobody really believed in it) but, rather, a kind of 'objective semblance,' a semblance materialized in the actual social functioning of the regime, in the way the ruling ideology was materialized in ideological rituals and apparatuses."[15]

Meanwhile, Correa responded to the deepening fiscal crisis of the state by accelerating the neoliberal reforms that were already under way, including the signing of a free trade agreement with the European Union, the passing of new laws promoting public-private partnerships and flexible labor contracts, and the return of the IMF to the country for the first time since its expulsion at the start of the Citizens' Revolution.[16] But rather than imposing a full austerity program, which would have been politically disastrous in the runup to the election, he chose to cover the growing gulf between state revenues and expenditures by plunging the country ever deeper into debt. A $1 billion bond issue was released in June 2016, followed by the sale of another $1 billion of bonds in September, a further $750 million in December, and $1 billion more in January 2017.[17] To regain the confidence of the credit markets from which Ecuador had been largely excluded since its partial default in 2008, Correa agreed to pay Occidental $980 million in compensation for its expulsion from Block 15 back in 2006.[18] And with a $650 million bond repayment falling due in December 2015, which coincided with the most critical moment in the fiscal crisis, he offered the French multinational Schlumberger a lucrative twenty-year contract for Block 61—one of the richest of Ecuador's mature oil fields—in exchange for an immediate $1 billion loan. The loan was made on the day of the bond repayment, thus saving the country from default through the further privatization of the oil industry.[19]

The main source of liquidity during the crisis, however, was China, in the form of an expansion of the loan-for-oil program discussed in the previous chapter. Over the course of the Correa administration, Ecuadorian debt to China rose from $7.1 million in 2007 to $17.4 *billion* in 2017, of which $8.3 billion was in the form of loan-for-oil contracts. Much of this credit was used to finance infrastructure projects built by Chinese companies, such as the Coca Codo Sinclair hydroelectric dam, which was constructed at a cost of $2.8 billion, with the aim of providing the electricity required by Ecuador's new industries. In the absence of any such industries, the resulting oversupply was diverted to the mining sector, which allowed the government to offer cheap electricity as an incentive to transnational capital.[20] Indeed, it was Chinese capital that stood to benefit most from this scheme, through the supply of electricity to the El Mirador copper and gold mine, and the Panantza-San Carlos Copper Project—a second open-pit mining concession that was now being developed near

El Mirador. Chinese credit was therefore funding projects built by Chinese capital that facilitated the Chinese exploitation of Ecuadorian minerals, while securing Chinese control over Ecuadorian hydrocarbon reserves. In the words of one commentator: "We have freed ourselves from Yankee imperialism . . . only to welcome Chinese imperialism with open arms. . . . We have escaped one form of dependency only to fall into another."[21]

At the same time, evidence began to emerge of a network of corruption at the heart of this process. In April 2016 the publication of the Panama Papers demonstrated that the managing directors of the state oil company had channeled at least $11.7 million into offshore accounts.[22] And in December 2016 the Brazilian construction firm Odebrecht—whose brief expulsion from Ecuador in 2008 had caused the withdrawal of Brazil from Manta-Manaus—was revealed to have paid $33 million in bribes to unnamed Ecuadorian officials between 2007 and 2016, in exchange for contracts with a combined value of $4.4 billion. These included the contract for the Refinery of the Pacific, which had already achieved notoriety as a white elephant on which over $1 billion of public funds had been spent on a process of earth removal in preparation for a project that was never executed.[23]

And all the while, the resource frontier continued to advance through acts of dispossession orchestrated by the state. In August 2016 the *Shuar* community of Nankints in the southern Amazon was evicted by the military to make way for the development of the Panantza–San Carlos Copper Project. As in the case of the eviction of the community of San Marcos from the site of El Mirador, their houses were destroyed and the wreckage buried to remove all trace of the existence of the community, while their crops were cut down and burned. In a press conference called to denounce these actions, the president of the CONAIE, Jorge Herrera, declared: "We will no longer continue to permit this kind of authoritarian brutality, [through which] the government of Rafael Correa is handing over the national territory to transnational companies." He was followed by the local leader of the *Shuar* federation, Agustín Wachapá, who vowed: "We are going to recuperate this territory. We will not retreat a single step. If this results in any deaths, then the government will be responsible."[24]

In November 2016 Correa and China's President Xi Jinping inaugurated Coca Codo Sinclair. The ceremony was held not at the remote site of the dam itself, but in a conference center in Quito, which was all that Xi's fleeting visit would allow. Standing on either side of a mock control panel mounted on a mahogany desk, the leaders pressed two big red plastic buttons, between which a pale green lightbulb flickered into life. It was a proud moment for Correa, and the final words of his speech were choked with emotion: "This is the new nation! Let no one place limits on our dreams!"[25] Three days after the ceremony, however, a group of *Shuar* militants seized control of the Chinese mining camp that had been constructed on the grounds of the displaced community of Nankints. Military reinforcements arrived; live rounds were exchanged and several police officers were injured. Security forces regained control of the camp the following day, while the *Shuar* took refuge in the jungle.[26] Three weeks later they attempted to reoccupy the camp, which remained under heavy military guard. Several people were injured in the ensuing shootout, and a police officer was killed.[27] In a repetition of his response to the *paro* in Dayuma in 2007, Correa declared a state of emergency and arrested Agustín Wachapá, before denouncing the *Shuar* as terrorists and insisting that "as long as I am president of Ecuador, everyone will respect public and private property!"[28]

But Correa's time as president was coming to an end. The constitution prevented him from running for reelection in 2017. He had attempted to amend it to be able to run indefinitely but had been forced to revise this amendment, which would now come into force only after the 2017 election. This still left the door open for Correa to run again in 2021, after which he could potentially govern the country for the rest of his life—an ambition that he strenuously denied. In the meantime, he chose Lenín Moreno, who had served as his vice president from 2007 to 2013, as the presidential candidate for Alianza PAIS in the 2017 election. Jorge Glas, who had replaced Moreno as Correa's vice-president, was selected as Moreno's running mate.[29]

In January 2017, one month before the election, Alianza PAIS staged a rally in the coastal city of Guayaquil. The event was held to celebrate the tenth anniversary of Correa's inauguration and to give a final push to Moreno's campaign. Addressing the huge crowd, which stretched into the distance down the central boulevard, Moreno declared: "During this decade we have lived a legend! A legend that one day you will all tell your children and grandchildren: 'I was part of the Citizens' Revolution! I rode alongside Correa! . . . I was part of the victorious decade!'" He was followed by Glas, who promised to continue "constructing this marvelous Ecuador that will never return to the past." Finally, Correa took the stage to rapturous applause: "Ten years ago we were just a handful of dreamers. But today we are thousands, hundreds of thousands, millions! And in only a decade we have managed to transform the country!" He went on to list the achievements of the Citizens' Revolution before drawing the event to a close with an emotional farewell to his loyal supporters, shouting at the top of his lungs over deafening cheers: "A thousand thanks to everyone for this victorious decade! For this collective dream! For the victories that we have achieved together! And finally, *compañeros*, may you never forget: *Hasta la victoria siempre!*"[30]

But for all the celebrations of the victorious decade, the government failed to win the first round of the election outright. Moreno was forced into a runoff against Guillermo Lasso, a banker who had served as finance minister during the devastating financial crisis of 1999, and who was running on an openly neoliberal platform. In the end, Moreno was narrowly elected. But in the Amazon, five of the six provinces voted for Lasso.[31] Ten years after entering the dreamworld of the Citizens' Revolution, they had chosen to return to the neoliberal night.

By this time, post-neoliberal regimes were in crisis throughout the continent—voted out of office in Argentina, mired in corruption scandals in Brazil, and spiraling into hyperinflation in Venezuela. Moreno's tenuous victory thus appeared to have sealed "Ecuador's position as the standard-bearer for '21st century socialism.'"[32] But despite his defeat of the neoliberal candidate, it soon became clear that Moreno would enact the return to neoliberalism that he had campaigned against. As we have seen, in practical terms this had already become the dominant trajectory of the Correa administration. But under Moreno this agenda was accelerated and made explicit. Upon his arrival in office in May 2017, Moreno dismissed René Ramírez and the other surviving Leftists of the Correa cabinet and replaced them with businessmen and neoliberal economists, including the finance minister, who promptly announced that the previous administration had "built the machine and now we have to start it up, and that is the responsibility of the private sector."[33]

There is a sense in which this destiny was inscribed into the post-neoliberal project from the outset, to the extent that it had limited its transformative ambitions to the ideological parameters of neostructuralism, which was premised precisely on "building the machine" of institutions and infrastructures required for systemic competitiveness. Indeed, Correa himself had ultimately justified the infrastructural investments of the Citizens' Revolution on the basis of their contribution to the conditions demanded by global capital, as illustrated by a speech he delivered in August 2016: "Now we have renewable energy, logistics, the road network, new ports and airports. . . . Now we have incentives, a good investment climate. . . . The public-private partnership law is proving a great success. . . . Businessmen recognize these advances. Now they can take full advantage of the platform of systemic competitiveness that we have generated. . . . Now foreign investment is coming, national private investment [is coming], and all thanks to the public works of the Citizens' Revolution!"[34]

But despite the essential continuity between Correa's post-neoliberal project and Moreno's subsequent embrace of a neoliberal agenda, Moreno sought to legitimate his rule by launching a concerted attack on the legacy of the Correa regime, which he had celebrated so effusively during his campaign. Correa, he claimed, had concealed the true extent of the national debt, which was over twice as high as official figures had suggested, and which would cost the country $10 billion in annual interest payments—more than the entire budget for health, education, and the military combined.[35] Moreno also set out to uncover "circles of corruption in state institutions,"[36] and by August 2017 no fewer than six ex-ministers were imprisoned or under investigation.[37] Further indictments followed, and before long the vice president and Correa loyalist Jorge Glas had been stripped of his office and imprisoned after being found guilty of receiving $13.5 million in bribes from Odebrecht.[38]

Moreno combined these investigations with an assessment of the infrastructural investments of the Correa administration. The resulting report found structural deficiencies and contractual inconsistencies in 640 projects and was accompanied by further revelations concerning many of the most iconic megaprojects of the Citizens' Revolution.[39] Following a visit to Yachay, for example, Moreno informed the nation of his astonishment with the vast expense and abject failure of the project: "There we have Yachay. Four massive buildings with structural flaws that mean that they must be abandoned. What? Have we gone crazy? Have we gone mad? What happened? Where did we lose our way?"[40] There was no choice, he argued, but to impose a "decree of austerity" to pay for the excesses of the Correa administration.[41] The Citizens' Revolution was finished. "These days," he concluded, "it seems that any old bullshit can be called a revolution [*Ahora llaman revolución a cualquier pendejada*]."[42]

The departure of Correa as the "subject supposed to believe" in the Citizens' Revolution, and his replacement with a president who clearly believed in no such thing, resulted in the final collapse of the entire ideological edifice. It was as if everyone could suddenly see what stood before their eyes. As one commentator observed: "As soon as its unifying leader was removed . . . the true face of the Citizens' Revolution was revealed, and the population has looked on in bewildered fascination."[43] Others denounced a "decadent decade" of "spectral illusions" fueled by the high price of crude, which had generated "the sensation of a country undergoing real transformation, the mirage of a nation on the move."[44] In the words of the journalist and activist Milagros Aguirre: "The famous revolution turned out to be a castle made of sand, of the kind that crumbles beneath the first rainstorm. It was enough for the leader to abandon his post for all the great achievements he had proclaimed . . . to be perceived in their true dimension."[45]

Such is the fate of spatial phantasmagorias, whose spell is sustained by the spectral presence of value. In its absence, "the decaying structures no longer hold sway over the collective imagination, [and] it is possible to recognize them as the illusory dream images they always were."[46] In the context of commodity booms—like the oil boom that fueled the Citizens' Revolution—value miraculously appears in the form of natural objects, which are alchemically transformed into money. As the controller of these resources, and the extractor of these rents, the state is endowed with the seemingly occult power to produce spectacular infrastructures that combine the commodity fetish of natural resource wealth with the utopian dream of instant modernity. But the end of the boom marks a jarring shift from the phantasmatic to the absurd, as these monuments to progress are revealed as highways without traffic, airports without flights, cities without people. The state, which had towered over society with a seemingly monolithic omnipotence, is shown to be a ramshackle contraption, cobbled together from fragmented and dysfunctional institutions, and fitfully spitting out half-baked schemes and hyperbolic slogans. And its representatives, who only yesterday were the heroic conductors of a magical dream machine, are exposed as charlatans and imposters, scrambling to maintain a semblance of coherence and control, as their dilapidated machinery is dismantled by the very hidden forces that had been holding it together.

Confronted with this scenario, Correa moved to Belgium. If his plan had been to govern from behind the scenes and to return to power in 2021, then this plan now lay in ruins. He responded to Moreno's betrayal by broadcasting a series of anguished monologues from his attic in Brussels, in a pale impression of his own presidential speeches to the nation. In the first of these messages, in August 2017, he appears hunched over his computer in a barren, windowless room, the low attic ceiling bearing down upon him:

> Greetings, my dear nation. An immense embrace to you all. . . . I thought I had left the nation in safe hands. But now I realize how naive I was. This is a nightmare! . . . They turned out to be wolves in sheep's clothing! And now I am confronted with an overwhelming avalanche of infamies. . . . We are confronting a state of lies. Lie after lie after lie! And all for political objectives. Enough! . . . This is how they are cheating the nation. . . . Ecuadorian people, it is time for us to

rebel! We must not lose all that we have gained! We must not
slide back into the past. . . . Not out of concern for myself,
but to protect the revolution. . . . Be strong, my dear compatriots, and *hasta la victoria siempre!*[47]

But his compatriots were no longer listening. Soon afterward, Moreno
announced a public consultation on a range of issues, chief among
which was the annulment of Correa's amendment to the constitution,
which would reimpose a two-term presidential limit and prevent Correa from running for president again. Correa briefly returned to Ecuador to campaign against the proposed reforms. But he was pelted with
garbage and rotten eggs, and the amendment was overwhelmingly
approved. Moreno then moved to ensure that Correa would not return to the country again by implicating him in a kidnapping and
obtaining a warrant for his arrest and pretrial detention.[48]

In the midst of this avalanche of infamies, I made a final journey
to the Amazon. I arrived in Coca in August 2017, not long after Correa had delivered his speech from his attic. The city had been gutted
by the oil crisis. Most of the bars and brothels had closed down, and
the hotels and restaurants were almost empty. The jungle was raven-
ously consuming an abandoned leisure complex on the outskirts of
town. A six-story shopping mall had recently been completed. But the
shops were vacant, the bowling alley was deserted, and no films were
showing in the multiscreen cinema. Even the Napo was lower than I
had ever seen it, exposing vast beaches strewn with broken trees.

Following the military repression in Dayuma at the start of the
Correa administration, the Citizens' Revolution had provided little to
the province of Orellana, which had voted for Lasso in the election: a
couple of Millennium Schools, the partial paving of some roads,
a hospital that was poorly equipped and critically understaffed, and a
huge bridge over the Napo, which was of more use to the oil industry

than to the local population. And yet this province was the source of the majority of the oil that had sustained the entire project, and the stronghold of the radical political movement that had helped make it possible. In the words of Enrique Morales of the ABP, who had played a key role in the August Uprising: "The Citizens' Revolution intervened in favor of the oil companies rather than the people [of the Amazon]. For us, this government has truly been a nightmare."[49]

This outcome might seem to suggest the conservative conclusion that all utopias are doomed to fail and fated to create even worse conditions than those they had attempted to escape. But this is not my intention. My aim in this book has been to demonstrate and explore the reality of dreams by illustrating the constitutive role of utopian fantasies in the production of social reality, and by tracing the ways in which such dreams are transformed through the process of their realization. These dreams give displaced expression to the desire for a radically different world. Their absurdity lies not in this desire itself, but in their tendency to express it in such a way that the conditions giving rise to it are not transcended but reproduced. This tendency is not necessarily inherent in social reality as such, but only in social reality under conditions of global capitalism. As we have seen, this is a reality filled with fetish objects, twisted into paradoxical inversions, and subordinated to inscrutable dynamics that human beings have created, but which "far from being under their control, in fact control them."[50] I have sought to develop a fantastical materialist approach to this surreal world in order to draw out its phantasmatic and absurd dimensions. And I have done so not as a dismissal of utopian dreams, but as a critique of the kind of world that needs such dreams to survive.

But there has also been a subplot to this story, composed of sudden moments of awakening, in which a different kind of utopia has sporadically exploded the established coordinates of social reality. The most momentous of these events was the August Uprising of 2005, in which the long-abandoned population of the northern Amazon responded to the destruction of their dreams by launching a wave of *paros* throughout the region, which succeeded in shutting down the entire oil industry and forcing significant concessions from the state and transnational capital. This was followed by further fleeting moments of a similar kind. Faced with displacement from their land for the construction of an eco-city, the members of Sumak Ñambi responded by defiantly creating their own urban space. Confronted with the defeat of their project for an indigenous oil company, the *comuneros* of Playas de Cuyabeno battled the military to prevent the state oil company from entering their land. And following the destruction of their community to make way for a foreign copper mine, the inhabitants of San Marcos rebuilt their humble town, inviting others to join them in the creation of a community of the dispossessed.

Each of these struggles was comprehensively defeated, and none corresponded to a conventional understanding of what constitutes utopia. But they all shared the qualities of an insurgent utopia, which erupts into existence through a sudden confrontation with the Real of capital, in which the phantasmatic coordinates of social reality are shattered, and the violence of global capitalism is revealed. An insurgent utopia has no plan or blueprint and is not based on a promise of progress or a vision for the future. Instead, it is a utopia of the present, which directly stages what Jacques Rancière has called "the equality of anyone at all with anyone else: in other words, in the final analysis, the sheer contingency of any social order."[51] As Susan Buck-Morss has argued, such events "surpass the confines of present constellations of power in perceiving the concrete meaning of freedom" and can be interpreted as moments, "however transitory, of the realization of absolute spirit."[52] As such, they possess an ecstatic dimension, despite the desperate conditions in which they occur. The August Uprising was described by its participants as an experience of collective euphoria, embodied in the burning of state buildings and the battles on the barricades. And the blockade in Playas de Cuyabeno took the form of a ludic festival, punctuated by pitched battles with the Ecuadorian army. Such acts stage a carnivalesque inversion of reality, in which the established order is abruptly inverted and the utopian dimension of egalitarian freedom is directly lived by those with nothing left to lose.

After spending a few days in Coca, I headed to Dayuma, where the utopian fantasy of the Citizens' Revolution had consolidated its victory over the insurgent utopia of the ABP. I had no reason to go there—the crackdown back in 2007 had crushed the last remnant of the movement, and there had been no further uprisings in the intervening decade. But Coca was dead. The dream had come to an end. And I had nothing else to do. I crossed the Napo at dawn. The river had risen overnight, erasing the beaches and sweeping the broken trees downstream in an endless logjam. I passed the military base on the far side of the bridge and turned onto the Savage Road. The mist hung low over the jungle on the fringes of the fields. The newly surfaced road was already disintegrating into a maze of deep shelves, sudden voids, and jagged edges. The old single-lane bridges had still not been replaced, and people still died on them. The road cut between the concrete huts of El Dorado and entered Block 61, the oil field that had been granted to Schlumberger in exchange for saving Ecuador from default. Immediately, the scene changed. The company was opening new wells throughout the block, and the roadsides were filled with drilling rigs, construction equipment, and surveillance cameras. But the road was strangely quiet, and the building sites were empty. I glimpsed a group of oil workers gathered beneath the narrow bridge at the entrance to Dayuma. Another group was standing outside the company gates in the center of town. They were demanding better wages and working conditions, and the company had locked a thousand workers inside to prevent them from joining the strike. The sun burned off the cloud, and the heat was intense. A convoy of police arrived, seized the leaders of the strike, and drove away at high speed toward Coca. The news spread fast. The workers burst the company gates and spilled onto the road. At the same time, a group of *Shuar* militants forced their way inside, kidnapped the company manager, hijacked a vehicle, and headed down the Savage Road, deep into the jungle. The army arrived to rescue him, but the road had been blocked by the workers and the people. The awakening had happened. The *paro* had begun.

Notes

Introduction

1. Correa, "Discurso." Throughout the text, translations from Spanish to English are the author's own.

2. Correa, in "Enlace ciudadano no. 294."

3. Berman, *All That Is Solid*, 74.

4. Buck-Morss, *Dreamworld*, ix.

5. Rancière, *Disagreement*, 113.

6. Jameson, *Archaeologies*, 289.

7. Marx Carrasco, "¿Por qué?" 76.

8. SENPLADES, *Buen vivir*, 34, 72, 20, 51, 54, 63.

9. Scott, *Seeing Like a State*.

10. Lefebvre, *Production of Space*.

11. Ferguson, *Anti-Politics Machine*.

12. Holston, *Modernist City*, 9.

13. Taussig, *Magic of the State*, 123, 144, 184.

14. Jackson, *Fantasy*, 48; Rose, *States of Fantasy*, 5.

15. Miéville, "Symposium: Marxism and Fantasy," 42.

16. McNally, *Monsters of the Market*, 5.

17. Benjamin, *Arcades Project*, 391.

18. Lund, "Concept of Phantasmagoria."

19. Cohen, "Walter Benjamin's Phantasmagoria."

20. Heinrich, *An Introduction to Karl Marx's Capital*; Postone, *Time, Labor, and Social Domination*.

21. Marx, *Capital*, 165.

22. Freud, *Interpretation of Dreams*.

23. Breton, "Manifesto of Surrealism (1924)," 9.

24. Benjamin, *Arcades Project*, 389.

25. Ibid., 24.

26. Ibid., 12. One of the chief inspirations for Benjamin's theory of the phantasmagoria was *Paris Peasant*, an experimental novel by Breton's fellow surrealist Louis Aragon, which depicted Paris as a dreamworld in which commodities were endowed with magical and sacred properties, as conveyed by this description of gas pumps at a filling station: "Here are great red gods, great yellow gods, great green gods. . . . Painted brightly with English or invented names, possessing just one long, supple arm, a luminous faceless head, a single foot and a numbered wheel in the belly, the petrol pumps sometimes take on the appearance of the divinities of Egypt or of those cannibal tribes which worship war and war alone. O Texaco motor oil, Esso, Shell, great inscriptions of human potentiality, soon we will cross ourselves before your fountains." Aragon, *Paris Peasant*, 117.

27. Fink, *Lacanian Subject*; Homer, *Jacques Lacan*.

28. Žižek, *Violence*, 11.

29. Marx and Engels, *Communist Manifesto*, 254–255.

30. Abensour, "History of Utopia," 21–22.

31. Žižek, *Sublime Object*, 126.

32. Jackson, *Fantasy*, 13.

33. Todorov, *The Fantastic*, 25.

34. Žižek, *Sublime Object*, 127.

35. Dolar, "Introduction," 10–11 (emphasis added).

36. Žižek, *Sublime Object*, 128.

37. Benjamin, *Arcades Project*, 486.

38. Žižek, "Reality of the Virtual."

39. Žižek, "The Need to Traverse" (emphasis in original).

40. Abensour, "History of Utopia," 34.

41. Bakhtin, *Rabelais*, 89. Fantastical materialism bears a certain resemblance to the "magical Marxism" of Andy Merrifield and the "enchanted materialism" of Jane Bennett. While these approaches are also concerned with the enchantment of modernity, however, they locate the source of this enchantment not in the social relations of capital itself, but in the joyful and marvelous dimensions of everyday life that escape or exceed the instrumental rationality of capitalist domination. See Merrifield, *Magical Marxism*; Bennett, *Enchantment*.

42. Esman, "Psychoanalysis and Surrealism," 174.

43. Eiland and Mclaughlin, "Translator's Foreword," xi.

44. Taussig, *Devil and Commodity Fetishism*, xiv.

45. Marx, *Capital*, 302, 353, 342.

46. Jameson, quoted in Eagleton, "Jameson and Form," 134.

47. Jameson, "Autobiografía."

48. Benjamin, quoted in Markus, "Walter Benjamin," 14.

49. Todorov, *The Fantastic*, 46, 26.

50. Thompson, *Happy Birthday*, 24; Thompson, *Fear and Loathing*, 47.

51. Bruce-Novoa, "Fear and Loathing," 42.

52. Ibid.

53. Thompson, *Happy Birthday*, 24.

54. E. T. A. Hoffman, quoted in Jackson, *Fantasy*, 123. Fantastic realism should not be confused with the more familiar literary genre of magical realism; see Bowers, *Magic(al) Realism*. Whereas magical realism is defined by the introduction of supernatural elements into material reality in a matter-of-fact way, fantastic realism is characterized by astonishment in the face of the fantastical nature of material reality itself.

55. Rancière, *Lost Thread*, 42.

56. Herzog, "Interview: Dreams and Burdens."

57. Ballard, *Atrocity Exhibition*, 156.

58. Oppenheimer, "Making the Invisible Visible."

Chapter 1. Enchanted Forest

1. Hecht and Cockburn, *Fate of the Forest*.

2. Herzog, *Conquest of the Useless*.

3. Grandin, *Fordlandia*, 6.

4. Wylie, "Introduction," 1.

5. Quoted in Koepnick, "Colonial Forestry," 136.

6. Da Cunha, *The Amazon*, 11.

7. Unnamed Brazilian explorer, quoted in Stepan, "Tropical Modernism," 79.

8. Smith, *Explorers of the Amazon*, 115.

9. Quoted in Hecht and Cockburn, *Fate of the Forest*, 63.

10. Ibid., 87.

11. Moore, *Capitalism*.

12. An official document of the time states: "The great lord or prince goes about continually covered in gold dust as fine as ground salt. He feels that it would be less beautiful to wear any other ornament. . . . His entire body is covered, from the soles of his feet to his head. So his looks are as resplendent as a gold object worked by the hands of a great artist. . . . If a chief does do this, then he must have very rich mines of the finest gold indeed"; quoted in Wood, *Conquistadors*, 184–185.

13. Smith, *Explorers of the Amazon*; Trujillo, *Utopías Amazónicas*.

14. Martínez, *El paraíso*; Muratorio, "Introduction."

15. Almeida, "El mito"; Restrepo, "El proceso."

16. Martínez, *El paraíso*, 103–118.

17. Cabodevilla, *Coca*, 183–226.

18. Quoted ibid., 222.

19. Ibid.

20. Quoted ibid., 266.

21. Almeida, "El mito"; Cepek, "Loss of Oil"; Galarza, *El festín*.

22. Quoted in Galarza, *El festín*, 126.

23. Viteri, *Petróleo*, 11, 14.

24. Ibid., 14.

25. Ibid., 11.

26. Ibid., 30.

27. Ibid., 49.

28. Watts, "Petro-Violence," 203.

29. Viteri, *Petróleo*, 50. As Fernando Coronil observes of the discovery of oil in Venezuela: "The mirage of El Dorado had haunted the early conquerors who were drawn ever deeper into the Amazonian jungle in their obsessive quest for the riches that indigenous people assured them lay just behind the next mountain. This mirage reappeared faintly with every discovery of mineral wealth throughout the succeeding centuries. With the gushing forth of oil, the submerged images of El Dorado shone again brightly, appearing as endless streams of black gold circulating through the vessels of the social body"; Coronil, *Magical State*, 389.

30. Cabodevilla *La selva*, 22; Galarza, *El festín*, 158.

31. Memoria Ecuador, "Primer barril."

32. Watts, "Petro-Violence," 200.

33. Deler, *Ecuador*; Larrea, "Extractivism"; Perreault and Valdivia, "Hydrocarbons."

34. Gerlach, *Indians, Oil, and Politics*, 38.

35. Kapuściński, *Shah of Shahs*, 34–35.

36. Carlos Añazco, son of Jorge Añazco, interview by the author, June 12, 2016, Lago Agrio, Ecuador.

37. Añazco, *Sucumbíos*, 131.

38. Ibid.

39. Ibid., 138.

40. Ibid., 145.

41. Restrepo, "El proceso"; Sawyer, *Crude Chronicles*, 44.

42. Añazco, *Sucumbíos*, 228.

43. Ibid., 167–168.

44. Diocles Zambrano, peasant farmer and human right activist, interview by the author, August 24, 2017, Coca, Ecuador.

45. Pablo Gallegos, Carmelite missionary, interview by the author, June 1, 2016, Coca.

46. Añazco, *Sucumbíos*, 207.

47. Ibid.

48. Ibid., 208.

49. Cabodevilla, *La selva*, 13, and *Coca*, 235. The entire right bank of the Napo from Coca to Pañacocha was dominated by the *Huaorani* during this period, following a series of violent confrontations with *hacendados* and their laborers. Before the discovery of oil in their territory, the total population of the *Huaorani* is estimated to have numbered between 500 and 1,000, and their territory stretched for over 7,000 square miles between the Napo and Curaray rivers; Deler, *Ecuador*, 108. At the time of Goldáraz's arrival, Coca was therefore regarded not only as the oil frontier, but as the boundary of "civilization" itself.

50. José Miguel Goldáraz, interview by the author, May 10, 2016, Coca.

51. Milton Noboa, president of the Orellana Chamber of Commerce, interview by the author, May 19, 2016, Coca.

52. Muratorio, "Introduction," 187; Martínez, *El paraíso*, 19. A ninth indigenous group, the *Teteté*, inhabited the region of the first oil wells, but they are believed to have died out in the early 1970s, following the arrival of the oil industry; Cabodevilla, *La selva*.

53. In many cases, the arrival of oil companies in the indigenous territories of the region was met with bewildered interest rather than resistance, and the process of dispossession was often facilitated by the most trifling of gifts, the presentation of which resembled scenes described by the chroniclers of the initial colonial invasion of the Americas. A leader of the *Cofán*, whose territory encompassed the Lago Agrio oil field, recalls that they did not know what oil was, or what the oil company was doing, and were initially happy to let the company fell trees and open roads because they received rice and wooden spoons in return: "That's why we now say that the companies bought the *Cofán* with a few spoons and other little things. No one worried about it and no one had the idea of defending our territory"; Roberto Aguinda, president of the *Cofán*, interview by the author, June 17, 2016, Cofán-Dureno, Ecuador. In his memoir, Viteri describes these early encounters with the *Cofán*, recalling, "We had to bring mirrors, torches, combs, hairbands, little penknives . . . biscuits, and sweets"; Viteri, *Petróleo*, 33.

54. José Miguel Goldáraz, interview by the author, May 10, 2016, Coca. Other evangelical missions operating in the region at the time had less emancipatory objectives. In contrast to Goldáraz, who made pragmatic pacts with the oil companies as a means of advancing the struggle for indigenous autonomy, the American missionaries of the Summer Linguistics Institute (ILV) were working directly in the interests of Texaco and other companies, relocating indigenous communities to facilitate oil exploration and exploitation throughout the region; Martínez, *El paraíso*.

55. Schaefer, "Engaging Modernity."

56. Aguirre, *Utopía*, 45.

57. José Miguel Goldáraz, interview by the author, May 10, 2016, Coca.

58. Grefa, *Maccuruchu*, 63.

59. Ibid., 55.

60. Otto Agosto Tapotapuy, president of El Edén, interview by the author, May 27, 2016, El Edén, Ecuador.

61. Aguirre, *Utopía*, 59.

62. Becker, *¡Pachakutik!*, 5; Sawyer, *Crude Chronicles*, 43.

63. Aguirre, *Utopía*, 92. The creation of the indigenous federations of the northern Ecuadorian Amazon took inspiration from the federation of the *Shuar*, the Local Association of Jivaro Centers, which was formed in 1961 in the southern region of the *Oriente*. Like the UNAE and the FCUNAE, the *Shuar* federation was formed in opposition to dispossession by settlers from the highlands and the coast; Becker, *¡Pachakutik!*, 6; Sawyer, *Crude Chronicles*, 42.

64. Quoted in Aguirre, *Utopía*, 163.

65. Žižek, *Plague of Fantasies*, 6.

66. Lefebvre, "Space," 214.

67. Harvey, *Spaces of Capital*, 247.

68. Polanyi, *Great Transformation*, 3.

69. Larrea, "Extractivism," 8; Kimerling, *Amazon Crude*, 31.

70. Diocles Zambrano, interview by the author, August 24, 2017, Coca.

71. Cepek, "Loss of Oil," 397; Sawyer, *Crude Chronicles* 101–103.

72. Cabodevilla, *La selva*, 36.

73. Ibid., 28.

74. Viteri, *Petróleo*, 202.

75. Jorge Viteri, interview by the author, April 25, 2016, Valle de los Chillos, Ecuador. Such costs were rarely reported in the national press, and the violence and destruction of the oil frontier were excluded from the triumphant official narrative of national development as "the hidden face of the supposedly brilliant oil moon. The

side that has never been seen or known, and that no one has wanted to discover";
Cabodevilla, "Prologo," 8. Though revealing of the plight of the oil workers in this
regard, Viteri's memoir does not tell the full story either, to the extent that it remains
silent regarding the many murders of *Huaorani, Tagaeri, and Taromenane* allegedly
committed by oil workers, illegal loggers, and the military.

76. Deler, *Ecuador*, 77; Purcell, Fernández, and Martínez, "Rents."

77. Gerlach, *Indians, Oil, and Politics*, 39.

78. The crash is widely believed to have been orchestrated by the CIA; see Perkins, *Confessions*, 153–157.

79. Quoted in Sawyer, *Crude Chronicles*, 11.

80. Larrea, "Extractivism"; Perreault and Valdivia, "Hydrocarbons."

81. Viteri, *Petróleo*, 50.

82. Añazco, *Sucumbíos*, 209.

83. Ibid., 207–208.

84. Viteri, *Petróleo*, 325.

85. Añazco, *Sucumbíos*, 256–258.

86. Viteri, *Petróleo*, 322–351.

87. Quoted in Cabodevilla, *La selva*, 15.

88. Fontaine, "Microconflictos," 38.

89. Añazco, *Sucumbíos*, 283.

90. Ibid., 284.

91. Ángel Sallo, interview by the author, June 16, 2016, Lago Agrio.

Chapter 2. The Politics of Awakening

1. Donald Moncayo, interview by the author, June 15, 2016, Lago Agrio.

2. Ibid.

3. Ibid.; Ángel Sallo, interview by the author, June 16, 2016, Lago Agrio; Julio González, interview by the author, June 18, 2016, Lago Agrio.

4. Quoted in "Termina 'larga noche neoliberal.'"

5. Alianza PAIS, *Plan de gobierno*, 3.

6. Conaghan and de la Torre, "Permanent Campaign," 272.

7. Becker, *¡Pachakutik!*; Gerlach, *Indians, Oil, and Politics*; Lucero "Crisis and Contention."

8. Espinosa, "Amazonía ecuatoriana," 29.

9. Martínez, "Ecuador," 66.

10. Julio González, interview by the author, June 18, 2016, Lago Agrio.

11. Becker, *¡Pachakutik!*, 54, 92.

12. Espinosa, "Amazonía ecuatoriana," 30–31.

13. Humberto Piaguaje, interview by the author, June 14, 2016, Lago Agrio.

14. Ibid.

15. Ángel Sallo, member of the Bi-Provincial Assembly of Orellana-Sucumbíos (ABP), who was working as a local journalist at the time, interview by the author, June 16, 2016, Lago Agrio.

16. In 1998 the continued expansion of the oil frontier resulted in the creation of the province of Orellana, adjacent to Sucumbíos, with Coca as the new provincial capital. At the time of its creation, Orellana contained both the highest poverty levels and the most productive oil wells of the country and was home to a population as diverse and rebellious as that of Sucumbíos.

17. MPD Sucumbíos, *Valerosas jornadas*, 24.

18. Asamblea Biprovincial, "Acuerdos."

19. MPD Sucumbíos, *Valerosas jornadas*, 28.

20. Ibid., 35–46.

21. In 2002 Congress approved a measure demanded by the IMF for the establishment of the Fund for Stabilization, Social and Productive Investment, and the Reduction of Public Debt (FEIREP), according to which 70 percent of all excess oil revenues (resulting from a higher oil price than that included in the annual budget) were automatically diverted toward foreign debt repayments. Twenty percent was dedicated to a stabilization fund, and a maximum of 10 percent was allocated for health and education expenditures; Ruiz, "Parte I," 47–50.

22. Julio González, a member of the ABP and congressman for Sucumbíos from 2003 to 2007, interview by the author, June 18, 2016, Lago Agrio.

23. Acosta and Falconi, "Otra política económica," 39, 70; Becker, *¡Pachakutik!*, 83–90.

24. Palacio faced a wave of *paros* across the country at the start of his presidency, though none was of the scale or significance of the Amazonian *paros biprovinciales*. Nineteen *paros* were recorded during the first 129 days of his presidency alone, many of them concentrated in the coastal region; "Gobierno de palacio."

25. Donald Moncayo, interview by the author, June 15, 2016, Lago Agrio.

26. Julio González, interview by the author interview, June 18, 2016, Lago Agrio.

27. Sallo, "Asamblea Biprovincial."

28. Ortiz Duran, "Dinero para carreteras."

29. Comité del Paro, "Boletín de prensa no. 1."

30. Enrique Morales, head of the Oil Policy Committee of the ABP, interview by the author, June 2, 2016, Coca.

31. Donald Moncayo, interview by the author, June 15, 2016, Lago Agrio.

32. MPD Sucumbíos, *Valerosas jornadas*, 56–57 (emphasis in original).

33. "Ecuador: Cronología mayo-agosto, 181; Sallo, "El paro toma fuerza."

34. Donald Moncayo, interview by the author, June 15, 2016, Lago Agrio.

35. Enrique Morales, interview by the author, June 22, 2016, Coca.

36. Ángel Sallo, interview by the author, June 16, 2016, Lago Agrio (emphasis added).

37. Ortiz, "Protestas locales."

38. Comité del Paro, "Boletín de prensa no. 3."

39. MPD Sucumbíos, *Valerosas jornadas*, 59–60; "Ecuador: Cronología mayo-agosto," 181.

40. Comité del Paro, "Boletines de prensa nos. 13–28."

41. Quoted in Comité del Paro, "Boletín de prensa no. 61."

42. "Sucumbíos y Orellana en manos de militares"; "Ecuador: Cronología mayo-agosto," 181.

43. The state of emergency declaration permitted detention without charge and the searching of homes without a warrant, and suspended freedom of association, freedom of speech, and freedom of movement; Herrera, "Represión militar."

44. MPD Sucumbíos, *Valerosas jornadas*, 60–61.

45. "Ecuador: Cronología mayo-agosto," 182.

46. MPD Sucumbíos, *Valerosas jornadas*, 61.

47. "Petroecuador dejó de producir petróleo."

48. "Sucumbíos y Orellana en manos de militares."

49. "Petroecuador dejó de producir petróleo."

50. "570 millones de pérdidas."

51. Ortiz, "Protestas locales."

52. On August 20 Palacio asked Venezuela to lend Ecuador the oil required to fulfill its international obligations. Chávez offered to lend Ecuador 88,000 barrels a day at no interest, while wryly noting that the United States would probably accuse him of being behind the uprising; "Paro con tácticas; Stratfor, "Ecuador: An Oil Strike."

53. Stratfor, "Ecuador: An Oil Strike."

54. "2 autoridades"; "Ecuador: Cronología mayo-agosto," 184; Sigcha, "Sucumbíos y Orellana."

55. Asamblea Biprovincial, "Acta de compromiso."

56. Congreso Nacional, *VVII Cumbre Amazónica*, 22; González, *Rendición de cuentas*, 26–29.

57. MPD Sucumbíos, *Valerosas jornadas,* 11 (emphasis added).

58. Žižek, "On Utopia."

59. Enrique Morales, interview by the author, June 22, 2016, Coca; Pablo Gallegos, interview by the author, May 22, 2016, Coca; Ángel Sallo, interview by the author, June 16, 2016, Lago Agrio.

60. Benjamin, "Surrealism," 55.

61. "Ecuador: Cronología mayo-agosto," 180.

62. Asamblea de los Pueblos de Sucumbíos, "Ecuador: Informe y declaración."

63. Ricardo Patiño, a key ally of Correa in the Citizens' Revolution, quoted in Harnecker, "Ecuador," 15.

64. Alberto Acosta, interview by the author, September 11, 2015, Quito. The central figures in these meetings were Correa, Acosta (subsequently appointed minister of energy and mines), Fander Falconí (who went on to lead the planning ministry), Ricardo Patiño (who became minister of foreign affairs), and Hugo Jacome (who would be appointed vice minister of economy and finance). All were academic economists specializing in heterodox economics; Harnecker, "Ecuador."

65. Alberto Acosta, interview by the author, September 11, 2015, Quito.

66. Acosta and Falconi, "Otra política económica," 29–33.

67. Alberto Acosta, interview by the author, September 11, 2015, Quito.

68. This image can be seen at http://abrebrecha-thisisit.blogspot.co.uk/2012/04/tu-decides-entre-el-oscuro-pasado-o.html (accessed March 5, 2017).

69. Alianza PAIS, *Plan de gobierno,* 9.

70. Alberto Acosta, interview by the author, September 11, 2015, Quito (emphasis added).

71. Correa, "Ejes del nuevo gobierno."

72. Gudynas, "Buen Vivir"; Walsh, "Development as Buen Vivir."

73. Correa, "Informe a la nación."

74. Leiva, *Latin American Neostructuralism,* xx.

75. Alianza PAIS, *Plan de gobierno,* 8; Presidencia de la República, *Constitución,* Article 284. According to Acosta, the manifesto of Alianza PAIS provided the "ideological and programmatic orientation" for the Citizens' Revolution; quoted in Harnecker, "Ecuador," 33. It is indicative of this orientation that the manifesto contains four mentions of "*buen vivir,*" one of "socialism," and none of "*sumak kawsay*" or "the rights of nature," compared to twenty-seven mentions of "competitiveness."

76. Alberto Acosta, interview by the author, September 11, 2015, Quito. Neostructuralism is an economic theory and policy paradigm promoted by the Economic Commission for Latin America and the Caribbean (ECLAC), which had a powerful

influence on Latin American policy makers looking for progressive alternatives to neoliberalism in the 1990s and 2000s. As Fernando Leiva has demonstrated, neostructuralism provided the policy foundation for the more moderate post-neoliberal projects in countries such as Brazil, Chile, and Uruguay, in contrast to the more radical experiments in Bolivia and Venezuela. Leiva, however, overlooks the influence of neostructuralism on the Citizens' Revolution and classifies Ecuador among the latter group; Leiva, *Latin American Neostructuralism*.

77. Abensour, "History of Utopia," 48.

78. Correa, "Otra economía," 70.

79. Ángel Sallo, interview by the author, June 16, 2016, Lago Agrio.

80. Ibid.

81. MPD Sucumbíos, *Valerosas jornadas*, 12.

82. Humberto Piaguaje, interview by the author, June 14, 2016, Lago Agrio.

83. Pablo Gallegos, interview by the author, June 1, 2016, Coca.

84. Donald Moncayo, interview by the author, June 15, 2016, Lago Agrio.

85. Becker, "Stormy Relations," 47.

86. SENPLADES, *Plan nacional para el buen vivir, 2009–2013*, 9.

87. "Cadena radial nro. 22."

88. "Cadena radial nro. 4."

89. Harvey, *Spaces of Hope*, 164–173. The fourth great Amazonian utopia of the Citizens' Revolution was Yasuní-ITT, which proposed to forego exploitation of the extensive oil reserves under a section of the Yasuní National Park in exchange for compensation for a proportion of the lost earnings from the "international community." This was a project of great significance at both national and international scales and was presented by the Correa administration as evidence of its adherence to the constitutional protection of the rights of nature; Arsel, "Between Marx and Markets"; Martin, "Global Governance." But unlike the other three utopian projects discussed here, Yasuní-ITT was not based on the vision of development articulated in the ABP Accords, and it was more reflective of the agenda of the middle-class environmental movement in Quito than the demands of the inhabitants of the Amazon. According to Milagros Aguirre, a journalist and activist who lived for years in the Amazon, "Yasuní-ITT was a utopia rooted in an imaginary idea of the jungle as a non-intervened space, and an idea of the noble savage"; interview by the author, April 20, 2016, Quito.

90. This process of historical erasure was applied not only to the ABP, but also to the entire network of social movements that had collectively opened the political space for the arrival of the Citizens' Revolution. According to a prominent activist

based in Quito: "From 1998 or 1999 onward, the movement kept growing, contributing imaginative and creative things, constructing many collective spaces. And now [the Correa administration] say that 'if it weren't for us, nothing would have happened'"; Alejandra Santillana, director of the Institute of Ecuadorian Studies (IEE), interview by the author, April 29 2016, Quito.

91. "Ikiam tendrá tres sedes"; "Quito y Brasilia"; "Correa: 'Pañacocha.'"

92. Coronil, *Magical State*, 5.

93. Milagros Aguirre, interview by the author, April 20, 2016, Quito.

94. Donald Moncayo, interview by the author, June 15, 2016, Lago Agrio.

95. Quoted in Nagera, *Basic Psychoanalytic Concepts*, 18 (emphasis added).

96. "570 millones."

97. Comisión de Prensa de Orellana, "Lo que la 'prensa seria.'"

98. "Cadena radial nro. 17."

99. "Resoluciones adoptadas en la asamblea entre las comunidades del bloque 14, 17 in Shiripuno, cuya operadora es PetroOriental." July 18, 2006 (unpublished document, personal archives of Enrique Morales). The demands of the *paro* were very modest, including hiring local women for washing the clothes of company staff; paying the minimum wage to local employees; and providing latrines, fencing, and roofing panels to local communities.

100. Jhon Rosero, political leader in the Vía Auca region and a key figure in the ABP, interview by the author, June 24, 2016, Dayuma, Ecuador; Comisión Ecuménica de Derechos Humanos, Represión militar a campesinos de Dayuma.

101. Quoted in Sigcha, "Pindo."

102. Diocles Zambrano, interview by the author, August 24, 2017, Coca.

103. The *paro* in Dayuma was calculated to have cut oil production by 190,791 barrels, at a cost to the state of $13,614,845. At this time the oil price stood at $71 per barrel. The economic cost of other major *paros biprovinciales* has been calculated as follows: 2002, 334,135 barrels lost at an average price of $22.06 per barrel; 2004, 17,178 barrels at $32.17 per barrel; 2005, 889,947 barrels at $42.84 per barrel; "En Orellana existen mafias."

104. Aguirre, *Dayuma*, 33–67; Obando, "Dayuma," 41–47.

105. Correa's speech can be heard in Aguirre, dir., *Dayuma nunca mas*.

106. Quoted in Obando, "Dayuma," 47.

107. Enrique Morales, interview by the author, August 22, 2017, Coca.

108. Quoted in "Correa advierte."

109. Enrique Morales, interview by the author, June 2, 2016, Coca.

110. Quoted in "Ecuador: Cronología del conflicto," 171.

111. Diocles Zambrano, Centro de Derechos Humanos de Orellana, interview by the author, August 24, 2017, Coca.

112. Ángel Sallo, interview by the author, June 16, 2016, Lago Agrio.

113. Untitled newspaper report, quoted in Aguirre, *Dayuma*, 33. Whether by accident or by design, the crackdown in Dayuma occurred on the morning of the inauguration of the Constituent Assembly, which was held on the distant Pacific coast. This was one of the key symbolic events of the Citizens' Revolution, in which social movements from across the country gathered to present their petitions for the drafting of the radical new post-neoliberal constitution. In contrast to the obscure conflict in Dayuma, the Constituent Assembly was followed live by millions of Ecuadorians on radios and televisions across the country. A few days later, a proposal was tabled for the repression in Dayuma to be addressed by the Assembly. At this point, however, Correa intervened, forbidding the Assembly to discuss Dayuma and threatening to resign if it did so. The proposal was dropped and the Assembly continued (ibid., 32).

114. "Cadena nacional 19 de diciembre." The documentary was one of a series of propaganda films that the Correa administration obliged all national networks to carry, using a broad interpretation of a law stipulating that television stations must provide the government with free air time for national public service broadcasts (Conaghan and de la Torre, "Permanent Campaign," 276).

Chapter 3. Amazon Unbound

1. A pseudonym has been used in this case. It refers to Carlos Fermín Fitzcarrald, the Peruvian rubber baron on whom Herzog based the character of Fitzcarraldo. On his way upriver in search of the mountain he must cross, Fitzcarraldo spends a night in a Jesuit mission. One of the monks asks what he is doing in this remote part of the Amazon. Fitzcarraldo responds, "I'm planning something geographical" (Herzog, *Fitzcarraldo*).

2. Carlos Fermín, interview by the author, February 9, 2015, Providencia, Ecuador.

3. "Enlace ciudadano 20 enero 2007."

4. Carlos Fermín, interview by the author, February 9, 2015, Providencia.

5. Koepnick, "Colonial Forestry"; Smith, *Explorers of the Amazon*.

6. Laboratorio Manta-Manaos, "Consultorio." The Vía Interoceánica was one of the axes on which Jorge Añazco located the site of Nueva Loja in 1969. In his memoir he describes how, after setting up camp on the bank of the Aguarico, a group of *colonos* "headed northeast in search of the track of the interoceanic highway, opened ten

years previously and surely by now transformed into undergrowth. We wanted to find this track in order to convert it into one of the axes of our cooperative project"; Añazco, *Sucumbíos*, 143.

7. Augusto Celís, interview by the author, March 3, 2015, Quito.

8. Carlos Fermín, interview by the author, February 9, 2015, Providencia.

9. Trajano Andrade, director of Manta Port Authority 2004–2007, and minister of transport and public works January–July 2007, interview by the author, March 16, 2015, Manta, Ecuador.

10. COSIPLAN, *Cartera de proyectos*, 69–94. These interoceanic corridors were part of the Amazon Hub of the IIRSA, which comprised ten infrastructural hubs spanning the entire continent. Through its planned reconfiguration of South American space in the image of transnational capital, the IIRSA embodied the logic of "planetary urbanization"; See Arboleda, "Spaces of Extraction"; Brenner, "Theses on Urbanization."

11. Autoridad Portuario de Manta, "Eje multimodal."

12. "Government Officials"; Medalla, "Pres-Elect."

13. Quoted in Medalla, "Manta-Manaus."

14. Colombo and Roark, "UNASUR."

15. COSIPLAN, *Cartera de proyectos*, 17.

16. Burbach, Fox, and Fuentes, *Latin America's Turbulent Transitions*, 26–37.

17. Leiva, *Latin American Neostructuralism*, 4.

18. COSIPLAN, *Cartera de proyectos*, 21, 17.

19. Quoted in Ministerio de Coordinación de la Producción, Empleo y Competitividad, *Plan comercial*, 13.

20. Nuestro Mar, "Puerto Providencia."

21. Jorge Marún, minister of transport and public works 2007–2009, interview by the author, March 13, 2015, Guayaquil, Ecuador.

22. COSIPLAN, *Cartera de proyectos*, 94.

23. Ministerio de Relaciones Exteriores, *Manta-Manaos*.

24. Bonilla, "Manta-Manaus"; "Proyecto Manta-Manaos."

25. *Colono* with land in Providencia, interview by the author, February 11, 2015, Shushufindi, Ecuador.

26. Elias Piaguaje, president of the *Sekoya*, interview by the author, February 10, 2015, Providencia.

27. "Barcaza ecuatoriana."

28. Correa's speech can be seen in Ministerio de Coordinación de la Producción, Empleo y Competitividad, "Primer viaje."

29. Carlos Fermín, interview by the author, February 2, 2015, Providencia.

30. Ministerio de Relaciones Exteriores, *Manta-Manaos.*

31. Quoted in Harvey, *Spaces of Capital*, 244.

32. Smith, *Uneven Development*, 158.

33. Harvey and Knox, "Enchantments," 534.

34. Harvey, *Limits*, 413–445; Moore, *Capitalism*, 2–3.

35. Marx, *Grundrisse*, 410 (emphasis in original).

36. Trajano Andrade, interview by the author, March 16, 2015, Manta.

37. Rumsey, "Ecuador to Seize Brazil's Odebrecht."

38. Trajano Andrade, interview by the author, March 16, 2015, Manta. Odebrecht was the first multinational to be expelled from Ecuador. Several foreign oil companies, however, including the Brazilian state oil company Petrobras, had already abandoned the country after Correa changed the terms of their contracts, and Correa had also had confrontations with other foreign companies; Rumsey, "Ecuador to Seize Brazil's Odebrecht"; Kueffner and Goodman, "Ecuador May Default."

39. According to an American intelligence brief disclosed by Wikileaks, "Hutchison's Managing Director told us that the change in the global economic environment, and the mercurial, anti-market behavior of the Ecuadorian government made the concession no longer viable." The brief refers to Manta-Manaus, noting that Hutchison "had planned to position Manta as the primary port of Ecuador and a redistribution center for other destinations," including "Brazil via an ambitious road and river development scheme"; Wikileaks, "Another One Bites the Dust."

40. Medalla, "Correa Conundrum."

41. "APM Launches"; Autoridad Portuaria de Manta, "Informe Anual."

42. Hapag-Lloyd, "Intra-Americas."

43. Trajano Andrade, interview by the author, March 16, 2015, Manta.

44. Vincent, *Operación Callao*, 81.

45. Medalla, "Times of Crisis"; COSIPLAN, *Cartera de proyectos*, 76. BNDES did not approve any further loans to Ecuador until 2012, when Correa granted Odebrecht the right to operate in the country again and signed several new contracts with the company; "Brazil to Finance Ecuador Project." The Ecuadorian government's dealings with Odebrecht would later be the subject of a series of corruption scandals.

46. By this point, Peru and Brazil were also collaborating in the construction of a second interoceanic corridor included in the Amazon Hub of the IIRSA, comprising a highway from the Peruvian port of Callao to the town of Pucallpa on the Ucayali River in the Peruvian Amazon, from which another *hydrovía* would lead to Manaus and Belém; COSIPLAN, *Cartera de proyectos*, 78; Gamarra, "Carretera IIRSA Sur."

47. Carlos Fermín, interview by the author, February 10, 2015, Providencia.

48. Medalla, "Correa Conundrum."

49. Ruiz, "Parte I," 69–99. Public investment in Ecuador rose from $1.1 billion in 2001 to $9.5 billion in 2011. Between 2007 and 2011 the government invested $5.3 billion on transport infrastructure; Dávalos and Albuja, "Ecuador," 157–158.

50. Official figures place road construction costs for Manta-Manaus at $876.481 million; Ministerio de Relaciones Exteriores, *Manta-Manaos*. Airport investments in Tena, Latacunga, and Manta totaled approximately $100 million, while state investment in the ports of Manta and Providencia amounted to $156 million; Ministerio de Transporte y Obras Públicas, "Proyecto multimodal." According to these figures, by 2015 total state expenditure on the infrastructure for Manta-Manaus stood at approximately $1,132,000,000.

51. Coronil, *Magical State*, 4.

52. Nataly Espinel, president of the Quevedo Chamber of Commerce, interview by the author, March 18, 2015, Quevedo, Ecuador.

53. Representative of the Ministry of Transport and Public Works, Municipality of Cotopaxi, interview by Manuel Bayón, May 5, 2015, Latacunga, Ecuador; member of the Autonomous Decentralized Government of Salcedo, interview by Manuel Bayón, May 5, 2015, Salcedo, Ecuador.

54. "Cadena radial nro. 22."

55. Carlos Fermín, interview by the author, February 9, 2015, Providencia.

56. Logistics consultant in the Ministry of Transport and Public Works, interview by the author, February 5, 2015, Quito.

57. Ministerio de Transporte y Obras Públicas, "Proyecto multimodal."

58. Junior minister, Ministry of Transport and Public Works, interview by the author, February 6, 2015, Quito.

59. Junior minister, SENPLADES, interview by the author, November 21, 2014, Quito.

60. Ministerial adviser with responsibility for rivers, Ministry of Transport and Public Works, interview by the author, March 13, 2015, Guayaquil; Marco González, managing director of Amazon Service, interview by the author, March 2, 2015, Quito.

61. Ministerio de Coordinación de la Producción, Empleo y Competitividad, *Plan comercial*, 4.

62. Logistics consultant, Ministry of Transport and Public Works, interview by the author, February 5, 2015, Quito.

63. Robin Draper, general manager, Conduto, interview by the author, February 24, 2015, Quito.

64. Ministerio de Transporte y Obras Públicas, "Proyecto multimodal," 6 (emphasis added).

65. Quoted in Laboratorio Manta-Manaos, "Consultorio," 31–32.

66. Marco González, interview by the author, March 2, 2015, Quito.

67. Son of Carlos Fermín, interview by the author, March 28, 2015, Providencia. See also Jacobs, "Amazon Shipping."

68. Inhabitant of Providencia no. 1, interview by the author, February 26, 2015, Providencia.

69. Inhabitant of Providencia no. 2, interview by the author, February 26, 2015, Providencia.

70. Augusto Celís, interview by the author, March 3, 2015, Quito.

71. Carlos Fermín, interview by the author, February 9, 2015, Providencia.

72. Correa, in Ministerio de Coordinación de la Producción, Empleo y Competitividad, "Primer viaje."

73. Aurora Valle, director of the Manta Chamber of Commerce, interview by the author, March 17, 2015, Manta.

74. Marco González, interview by the author, March 2, 2015, Quito.

75. Ibid.

76. "El embarque por la ruta Manta-Manaos."

77. Guadalupe Llori, prefect of Orellana, interview by the author, March 24, 2015, Coca.

78. Prager, "Werner Herzog," 23.

79. Kapuściński, Shah of Shahs, 56.

80. Keller Easterling, interview by the author, April 9, 2016, Detroit.

81. Easterling, "Geopolitics," 5.

82. Easterling, Subtraction, 67, 74.

83. Easterling, "Split Screen," 272.

84. Easterling, "Geopolitics"; Subtraction, 68–72.

85. South America Project, "IIRSA Workshops."

86. Cuff and Sherman, Fast-Forward Urbanism.

87. South America Project, "IIRSA Workshops."

88. Santiago del Hierro, interview by the author, May 29, 2015, Quito.

89. Carlos Fermín, interview by the author, February 10, 2015, Providencia.

90. Cuff and Sherman, Fast-Forward Urbanism, 27 (emphasis in original).

91. Kasarda and Lindsay, Aerotropolis.

92. Lindsay, "Rise." Aerotropolis has been described by the author and journalist Will Self as "a classic example of the Fin de Siècle scientific romance in its utopian

guise. It aims, like its predecessors, to resolve the contradictions and divisions of the present by thrusting its readers . . . into a future typified by plenty, social accord and clean, green cities linked together by clean, green jets"; Self, "Frowniest."

93. CityLab, "Divining Providencia," 48, 149.

94. Ibid, 87, 150.

95. Roger Sherman, interview by the author, June 12, 2015, Los Angeles (via Skype).

96. Adams, "Longing," 7.

97. Roger Sherman, interview by the author, June 12, 2015, Los Angeles.

98. Member of the Amazon master plan design team, SENPLADES, interview by the author, October 30, 2014, Quito.

99. Ecuadorian representative of UNASUR, interview by the author, March 3, 2015, Quito.

100. Santiago del Hierro, interview by the author, October 22, 2014, Quito.

101. Lindsay, "'Divining Providencia'"; Sherman, "Uncovering Providencia"; Easterling, "Geopolitics," 3.

102. The decision to exploit Block 43 was condemned by international environmental organizations, and in Ecuador a petition was submitted with over 750,000 signatures opposing exploitation and demanding a public consultation on the issue. The National Electoral Board, however, questioned the validity of hundreds of thousands of these signatures and refused to hold the consultation; Economist Intelligence Unit, "CNE."

103. Marco González, interview by the author, March 2, 2015, Quito.

104. Robin Draper, interview by the author, February 24, 2015, Quito.

105. Member of the parish council of Limoncocha, the parish in which Providencia is located, interview by the author, February 25, 2015, Limoncocha, Ecuador.

106. Inhabitant of Providencia no. 1, interview by the author, February 26, 2015, Providencia.

107. Inhabitant of Providencia no. 3, interview by the author, February 26, 2015, Providencia.

108. Elias Piaguaje, interview by the author, February 10, 2015, Providencia.

109. Nelson Castillo, speech delivered at an assembly of Sumak Ñambi, March 29, 2015, Providencia.

110. CityLab, "Divining Providencia," 3, 48, 66.

111. Roger Sherman, interview by the author, June 12, 2015, Los Angeles.

112. ECLAC 2006, *Hacia un desarrollo sustentable*, 60.

113. Ibid., 56. By the time of Correa's triumphant inauguration of Manta-Manaus in 2011, politicians at the highest levels of government had been provided with direct experience of its geographical unviability. Several months before the inauguration, the foreman of one of the main shipping companies on the Napo was commissioned to provide a prominent minister with a tour of the river, so that the minister and his advisers could judge its navigability for themselves. "They said that they wanted to bring vessels with a six-hundred-, eight-hundred-, one-thousand-ton capacity," he recalled. "And that depth won't enter here. [The minister] saw that the conditions here aren't appropriate. Everyone was a bit disillusioned because they saw that things were not as they had thought"; manager of operations, Servicios Petroleros Galeth (SEPEGA), interview by the author, March 26, 2015, Puerto Miranda, Ecuador. And yet the maiden voyage went ahead as planned . . .

114. Guadalupe Llori, interview by the author, March 24, 2015, Coca.

115. Grinberg and Starosta, "Global Capitalism," 240; Postone, *Time, Labor, and Social Domination*, 17.

116. Juan Carlos Hidalgo, owner of the Hidalgo Shipping Co., interview by the author, March 24, 2015, Coca.

117. Rafael Galeth, owner of SEPEGA, interview by the author, April 6, 2015, Coca.

118. Luis Cordobillo, vice mayor of Aguarico, interview by the author, March 26, 2015, Tiputini, Ecuador.

119. Marx, quoted in Harvey, *Companion*, 70.

120. Carlos Fermín, interview by the author, February 10, 2015, Providencia.

121. Inhabitant of Providencia no. 3, interview by the author, February 26, 2015, Providencia.

122. Member of the parish council of Limoncocha, interview by the author, February 25, 2015, Limoncocha.

123. Marco González, interview by the author, March 2, 2015, Quito.

124. Entrepreneur operating in Providencia, interview by the author, February 11, 2015, Shushufindi.

125. Operator of an oil port in Providencia, interview by the author, February 24, 2015, Quito.

126. Logistics consultant, Ministry of Transport and Public Works, interview by the author, February 5, 2015, Quito.

127. Operator of an oil port in Providencia, interview by the author, February 24, 2015, Quito.

128. Inhabitant of Providencia no. 4, interview by the author, February 26, 2015, Providencia.

129. Ex-member of the parish council of Limoncocha, interview by the author, February 25, 2015, Limoncocha.

130. Marco González, interview by the author, March 3, 2015, Quito.

131. Son of Carlos Fermín, interview by the author, March 28, 2015, Providencia.

132. Marx, *Capital*, 342.

133. Partlow, "Can a Chinese Billionaire"; Fonseca, "Nicaragua Constructs."

134. Harvey, *Limits*.

135. Žižek, *Plague of Fantasies*, 14.

136. The phrase has a different meaning in *Fitzcarraldo,* referring not to the fate of modernizing utopias such as that of the protagonist, but to the purported beliefs of the indigenous people of the region. At the Jesuit mission at which Fitzcarraldo passes the night on his way upriver to the mountain he must cross, a monk tells him that the missionaries "can't seem to cure them of the idea that our everyday life is only an illusion, behind which lies the reality of dreams."

137. Nelson Castillo, speech delivered at an assembly of Sumak Ñambi, March 29, 2015, Providencia.

138. Sumak Ñambi's implicit assertion of the right to the city resonates with Lefebvre's insistence that "the *right to the city* . . . can only be formulated as a transformed and renewed *right to urban life*. It does not matter whether the urban fabric encloses the countryside and what survives of peasant life, as long as the 'urban,' place of encounter, priority of use value, inscription in space . . . finds its morphological base and its practico-material realization"; Lefebvre, "Right to the City," 158 (emphasis in original).

139. Badiou, *Rebirth*, 56.

140. Easterling, "Split Screen," 268.

141. Easterling, "Geopolitics," 2.

142. Sherman, "Uncovering Providencia."

143. Ibid.

144. Žižek, "Greece" (paraphrasing Gilles Deleuze).

Chapter 4. Cities of Black Gold

1. Marx Carrasco, "Acumulación originaria (Parte 1)"; Marx Carrasco, "Acumulación originaria (Parte 2)"; Marx Carrasco, "¿Por qué una nueva economía?"

2. Marx, *Capital*, 873–970.

3. Marx Carrasco, "Acumulación originaria (Parte 2)."

4. Escribano, "Ecuador's Energy Policy"; Ruiz, "Parte I."

5. Correa, "Comunidad."

6. Jameson, *Archaeologies*, 10.

7. Bloch, *Principle of Hope*, 99, 102.

8. Freud, *Interpretation of Dreams*, 5.

9. Calvino, *Invisible Cities*, 44.

10. Freud, *Interpretation of Dreams*, 70.

11. Ecuador Estratégico, *Recursos*.

12. Kaika, *City of Flows*, 40.

13. Ecuador Estratégico, *Estratégico* no. 1, 2.

14. Ibid., 3.

15. Ecuador Estratégico, *Estratégico* no. 3, 3.

16. Ecuador Estratégico, *Estratégico* no. 1, 3.

17. Quoted in Ecuador Estratégico *Estratégico* no. 3, 41.

18. The Pañacocha oil field lies between the Napo and Aguarico rivers. At the time of its inauguration it was estimated to contain 42 million barrels of crude (Petroamazonas, *Proyecto Pañacocha*).

19. In 2000 Occidental had sold a stake in one of its Ecuadorian oil fields, in violation of the terms of its concession. But the United States had threatened to cancel its free trade agreement with Ecuador if action was taken against the company, and popular demands for its expulsion had consequently gone unmet. On May 9, 2006, however, the ABP organized a demonstration of over forty thousand people in Quito, opposing the free trade agreement and threatening a paralyzation of the entire Amazon if Occidental was not expelled immediately. Six days later, the government finally canceled Occidental's contract and seized control of its oil fields; González, *Rendición de cuentas*, 2; Congreso Nacional, *VVII Cumbre Amazónica*, 107–114.

20. Correa, in Visión 360, *Ciudades del Milenio* (a documentary broadcast by the Ecuadorian national television program Vision 360 that was inspired by the research presented in this chapter).

21. Sandoval, "Régimen."

22. Correa, in Visión 360, *Ciudades del Milenio*.

23. "Ecuador, con petróleo."

24. Ecuador Estratégico, "Ecuador Estratégico," 41.

25. SENPLADES, *Buen vivir*, 20.

26. "Petróleo para el buen vivir."

27. "Comuneros."

28. Correa, "Ejes del nuevo gobierno."

29. SENPLADES, *Plan nacional de desarrollo*, 64.

30. Ángel Sallo, director of Ecuador Estratégico in the Amazon, interview by the author, June 16, 2016, Lago Agrio.

31. Scott, *Seeing Like a State*, 4, 88.

32. Correa, in Visión 360, *Ciudades del Milenio*.

33. Holston, *Modernist City*, 5.

34. Dávalos, "Geopolítica."

35. Cielo, Coba, and Vallejo, "Women"; Ospina, "Crisis."

36. Quoted in "Comuneros."

37. Quoted in "Si llegan obras."

38. Olmedo Torres, interview by the author, June 24, 2015, Pañacocha, Ecuador.

39. Manuel Bustos, interview by the author, June 22, 2015, Pañacocha.

40. Correa, "Comunidad."

41. Ecuador Estratégico, "Ecuador Estratégico," 41.

42. This account of the Millennium Cities is based on interviews with teachers, nurses, police officers, local politicians, and inhabitants of Pañacocha and Playas de Cuyabeno, as well as field notes from a period spent living in each city.

43. Correa, "Discurso."

44. Inhabitant of Pañacocha no. 1, interview by the author, June 22, 2015, Pañacocha.

45. Member of the parish council of Pañacocha, interview by the author, June 24, 2015, Pañacocha.

46. Jameson, *Archaeologies*, 73.

47. Member of the *comuna* of Playas de Cuyabeno, interview by the author, July 20, 2015, Playas de Cuyabeno, Ecuador.

48. Inhabitant of Pañacocha no. 1, interview by the author, June 22, 2015, Pañacocha.

49. Stites, *Revolutionary Dreams*, 22.

50. Inhabitant of Playas de Cuyabeno no. 1, interview by the author, July 17, 2015, Playas de Cuyabeno.

51. Inhabitant of Pañacocha no. 1, interview by the author, June 22, 2015, Pañacocha.

52. Ibid.

53. Correa, "Discurso."

54. Inhabitant of Pañacocha no. 1, interview by the author, June 22, 2015, Pañacocha.

55. Member of the *comuna* of Edén, interview by the author, October 2, 2015, Edén.

56. Felipe Borman, president of the parish council of Cuyabeno, interview by the author, July 17, 2015, Playas de Cuyabeno.

57. Inhabitant of Pañacocha no. 2, interview by the author, June 23, 2015, upriver from Pañacocha.

58. Inhabitant of Pañacocha no. 3, interview by the author, June 25, 2015, upriver from Pañacocha.

59. Member of the parish council of Pañacocha, interview by the author, June 24, 2015, Pañacocha.

60. Petroamazonas, *Proyecto Pañacocha*, 10.

61. Following its creation in December 2007, Petroamazonas assumed control of the majority of state oil production, and Petroecuador focused primarily on the commercial side of the industry.

62. Sacha Petrol took inspiration from indigenous oil companies in Canada, some of which advised the company in its negotiations with the Ecuadorian government and foreign corporations that included the Canadian company Talisman. Canada's indigenous peoples have pioneered this form of engagement with extractive industries in their territories; see Anderson, Dana, and Dana, "Indigenous Land Rights"; Anderson and Giberson, "Aboriginal Entrepreneurship".

63. Alian Petrol, "Plan de desarrollo." In 2007 Rafael Alvarado changed the name of Sacha Petrol to the more overtly political name of Alian Petrol—standing for *Alianza Indígena* (Indigenous Alliance). However, the company continued to be known locally by the name of Sacha Petrol, and this name has been retained here.

64. Rafael Alvarado, interview by the author, July 22, 2015, Quito.

65. Presidents of the *comunas* of Pañacocha, Pukapeña, and Playas de Cuyabeno to Rafael Correa and Alberto Acosta, the minister of energy and mines, February 22, 2007 (archives of the *comuna* of Playas de Cuyabeno).

66. President, vice president, and treasurer of the parish council of Cuyabeno to Carlos Pareja, president of Petroecuador, April 20, 2007 (archives of the *comuna* of Playas de Cuyabeno).

67. CONFENIAE, "Resolución."

68. Valerio Grefa, ex-president of the FICCKAE, interview by the author, July 15 2015, Coca.

69. Tomšič, *Capitalist Unconscious*, 5.

70. Act of the Assembly of the Province of Orellana, October 3, 2007 (archives of the *comuna* of Playas de Cuyabeno).

71. Resolution signed by the presidents of the parish councils of Cuyabeno, San Roque, and Pañacocha, and by the presidents of the corresponding *comunas* of Playas

de Cuyabeno, Pukapeña and Pañacocha, October 3, 2007 (archives of the *comuna* of Playas de Cuyabeno).

72. "Explotarán otro campo."

73. Bercelino Noteño, president of the Playas de Cuyabeno *comuna*, interview by the author, July 17, 2015, Playas de Cuyabeno.

74. Rosa Capinoa, ex-president of the Pañacocha *comuna*, interview by the author, June 24, 2015, Pañacocha.

75. Presidents of the *comunas* of Pañacocha, Playas de Cuyabeno, and Pukapeña to Tania Masson, minister of the Amazon and executive secretary of ECORAE, March 18, 2008 (archives of the *comuna* of Playas de Cuyabeno).

76. Inhabitant of Playas de Cuyabeno no. 2, interview by the author, July 20, 2015, Playas de Cuyabeno.

77. Inhabitant of Playas de Cuyabeno no. 4, interview by the author, July 18, 2015, Playas de Cuyabeno.

78. The footage of the battle can be seen in Visión 360, *Ciudades del Milenio*.

79. This scene was described by Nancy Morocho, the governor of Sucumbíos at the time (interview by Manuel Bayón, November 9, 2015, Coca), and Pablo Gallegos, the Carmelite priest who played a key role in the struggles of the ABP, and who participated in the negotiations in Playas de Cuyabeno (interview by the author, June 1, 2016, Coca).

80. Bercelino Noteño, president of the Playas de Cuyabeno *comuna*, interview by the author, July 17, 2015, Playas de Cuyabeno.

81. Žižek, *For They Know Not*, 193.

82. Member of the parish council of Pañacocha, interview by the author, June 24, 2015, Pañacocha.

83. Freud, *Interpretation of Dreams*, 70.

84. Felipe Borman, interview by the author, July 17, 2015, Playas de Cuyabeno.

85. "Si llegan obras."

86. "El Oriente."

87. Vallejo and Duhalde, "Chamanismo," 5.

88. This story was reported to me by Angus Lyall, an anthropologist researching Playas de Cuyabeno.

89. Marx, *Theories*, 30–37.

90. Grinberg and Starosta, "Global Capitalism"; Labban, *Space, Oil and Capital*.

91. Marx, *Theories*, 31.

92. Coronil, *Magical State*, 2.

93. Enrique Morales, interview by the author, August 22, 2017, Coca. Ecuador Estratégico also incorporated leaders of the ABP into its management. Ángel Sallo, for example, who had been a leading figure in the ABP, was appointed director of Ecuador Estratégico in Sucumbíos. He claims that he had initially hoped that Ecuador Estratégico could take lessons from the horizontal organization and participatory democracy of the ABP, and that he had proposed that the company should "empower the population through public works." In response, the management team had told him: "No, no, no, no. We are technocrats. [Ecuador Estratégico] isn't political, it's technical"; interview by the author, June 16, 2016, Lago Agrio.

94. Cristian Torres, assistant manager of planning, Ecuador Estratégico, interview by the author, December 12, 2014, Quito.

95. Ibid.

96. Ramon Grefa, president of Pukapeña, interview by the author, July 20, 2015, Pukapeña.

97. Freud, *Interpretation of Dreams*, 68 (emphasis and parentheses in original).

98. Rosa Capinoa, ex-president of the Pañacocha *comuna*, interview by the author, June 24, 2015, Pañacocha.

99. Kouvelakis, "Henri Lefebvre," 711.

100. Rafael Alvarado, interview by the author, July 22, 2015, Quito.

101. Valerio Grefa, ex-president of the FICCKAE, interview by the author, July 15, 2015, Coca.

102. Ramon Grefa, interview by the author, July 20, 2015, Pukapeña.

103. Valerio Grefa, interview by the author, July 15, 2015, Coca.

104. Dolar, "German Idealism."

Chapter 5. The Mirage Laboratory

1. Alianza PAIS, *Plan de gobierno*, 25.

2. Ramírez, *Socialismo del sumak kawsay*.

3. Beaumont, *Utopia Ltd.*, 45.

4. Ramírez, "Izquierda," 2; Ramírez, "Otra ética," 36; Ramírez, "Entre la transición y la transformación," 13.

5. Correa, "Ecuador y sus transformaciones."

6. Wilson, *Jeffrey Sachs*.

7. Todorov, *The Fantastic*, 26.

8. Jameson, *Marxism and Form*, 309.

9. Ramírez, "Otra ética," 35.

10. Correa, "Prologo," 16.

11. Harnecker, "Ecuador," 31.

12. De la Torre, "Tecnopopulismo," 34, 38.

13. Ibid., 38.

14. Quoted in Ramírez, *Socialismo del sumak kawsay*, 23.

15. SENPLADES, *Plan nacional para el buen vivir, 2009–2013*, 5.

16. Ramírez, *Socialismo del sumak kawsay*, 23.

17. Ramírez, "Izquierda," 7; Ramírez, "Más allá."

18. Ramírez, "Otra ética."

19. Ramírez, *Socialismo del sumak kawsay*, 38.

20. Ramírez, "Interview."

21. Ramírez, *Socialismo del sumak kawsay*, 8; Ramírez, "Otra ética."

22. Ramírez, "Interview."

23. SENPLADES, *Buen vivir*, 15.

24. Ramírez, "La disputa."

25. Correa, "Ecuador y sus transformaciones," 25.

26. "La Universidad Ikiam"; "Ikiam fusiona."

27. Member of the Ikiam architectural team no. 1, interview by the author, August 18, 2015, Quito.

28. Ramírez, "Interview."

29. Vallas and Kleinman, "Contradiction"; Zeller, "From the Gene."

30. Ramírez, "La disputa"; Ramírez, "La idea."

31. Ramírez, "La idea."

32. Ramírez, *La vida (buena)*, 43.

33. SENPLADES, *Plan nacional para el buen vivir, 2009–2013*, 17.

34. Hecht and Cockburn, *Fate of the Forest*, 15.

35. Smith, *Explorers of the Amazon*, 182.

36. Ramírez, in CIESPAL, "Clausura."

37. Ikiam, "Ikiam Memoirs." The entire event was transcribed and published as a set of books that were distributed to the workshop participants. The quotations from the workshop that appear in this chapter are all taken from the unnumbered pages of the transcripts on which these books were based.

38. The team comprised biologists, chemists, and physicists engaged in research projects including the creation of an inventory of the flora and fauna of the region, the cataloguing of the variety of bacteria in the soil, and the investigation of the molecular structures of Amazonian bird eggs and the potential for their artificial reproduction through "bio-mimesis," with the aim of creating "bio-ceramics" with

industrial applications. A team of linguists, anthropologists, agronomists, and ethnobotanists was also working with the indigenous communities of the region in the identification of plants with potential medicinal or nutritional properties.

39. Ikiam scientist no. 1, interview by the author, November 11, 2015, Ikiam, Ecuador.

40. Ikiam scientist no. 2, interview by the author: November 7, 2015, Ikiam.

41. Leiva, *Latin American Neostructuralism.*

42. ECLAC, *Cambio estructural.*

43. SENPLADES, *Buen vivir,* 35; Arauz, "Cambio de la matriz productiva," 297; SENESCYT, *Yachay,* 13; SENPLADES, *Buen vivir,* 42.

44. Boyd, Prudham, and Schurman, "Industrial Dynamics," 18, 24. According to Marx, capitalism emerges with the formal subsumption of labor to capital, understood as the subordination of preexisting forms of production under the reign of wage labor. Intercapitalist competition, however, drives toward the real subsumption of labor to capital, through which the labor process is transformed by technologies that increase productivity and the rate of surplus value extraction (Marx, *Capital,* 1019–1038). Like labor, nature is formally subsumed to the extent that it is directly exploited in the conditions in which it is found, confronting capital as "an exogenous set of material properties and bio/geophysical processes"; Boyd et al., 3. Under conditions of real subsumption, by contrast, "natural" biological processes are manipulated to increase yields, enhance metabolisms, and intensify industrial productivity; Birch, Levidow, and Papaioannou, "Sustainable Capital."

45. These included Alexis Mera (who served in the administration of León Febres Cordero), Vinicio Alvarado (who served in the government of Abdalá Bucaram), and Nathalie Cely (who served in the government of Jamil Mahuad). All went on to be influential figures in Correa's cabinet; "Vinicio Alvarado."

46. Julio Peña, president of the Administrative Council of the International Center of Higher Education in Communication for Latin America (CIESPAL) and adviser to René Ramírez, interview by the author, April 2, 2016, Quito.

47. Alberto Acosta, interview by the author, September 30, 2014, Quito.

48. "Mañana."

49. Correa, "Ecuador y sus transformaciones," 36.

50. Wilson, *Jeffrey Sachs,* 112–117.

51. Correa's speech could previously be seen at https://www.youtube.com/watch?v=RGVyEYC72ks (accessed April 12, 2016). The link is no longer functioning.

52. SDSN, *SDSN—Amazonia Launch.*

53. Milstein, "The Private Sector."

54. Cely, "El papel del sector privado"; Zhang, "Ecuador's Galapagos Islands."

55. SENESCYT, *Yachay*. Like Ikiam, Yachay's name was drawn from the language of one of Ecuador's indigenous nationalities, meaning "knowledge" in *Kichwa*; see Howard, "Yachay."

56. Arturo Villavicencio, interview by the author, November 25, 2015, Quito.

57. Ibid.

58. Ibid.

59. Villavicencio, *Innovación*, 16.

60. Carlos Ávila, interview by the author, October 23, 2015, Quito.

61. The contract was signed with the Office of the Incheon Free Economic Zone. Incheon is known as the Silicon Valley of South Korea; Quiroz and Heredia, "Yachay no paso." The circumstances in which the contract was allegedly negotiated were relayed by a family member of one of the Leftist ministers in the Correa cabinet (informal conversation, December 15, 2015).

62. Ikiam, "Ikiam Memoirs." Subsequent quotes from the conference are all taken from this document.

63. Member of the Ikiam architectural team no. 2, interview by the author, October 22, 2014, Quito.

64. Larkin, "Politics and Poetics."

65. Resident of Alto Tena, focus group, November 8, 2015, Alto Tena, Ecuador.

66. This section draws on interviews with Ikiam staff and field notes from several visits to the site in 2015.

67. Before the arrival of Ikiam, the Ecuadorian Amazon had only one public university, which was underfunded, oversubscribed, and located hundreds of miles farther south, in the city of Puyo. This obliged most prospective students from the northern Amazon to travel to universities in the Andean and coastal regions of the country, imposing travel and accommodation costs that few families could afford. Families throughout the Amazon were therefore hopeful that Ikiam would at last provide an opportunity for their children to attend a "first-class" university.

68. Member of the municipal government of Tena, interview by the author, November 5, 2015, Tena, Ecuador.

69. Headmaster of a college in the Tena region, interview by the author, November 5, 2015, Tena.

70. Representative of the Ministry of the Environment, interview by the author, November 6, 2015, Tena.

71. Ibid.

72. Resident of Alto Tena, a community near the Colonso-Chalupas reserve, focus group, November 8, 2015, Alto Tena.

73. Ex-adviser to Carlos Ávila, interview by the author, October 14, 2015, Quito.

74. Member of the Ikiam architectural team no. 1, interview by the author, August 18, 2015, Quito.

75. Member of Mushuk Kawsay, community assembly, November 8, 2015, Mushuk Kawsay, Ecuador.

76. SENPLADES, *Buen vivir*, 52.

77. Member of the Ikiam architectural team no. 1, interview by the author, August 18, 2015, Quito.

78. Member of the Ikiam architectural team no. 2, interview by the author, October 22, 2014, Quito.

79. St. Angelo, "Ecuador Gutted." The price referred to is that of Brent Crude, the leading indicator of the international oil price. Ecuadorian crude trades at a slightly lower price than Brent, which implies an even deeper crisis for the Ecuadorian state.

80. Ex-consultant to the rector of Ikiam, interview by the author, October 14, 2015, Quito.

81. CEO of a biotechnology start-up company, interview by Manuel Bayón, October 8, 2015, Ibarra, Ecuador.

82. Carlos Ávila, interview by the author, October 23, 2015, Quito. The majority of toilet paper consumed in Ecuador at this time was imported, and the few Ecuadorian factories producing toilet paper did so with imported materials; "Otro actor."

83. Ikiam scientist no. 1, interview by the author, November 4, 2015, Ikiam.

84. Government consultant working on the productive matrix, interview by the author, October 7, 2015, Quito.

85. Ikiam scientist no. 1, interview by the author, November 4, 2015, Ikiam.

86. Domingo Tangay Cerda, interview by the author, November 7, 2015, Atacapi, Ecuador.

87. Correa, "Ecuador y sus transformaciones," 31.

88. Maggie Cavendish, interview by the author, December 3, 2015, Quito. A pseudonym has been used in this case. The pseudonym refers to Margaret Cavendish, author of *The Description of a New World, Called the Blazing-World*—a pioneering work of utopian science fiction published in 1666. The "new world" imagined in the book is precisely that of the recently "discovered" world of the Americas.

89. Ikiam, "Code of Ethics."

90. Ramírez, *La vida (buena)*, 108.

91. Ikiam, "Code of Ethics."

92. Maggie Cavendish, interview by the author, December 3, 2015, Quito.

93. Ibid.

94. Rodrigo de la Cruz, Department of Ancestral Knowledge, SENESCYT, Ikiam Code of Ethics Workshop, November 26, 2015. The dialogue reported in the following paragraphs was recorded at the Code of Ethics workshop on November 26 and 27, 2015. Manuel Bayón and I were participating in the workshop as representatives of CENEDET. The descriptions of the event are based on my observations.

95. Quoted in Larrea, "Buen vivir," 68.

96. Ramírez, "La disputa."

97. Swyngedouw, "Apocalypse," 227, 225.

98. Franklin Sharupi, interview by Manuel Bayón, November 29, 2015, Quito.

99. Robertson, "Discovering Price," 500.

100. Ramírez, *Socialismo del sumak kawsay*, 36.

101. Ramírez, "Izquierda," 7.

102. Correa, in "Enlace Ciudadano Nro. 445."

103. Escribano, "Ecuador's Energy Policy"; Iturralde, "Apuntes."

104. Davidov, "Mining versus Oil Extraction"; Rosales, "Going Underground."

105. Don Pazmiño, informal conversation, November 10, 2015, near El Eno, Ecuador.

106. Patricia Garcia, president of the parish council of El Eno, interview by the author, November 9, 2015, El Eno.

107. "Ecuador to Sign Contracts"; "French Oil Company"; Petroamazonas, "Consorcio."

108. President of the *comuna* of Sinchi Urku, interview by the author, November 9, 2015, Vía Guanta, Ecuador.

109. Jairo Herrera, mayor of El Pangui, interview by the author, December 9, 2015, El Pangui, Ecuador.

110. Escribano, "Ecuador's Energy Policy"; Purcell and Martínez, "Post-Neoliberal Energy"; Sacher et al., *Entretelones*. Following the signing of the contract for El Mirador, the Correa administration intensified its efforts to attract foreign investment to the mining industry. In October 2015 the government announced its intention of attracting $750 million of foreign mining investment with a combination of mining incentives and tax benefits. This resulted in the signing of a twenty-five-year contract in January 2016 with the Canadian mining company Lundin Gold, for the development of the Fruta del Norte gold mine, south of El Mirador—the mine was discovered in 2006 and was one of the largest recent gold discoveries in the world, containing an estimated 6.7 million ounces of gold and 9 million ounces of silver; Jamasmie, "Ecua-

dor Aims to Attract"; Jamasmie, "Ecuador, Lundin Gold." Commenting on the story online, one anonymous investor mocked the evident contradiction with the Ecuadorian government's stated commitment to the rights of nature: "Is the mountain still a living being, and mining is stealing from the mountain gods? . . . The whole world is a connected thinking being, but it makes for very, very poor business confidence"; Jamasmie, "Ecuador Aims to Attract").

111. Becker, "Stormy Relations," 58; Iturralde, "Apuntes," 173.

112. "EcuaCorriente"; "Ikiam tiene aprobación."

113. Correa, in "Enlace Ciudadano Nro. 445." This section also draws on interviews conducted with local politicians and government functionaries in the region of El Pangui.

114. Carlos Tendetza, interview by the author, December 12, 2015, Yanua, Ecuador.

115. Collyns, "Was This Indigenous Leader Killed?"; Sacher, *Entretelones*. Two local ECSA employees were accused of Tendetza's murder but were found not guilty. ECSA denied any involvement in the affair.

116. As in the northern Amazon, the government had designated the entire region as *terrenos baldios* (vacant lands), although it was in fact the historical territory of the indigenous inhabitants of the region—in this case the *Shuar*; Benham, "On the Edge," 26.

117. Diego Fernando Esparza, governor of Zamora Chinchipe, interview by the author, December 11, 2015, Zamora, Ecuador.

118. Ex-inhabitant of San Marcos, interview by the author, December 13, 2015, Gualaquiza, Ecuador.

119. Quoted in Benham, "On the Edge," 42.

120. Member of CASCOMI, interview by the author, December 12, 2015, Gualaquiza.

121. Ángel Arevalo, president of the Parish Council of Tundayme, interview by the author, December 9, 2015, Tundayme, Ecuador. The government disputed this version of events, claiming that most of the land had been illegally invaded, that the displacements were peaceful and respectful of human rights, and that the displaced families had been compensated and rehoused elsewhere; Diego Fernando Esparza, governor of Zamora-Chinchipe, interview by the author, December 11, 2015, Zamora; see also ARCOM, "Cerca"; Gobernación de Zamora, "La verdad." As the *Shuar* leader and prefect of Zamora, Salvador Quishpe, observed: "[The evictions in San Marcos] were done in broad daylight. The media were there, people were present. It was public. But it's astonishing to see the government authorities claiming that it didn't happen"; interview by the author, December 11, 2015, Zamora.

122. Leonardo Elizalde, representative of ECSA, interview by the author, December 9, 2015, Tundayme.

123. Wilson, "Perplexing Entanglements."

124. Wilson and Bayón, in CIESPAL, "Panel 1."

125. Ramírez, in CIESPAL, "Clausura."

Conclusion

1. Ecuador Estratégico, "País de sueños cumplidos."

2. Domingo Tangay Cerda, interview by the author, November 7, 2015, Atacapi (emphasis added).

3. Purcell and Martínez, "Post-neoliberal Energy"; Sosa, "El sector externo."

4. Becker and Riofrancos, "Souring Friendship"; Gill, "Ecuador Enters Recession."

5. Todorov, *The Fantastic*, 173–174.

6. Bonilla, "Caricaturas."

7. "Enlace ciudadano 460."

8. "Enlace ciudadano 502."

9. "Enlace ciudadano 481."

10. "Enlace ciudadano 460."

11. Member of the municipal government of Cuyabeno, interview by the author, July 16, 2015, Tarapoa.

12. Minister in the Correa government, informal conversation, November 9, 2014, Quito.

13. Žižek, *For They Know Not*, lxxiv.

14. Žižek, *Plague of Fantasies*, 136.

15. Ibid., 157.

16. "Crédito del FMI"; Ospina, "¿Por quién doblan las campanas?"

17. Palacios, "Ecuador colocó"; "Dos emisiones."

18. "Ecuador to Pay."

19. "Petrolera estatal."

20. Maldonado, "1000 millones"; Purcell and Martínez, "Post-Neoliberal Energy Modernity."

21. Mantilla, "Los dilemas."

22. Ortiz and El Comercio Data, "Conozca el estado."

23. "Constructora Odebrecht"; Ospina, "Orden de prisión."

24. CONAIE, "No somos invasores."

25. "Enlace ciudadano 502."

26. Márquez and Heredia, "División en la provincia."

27. Agencia AFP, "Indígenas piden mediación."

28. "Enlace ciudadano 505." According to Correa, the members of the community of Nankints were opportunistic squatters with no legitimate claim to the land. The same accusation was made against the community of San Marcos in relation to the displacement to make way for the El Mirador mine, and a similar strategy was deployed in official representations of the repression in Dayuma, which was justified as the response to mysterious crimes. Michael Taussig has characterized this form of ideology as the generation of "epistemic murk," which operates through creating "an uncertain reality out of fiction, a nightmarish reality in which the unstable interplay of truth and illusion becomes a social force of horrendous and phantasmatic dimensions . . . and a principle medium of political practice"; Taussig, "Culture of Terror," 492.

29. Becker, "Ecuador"; Coffey, "Time."

30. "Enlace ciudadano 508." As public support for the Citizens' Revolution declined, the audiences that attended Correa's weekly television addresses, and the crowds at pro-government demonstrations such as this one, were increasingly composed of unemployed people, bused in from other provinces and paid a small fee to attend, and government employees, who were obliged by their superiors to do so. One such employee told me that she had frequently been instructed to attend demonstrations at which Correa was speaking. According to her, attendance was taken, state employees were kept under observation to ensure that they actively participated in the pro-government chants and celebrations, and anyone who failed to do so was fined or dismissed; legal adviser to the president of the National Assembly, interview by the author, February 11, 2016, Quito.

31. Becker, "Ecuador"; Puente, "El fortín electoral."

32. Collyns, "Polarised Ecuador."

33. Quoted in Angulo and Orozco, "Carlos de la Torre."

34. Correa, in "Enlace ciudadano 487."

35. "Lenín Moreno."

36. Quoted in Becker and Riofrancos, "Souring Friendship," 124.

37. "Seis exministros."

38. Ospina, "Orden de prisión." The evidence of systemic corruption within the Correa administration led one commentator to identify a third influential group in the government, in addition to the Leftists and the Pragmatists. This group was allegedly centered on Glas and dedicated to the embezzlement of public funds through the corrupt mismanagement of large-scale government contracts with

foreign companies in the construction of the infrastructural megaprojects of the Citizens' Revolution; ibid.

39. Pacheco, "El presidente."

40. Quoted in "Seis exministros."

41. Quoted in "Desde el 1 de septiembre."

42. Quoted in Cuvi, "Cualquier pendejada."

43. Flores, "Exorcizar el correísmo."

44. "Una década decadente"; Torres, "El desgaste."

45. Aguirre, "Castillos de arena."

46. Buck-Morss, *Dialectics of Seeing*, 159.

47. Correa, in "Enlace digital no. 1."

48. Becker and Riofrancos, "Souring Friendship"; Long, "Ecuador's Correa"; Ospina, "Orden de prisión."

49. Enrique Morales, interview by the author, June 22, 2016, Coca.

50. Marx, quoted in Heinrich, *An Introduction to Karl Marx's Capital*, 75.

51. Rancière, *Disagreement*, 15.

52. Buck-Morss, *Hegel*, 75.

References

Abensour, Miguel. "The History of Utopia and the Destiny of Its Critique." In *Political Uses of Utopia: New Marxist, Anarchist, and Radical Democratic Perspectives*, edited by S. D. Chrostowska and James D. Ingram, 3–57. New York: Colombia University Press, 2016.

Acosta, Alberto, and Fander Falconí Benítez. "Otra política económica, deseable y posible." In *Asedios a lo imposible: Propuestas económicas en construcción*, edited by Alberto Acosta and Fander Falconí, 17–38. Quito: FLACSO, 2005.

Adams, Ross. "Longing for a Greener Present: Neoliberalism and the Eco-City." *Radical Philosophy* 163 (2010): 2–7.

Agencia AFP. "Indígenas piden mediación de la OEA y ONU en conflicto minero." *El Comercio*, December 15, 2016.

Aguirre, Milagros. "Castillos de arena." *El Comercio,* September 9, 2017.

———. *Dayuma: ¡Nunca mas!* Quito: CICAME, 2008.

———. *La utopía de los pumas.* Quito: CICAME, 2007.

———, director. *Dayuma Nunca Mas.* Quito: Urbano Films, 2008. https://www.youtube.com/watch?v=jUN-gcjvxTo (accessed March 5, 2020).

"Alcaldesa de Orellana rechazo la militarización de campos petroleros." *Ecuador Inmediato*, May 13, 2007.

Alian Petrol. "Plan de desarrollo campo Pañacocha." Unpublished document, 2007 (archives of the *comuna* of Playas de Cuyabeno, Ecuador).

Alianza PAIS. *Plan de gobierno del Movimiento PAIS, 2007–2011.* Quito: Alianza PAIS, 2006.

Almeida, José. "El mito de la Amazonía en la construcción de la identidad ecuatoriana." *Revista Memoria* 4 (1994): 201–224.

Añazco Castillo, Jorge. *Sucumbíos: Quinta provincia amazónica*. Quito: Gobierno Provincial de Sucumbíos, 2008.

Anderson, Robert B., Leo Paul Dana, and Teresa Dana. "Indigenous Land Rights, Entrepreneurship, and Economic Development in Canada: 'Opting-in' to the Global Economy." *Journal of World Business* 41 (2006): 44–45.

Anderson, Robert B., and Robert J. Giberson. "Aboriginal Entrepreneurship and Economic Development in Canada: Thoughts on Current Theory and Practice." *International Research in the Business Disciplines* 4 (2003): 139–165.

Angulo, Sebastián, and Mónica Orozco. "Carlos de la Torre: 'El sector privado será el motor de la economía.'" *El Comercio*, May 28, 2017.

"APM Launches $300mn Manta Port Concession Tender." *Business News Americas*, May 9, 2012.

Aragon, Louis. *Paris Peasant*. Translated by Simon Watson Taylor. 1971. Reprint, Boston: Exact Change, 1994.

Arauz, Andrés. "Cambio de la matriz productiva." In *La nueva economía en la nueva constitución del Ecuador*, edited by Alfredo Serrano Mancilla, 221–286. Quito: Servicio de Rentas Internas, 2015.

Arboleda, Martín. "Spaces of Extraction, Metropolitan Explosions: Planetary Urbanization and the Commodity Boom in Latin America." *International Journal of Urban and Regional Research* 40, no. 1 (2015): 96–112.

ARCOM. "Cerca de dos millones de dólares para 14 procesos de servidumbre en el proyecto Mirador." December 17, 2015. http://www.control minero.gob.ec/?p=3226 (accessed March 1, 2016).

Arsel, Murat. "Between Marx and Markets? The State, the 'Left Turn' and Nature in Ecuador." *Tijdschrift voor Economische en Sociale Geografie* 10, no. 2 (2012): 150–163.

Asamblea Biprovincial. "Acta de compromiso entre las empresas petroleras con el gobierno nacional y la participación de la Asamblea Biprovincial Sucumbíos-Orellana." Unpublished document, August 30, 2005 (personal archives of Enrique Morales).

———. "Acuerdos entre la Asamblea Biprovincial de Sucumbíos y Orellana y el gobierno nacional." Unpublished document, May 9, 2004 (personal archives of Julio González).

Asamblea de los Pueblos de Sucumbíos. "Ecuador: Informe y declaración de la asamblea de los Pueblos de Sucumbíos y la red amazónica por la vida." Press release, August 20, 2005. http://www.rebelion.org/noticia.php?id=19127 (accessed September 21, 2017).

Autoridad Portuaria de Manta. "Eje multimodal Pacífico-Atlántico Ecuador-Brasil." Unpublished PowerPoint presentation, 2006.

————. "Informe anual 2014." Unpublished document, 2015.

Badiou, Alain. *The Rebirth of History: Times of Riots and Uprisings.* London: Verso, 2012.

Bakhtin, Mikhail. *Rabelais and His World.* Translated by Hélène Iswolsky. 1968. Reprint, Bloomington: Indiana University Press, 1984.

Ballard, J. G. *The Atrocity Exhibition.* 1970. Reprint, London: Fourth Estate, 2014.

————. *Vermilion Sands.* 1973. Reprint, London: Vintage, 2016.

"Barcaza ecuatoriana abre la hidrovía del río Napo." *El Telégrafo,* July 16, 2011.

Beaumont, Matthew. *Utopia Ltd.: Ideologies of Social Dreaming in England, 1870–1900.* Leiden: Brill, 2005.

Becker, Marc. "Ecuador: Slowing a Conservative Restoration." *NACLA Report on the Americas* 49, no. 2 (2017): 127–131.

————. *¡Pachakutik! Indigenous Movements and Electoral Politics in Ecuador.* Lanham, Md.: Rowman and Littlefield, 2011.

————. "The Stormy Relations between Rafael Correa and Social Movements in Ecuador." *Latin American Perspectives* 40 (2013): 43–62.

Becker, Marc, and Thea N. Riofrancos. "A Souring Friendship, a Left Divided." *NACLA Report on the Americas* 50, no. 2 (2018): 124–127.

Benham, Elaine. "On the Edge of an Open Pit: Access to Land and Natural Resources in Tundayme, Ecuador." Master's diss., Norwegian University of Life Sciences, 2015.

Benjamin, Walter. *The Arcades Project.* Translated by Howard Eiland and Kevin McLaughlin. Cambridge: Harvard University Press, 1999.

————. "The Author as Producer." *New Left Review* 62 (1970): 83–96.

————. "Surrealism: The Last Snapshot of the European Intelligentsia." *New Left Review* 108 (1978): 47–56.

Bennett, Jane. *The Enchantment of Modern Life*. Princeton: Princeton University Press, 2001.

Berman, Marshall. *All That Is Solid Melts into Air*. London: Penguin, 1982.

Birch, Kean, Les Levidow, and Theo Papaioannou. "Sustainable Capital? The Neoliberalization of Nature and Knowledge in the European 'Knowledge-based Bio-economy.'" *Sustainability* 2 (2010): 2898–2918.

Bloch, Ernst. *The Principle of Hope*, vol. 1. Cambridge: MIT Press, 1986.

Bonilla, Omar. "The Manta-Manaus Project: Nature, Capital and Plunder." In *The CEECEC Handbook: Ecological Economics from the Bottom Up*, 7–23. CEECEC, 2010. http://www.ceecec.net/wp-content/uploads/2010/09/HANDBOOK_v2.pdf (accessed May 21, 2015).

Bonilla, Xavier [Bonil]. "Caricaturas." *El Universo*, January 27, 2016.

Bowers, Maggie Ann. *Magic(al) Realism*. London: Routledge, 2004.

Boyd, William, Scott Prudham, and Rachel Schurman. "Industrial Dynamics and the Problem of Nature." Working paper, 2008. http://geography.utoronto.ca/wp-content/uploads/2013/10/SNR2001final.pdf (accessed December 11, 2014).

"Brazil to Finance Ecuador Project for 1st Time since 2008 Clash." Reuters, November 12, 2012.

Brenner, Neil. "Theses on Urbanization." In *Implosions/Explosions: Towards a Study of Planetary Urbanization*, edited by Neil Brenner, 181–202. Berlin: Jovis, 2014.

Breton, André. "Manifesto of Surrealism (1924)." In *Manifestoes of Surrealism*, by André Breton, 1–48. Ann Arbor: University of Michigan Press, 1969.

Bruce-Novoa. "Fear and Loathing on the Buffalo Trail." *Non-Traditional Genres* 6, no. 4 (1979): 39–50.

Buck-Morss. Susan. *The Dialectics of Seeing: Walter Benjamin and the Arcades Project*. Cambridge: MIT Press, 1989.

———. *Dreamworld and Catastrophe: The Passing of Mass Utopia in East and West*. Cambridge: MIT Press, 2002.

———. *Hegel, Haiti, and Universal History*. Pittsburgh: University of Pittsburgh Press, 2009.

Burbach, Roger, Michael Fox, and Federico Fuentes. *Latin America's Turbulent Transitions: The Future of Twenty-First-Century Socialism.* London: Zed, 2013.

Cabodevilla, Miguel Ángel. *Coca: Le región y sus historias.* Quito: CICAME, 2007.

———. "Prologo." In *Petróleo, lanzas y sangre,* by Jorge Viteri Toro, 7–10. Quito: La Palabra, 2008.

———. *La selva de los fantasmas errantes.* Pompeya, Ecuador: CICAME, 1997.

"Cadena nacional 19 de diciembre de 2007." Enlace Ciudadano, December 19, 2007. https://www.youtube.com/watch?v=cUXCbYk1lJA (accessed June 11, 2017).

"Cadena radial nro. 4 desde Tena, Napo." Enlace Ciudadano, February 10, 2007. https://www.youtube.com/watch?v=nBJPDu81M2s (accessed September 26, 2017).

"Cadena radial nro. 17." Enlace Ciudadano, May 12 2007. https://www.youtube.com/watch?v=X5IM6 WRCs3E (accessed September 26, 2017).

"Cadena radial nro. 22 desde El Coca, provincia de Orellana, 16 de junio 2007." Enlace Ciudadano, June 16, 2007. https://www.youtube.com/watch?v=tdVGWilybU8 (accessed September 26, 2017).

Calvino, Italo. *Invisible Cities.* Translated by William Weaver. New York: Harcourt Brace Jovanovich, 1974.

Cavendish, Margaret. *The Description of a New World, Called the Blazing-World.* 1666. Reprint, Marston Gate, U.K.: Amazon, 2006.

Cely, Nathalie. "El papel del sector privado en el desarrollo sostenible." Lecture delivered at the International Conference on Sustainable Development, Quito, June 30, 2015. https://sdsnandes.files.wordpress.com/2015/07/nathalie-cely.pdf (accessed March 12, 2020).

Cepek, Michael. "The Loss of Oil: Constituting Disaster in Amazonian Ecuador." *Journal of Latin American and Caribbean Anthropology* 17, no. 3 (2012): 393–412.

Cielo, Cristina, Lisset Coba, and Ivette Vallejo. "Women, Nature, and Development in Sites of Ecuador's Petroleum Circuit." *Economic Anthropology* 3 (2016): 119–132.

CIESPAL. "Clausura: Pensamiento crítico y teoría del valor." Closing speeches delivered at the International Seminar on Value Theory, Communication, and Territory, CIESPAL, Quito, January 26, 2016. https://www.youtube.com/watch?v=L973bHCouks (accessed March 10, 2020).

———. "Panel 1: Comunicación, cultura urbana y desarrollo local." Panel session at the International Seminar on Value Theory, Communication, and Territory, CIESPAL, Quito, January 25, 2016. https://www.you tube.com/watch?v=fVh9lDw1RmA (accessed March 10, 2020).

CityLab. "Divining Providencia: Building a Bio-Cultural Capitol for the Amazon." Los Angeles: University of California. Unpublished planning document, 2013.

Coffey, Gerard. "Time for a New Ecuador?" *Open Democracy*, February 9, 2018.

Cohen, Margaret. "Walter Benjamin's Phantasmagoria." *New German Critique* 48 (1989): 87–107.

Collyns, Dan. "Polarised Ecuador Puts President-Elect's Big Promises to the Test." *Guardian*, April 7, 2017.

———. "Was This Indigenous Leader Killed Because He Fought to Save Ecuador's Land?" *Guardian*, June 2, 2015.

Colombo, Sandra, and Mariano Roark. "UNASUR: Integración regional y gobernabilidad en el siglo XXI." *Densidades* 10 (2012): 21–40.

Comisión de Prensa de Orellana. "Lo que la 'prensa seria' nunca contara." Press release, June 30, 2007. http://www.llacta.org/organiz/coms/2007/com0160.htm (accessed June 16, 2017).

Comisión Ecuménica de Derechos Humanos. "Represión militar a campesinos de Dayuma." July 4, 2007. http://www.llacta.org/organiz/coms/2007/com0179.htm (accessed June 16, 2017).

Comité del Paro. "Boletín de prensa no. 1." Press release, August 14, 2005. https://www.nadir.org/nadir/initiativ/agp/free/imf/ecuador/txt/2005/0815petroleras.htm (accessed June 16, 2017).

———. "Boletín de prensa no. 3." Press release, August 15, 2005. http://llacta.org/organiz/coms/2005/com0373.htm (accessed September 21, 2017).

————. "Boletines de prensa nos. 13–28." Press release, August 16, 2005. http://llacta.org/organiz/coms/2005/como357.htm (accessed September 21, 2017).

————. "Boletín de Prensa no. 61." Press release, August 20, 2005. https://www.nadir.org/nadir/initiativ/agp///free/imf/ecuador/txt/2005/0820actualizaciones.htm (accessed October 3, 2017).

"Comuneros acceden gratuitamente a viviendas." *El Telégrafo*, October 2, 2013.

Conaghan, Catherine, and Carlos de la Torre. "The Permanent Campaign of Rafael Correa: Making Ecuador's Plebiscitary Presidency." *Press/Politics* 13, no. 3 (2008): 267–284.

CONAIE. "No somos invasores—desalojo Nankints—rueda de prensa 23/08/2016." Press conference, August 23, 2018. https://www.youtube.com/watch?v=plA5veCFNIg (accessed December 17, 2018).

CONFENIAE. "Resolución de la XIII Asamblea Ordinaria de la CONFENIAE y VI del Parlamento indio Amazónico, puyo del 26 al 29 de Noviembre de 2007." Unpublished document, archives of the *comuna* of Playas de Cuyabeno, Ecuador.

Congreso Nacional. *VVII Cumbre Amazónica: Por una Amazonía ecuatoriana unida y solidaria*. Quito: Congreso Nacional, 2006.

Conrad, Joseph. *Heart of Darkness*. 1899. Reprint, New York: Dover, 1990.

"Constructora Odebrecht pagó sobornos en Ecuador, anuncia Departamento de Justicia de EE.UU." *El Universo*, December 21, 2016.

Coronil, Fernando. *The Magical State: Nature, Money, and Modernity in Venezuela*. Chicago: University of Chicago Press, 1997.

"Correa: 'Pañacocha ya no es una comunidad en extrema pobreza.'" *El Telégrafo*, January 16, 2014.

Correa, Rafael. "Comunidad del Milenio Playas de Cuyabeno." Speech delivered at the inauguration of the Millennium City of Playas de Cuyabeno, October 10, 2013. https://www.presidencia.gob.ec/wp-content/uploads/downloads/2013/10/2013-10-01-ComunidadMilenioCuyabeno.pdf (accessed May 10, 2020).

————. "Discurso en la inauguración de la Comunidad del Milenio de Pañacocha." Speech delivered at the inauguration of the Millennium

City of Pañacocha, January 16, 2014. http://www.ivoox.com/16-01-2014-discurso-del-presidente-eco-rafael-correa-en-audios-mp3_rf_2720714_1.html (accessed November 29, 2015).

———. "Ecuador y sus transformaciones en política, ciencia y tecnología." Speech delivered at Yale University, October 4, 2014. https://www.presidencia.gob.ec/wp-content/uploads/downloads/2016/11/2014.04.10-Conferencia-Magistral-Yale-ESP.pdf (accessed May 10, 2020).

———. "Los ejes del nuevo gobierno: Discurso completo de la toma de posesión de Rafael Correa como presidente de Ecuador." Inaugural speech as president of Ecuador, January 15, 2007. http://www.democraciasur.com/documentos/EcuadorCorreaTomaPresidencial.htm (accessed September 21, 2017).

———. "Enlace digital no. 1 Rafael Correa." August 12, 2017. https://www.youtube.com/watch?v=9PNuvOdo_V4 (accessed December 16, 2018).

———. "Informe a la nación 2016: La década ganada." Speech delivered in Quito, June 24, 2016. http://www.presidencia.gob.ec/wp-content/uploads/downloads/2016/05/INFORME-A-LA-NACIÓN.pdf (accessed September 21, 2017).

———. "Otra economía es posible." In *Asedios a lo imposible: Propuestas económicas en construcción*, edited by Alberto Acosta and Fander Falconí, 69–78. Quito: FLACSO, 2005.

———. "Prologo: ¿Por qué es necesario cuestionar la disciplina económica para transformar la sociedad?" In *La vida (buena) como riqueza de los pueblos: Hacia una socioecologia política del tiempo*, by René Ramírez, 13–21. Quito: IAEN, 2012.

"Correa advierte a Asamblea no tratar tema Dayuma." *El Univserso*, December 9, 2007.

COSIPLAN. *Cartera de proyectos*. Santiago: COSIPLAN, 2013. http://www.iirsa.org/Document/Detail?Id=3716 (accessed December 11, 2014).

"Crédito del FMI está en función de la cuota del país." *El Comercio*, April 29, 2016.

Cuff, Dana, and Roger Sherman, eds. *Fast-Forward Urbanism: Rethinking Architecture's Engagement with the City*. New York: Princeton Architectural Press, 2011.

Cunha, Euclides da. *The Amazon: Land without History*. Translated by Ronald Sousa. Oxford: Oxford University Press, 2006.

Cuvi, Pablo. "Cualquier pendejada." *El Comercio*, August 11, 2018.

Dávalos, Pablo. "Geopolítica de la acumulación de capital: Ecuador en la Iniciativa IIRSA-COSIPLAN." *América Latina en Movimiento*, February 11, 2014. http://www.alainet.org/images/Ecuador%20en%20la%20 Iniciativa%20IIRSA-COSIPLAN.pdf (accessed November 29, 2015).

Dávalos, Pablo, and Verónica Albuja. "Ecuador: Extractivist Dynamics, Politics and Discourse." In *The New Extractivism: A Post-Neoliberal Development Model or Imperialism of the Twenty-First Century?* edited by Henry Veltmeyer and James Petras, 144–171. London: Zed, 2014.

Davidov, Veronica. "Mining versus Oil Extraction: Divergent and Differentiated Environmental Subjectivities in 'Post-Neoliberal' Ecuador." *Journal of Latin American and Caribbean Anthropology* 18, no. 3 (2013): 485–504.

"Una década decadente." *El Expreso*, January 15, 2017.

De la Torre, Carlos. "El tecnopopulismo de Rafael Correa ¿Es compatible el carisma con la tecnocracia?" *Latin American Research Review* 48, no. 1 (2013): 24–43.

Deler, Jean Paul. *Ecuador: Del espacio al estado nación*. Quito: Universidad Andina Simón Bolívar, 2007.

"Desde el 1 de septiembre rige el decreto de austeridad en Ecuador." *El Universo*, September 6, 2017.

Dolar, Mladen. "German Idealism and Psychoanalysis: A Lacanian Perspective." Lecture delivered at New York University, April 20, 2012. https:// www.youtube.com/watch?v=wrXhkvUqzA4 (accessed November 30, 2015).

———. "Introduction: Awakening." Unpublished manuscript, 2017.

"Dos emisiones de bonos en menos de un mes." *El Comercio*, January 11, 2017.

Eagleton, Terry. "Jameson and Form." *New Left Review* 59 (2009): 123–137.

Easterling, Keller. "The Geopolitics of Subtraction." *Domus* 963 (2012): 2–6.

———. "Split Screen." In *Infrastructure Space*, edited by Ilka Ruby and Andreas Ruby, 264–272. Berlin: Ruby, 2017.

————. *Subtraction*. Berlin: Sternberg, 2014.

ECLAC. *Cambio estructural para la igualdad: Una visión integrada del desarrollo*. Santiago: ECLAC, 2012.

————. *Hacia un desarrollo sustentable e integrado de la Amazonía*. Santiago: ECLAC, 2006.

Economist Intelligence Unit. "CNE Rejects Yasunidos Petition." *Economist*, May 7, 2014.

"EcuaCorriente ha estregado $US70 millones por concepto de regalías anticipadas del proyecto Mirador." *Ecuador Inmediato*, August 3, 2015.

"Ecuador, con petróleo para 20 años más." *El Comercio*, July 16, 2012.

"Ecuador: Cronología del conflicto social junio–diciembre 2007." Quito: OSAL, 2007. http://www.flacsoandes.edu.ec/libros/digital/39949.pdf (accessed September 26, 2017).

"Ecuador: Cronología mayo–agosto 2005." *OSAL* 17 (2005): 177–185.

Ecuador Estratégico. "Ecuador Estratégico lleva desarrollo integral a 11 provincias del país." October 2, 2013. https://www.ekosnegocios.com/articulo/ecuador-estrategico(2) (accessed November 3, 2020).

————. *Estratégico no. 1*. January 2016. https://issuu.com/eestrategico/docs/enero_revista (accessed February 23, 2018).

————. *Estratégico no. 3*. March 2016. https://issuu.com/eestrategico/docs/marzo_revista (accessed February 23, 2018).

————. "País de sueños cumplidos." April 27, 2016. https://www.youtube.com/watch?v=K_TlP9uR7p4 (accessed December 15, 2018).

————. *Recursos que construyen felicidad*. Quito: Ecuador Estratégico, 2015.

"Ecuador's $300mn Manta Port Concession Process to Be Relaunched in September." *Business News Americas*, July 8, 2013.

"Ecuador to Pay $980 Million to Occidental for Asset Seizure." Reuters, January 13, 2016.

"Ecuador to Sign Contracts for Two Controversial Oil Blocks." Amazon Watch, January 20, 2016. https://amazonwatch.org/news/2016/0120-ecuador-to-sign-contracts-for-two-controversial-amazonian-oil-blocks (accessed June 20, 2018).

Eiland, Howard, and Kevin McLaughlin. "Translators' Foreword." In *The Arcades Project*, by Walter Benjamin, ix–xiv. Cambridge: Harvard University Press, 1999.

"El embarque por la ruta Manta-Manaos llegó a Leticia." *El Comercio*, August 3, 2011.

"En Ecuador, los sueños se convierten en obras." *El Ciudadano*, September 17, 2014.

"Enlace ciudadano 20 Enero 2007." Enlace Ciudadano, January 20, 2007. https://www.youtube.com/watch?v=cvOIwRlbBcA (accessed November 10, 2017).

"Enlace ciudadano no. 294." *El Comercio*, October 20, 2012.

"Enlace ciudadano no. 445 desde Quito, Pichincha." Enlace Ciudadano, October 10, 2015. https://www.youtube.com/watch?v=-K3_LSH9PwE (accessed March 10, 2020).

"Enlace ciudadano 460 desde La Libertad." Enlace Ciudadano, January 30, 2016. https://www.youtube.com/watch?v=nG8LvyHQz70 (accessed December 15, 2018).

"Enlace ciudadano 481 desde Manta." Enlace Ciudadano, June 25, 2016. https://www.youtube.com/watch?v=2lQmMq1XXYs (accessed October 20, 2018).

"Enlace ciudadano 487 desde Pujilí." Enlace Ciudadano, August 6, 2016. https://www.youtube.com/watch?v=32vsQBOEOOs (accessed October 20, 2018).

"Enlace ciudadano 502 desde Catamayo." Enlace Ciudadano, November 26, 2016. https://www.youtube.com/watch?v=0007mWztTzs (accessed October 20, 2018).

"Enlace ciudadano 505 desde Quito." Enlace Ciudadano, December 17, 2016. https://www.youtube.com/watch?v=4Q4ltUqhoYg (accessed December 16, 2018).

"Enlace ciudadano 508 desde Rumiñahui." Enlace Ciudadano, January 14, 2017. https://www.youtube.com/watch?v=eMDEk9BiZd8 (accessed December 16, 2018).

"En Orellana existen mafias dice Correa." *La Hora*, December 15, 2007.

Escribano, Gonzalo. "Ecuador's Energy Policy Mix: Development versus Conservation and Nationalism with Chinese Loans." *Energy Policy* 57 (2013): 152–159.

Esman, Aaron. "Psychoanalysis and Surrealism: André Breton and Sigmund Freud." *Journal of the American Psychoanalytic Association* 59, no. 1 (2011): 173–181.

Espinosa, María Fernanda. "La Amazonía ecuatoriana: Colonia interna." *Iconos* 5 (1998): 28–34.

"Explotarán otro campo petrolero." *La Hora*, October 4, 2007.

Ferguson, James. *The Anti-Politics Machine: "Development," Depoliticization, and Bureaucratic Power in Lesotho*. Minneapolis: University of Minnesota Press, 1994.

Fink, Bruce. *The Lacanian Subject: Between Language and Jouissance*. Princeton: Princeton University Press, 1995.

"570 millones de pérdidas por paro Amazónico." *Ecuador Inmediato*, August 19, 2005.

Flores, Thalía. "Exorcizar el correísmo." *El Comercio*, March 15, 2018.

Fonseca, Pablo. "Nicaragua Constructs Enormous Canal, Blind to Environmental Cost." *Scientific American*, February 11, 2015.

Fontaine, Guillaume. "Microconflictos ambientales y crisis de gobernabilidad en la Amazonía ecuatoriana." *Iconos: Revista de Ciencias Sociales* 21 (2005): 35–46.

"French Oil Company to Invest More Than $4.9 Billion in Ecuador." *Andes*, December 15, 2015.

Freud, Sigmund. *The Interpretation of Dreams*. Translated by A. A. Brill. 1913. Reprint, Ware, U.K.: Wordsworth, 1997.

Galarza Zavala, Jaime. *El festín del petróleo*. Quito: Sur Editores, 2012.

Gamarra, Luis Felipe. "Carretera IIRSA Sur: Símbolo de unión entre dos países." *La Republica*, June 5, 2013.

Gerlach, Allen. *Indians, Oil, and Politics: A Recent History of Ecuador*. Wilmington, Del.: Scholarly Resources, 2003.

Gill, Nathan. "Ecuador Enters Recession as China Loans Fail to Offset Oil." *Bloomberg News*, September 30, 2015.

Gobernación de Zamora Chinchipe. "La verdad sobre San Marcos." Video broadcast, October 8, 2015. https://www.youtube.com/watch?v=Nkd__ WIDCL4 (accessed March 10, 2020).

"Gobierno de Palacio: 19 paros en 129 días." *Hoy*, August 25, 2005.

González, Julio. *Rendición de cuentas*. Quito: Congreso Nacional, 2007.

"Government Officials Discuss Manta-Manaus Corridor Financing." *Business News Americas*, April 20, 2007.

Grandin, Greg. *Fordlandia: The Rise and Fall of Henry Ford's Forgotten Jungle City*. New York: Picador, 2009.

Grefa, Fredy Rafael. *Maccuruchu: Acercamiento al conocimiento indígena y la planificación en la Amazonía norte del Ecuador*. Quito: Abya Yala, 2014.

Grinberg, Nicolas, and Guido Starosta. "From Global Capitalism to Varieties of Centre-Leftism in South America: The Cases of Brazil and Argentina." In *Crisis and Contradiction: Marxist Perspectives on Latin America in the Global Political Economy*, edited by Susan J. Spronk and Jeffrey Webber, 236–273. Leiden: Brill, 2015.

Gudynas, Eduardo. "Buen Vivir: Today's Tomorrow." *Development* 54, no. 4 (2011): 441–447.

Hapag-Lloyd. "Intra-Americas Service Improvement—New ASW Service and Revised MXP Service" (press release). April 12, 2012. (This press release is no long available online).

Harnecker, Marta. *Ecuador: Una nueva izquierda en busca de la vida en plenitud*. Quito: Abya Yala, 2011.

Harvey, David. *A Companion to Marx's Capital*, vol. 2. London: Verso, 2013.

———. *The Limits to Capital*. Oxford: Blackwell, 1982.

———. *Spaces of Capital: Towards a Critical Geography*. Edinburgh: Edinburgh University Press, 2001.

———. *Spaces of Hope*. Berkeley: University of California Press, 2000.

Harvey, Penny, and Hannah Knox. "The Enchantments of Infrastructure." *Mobilities* 7, no. 4 (2012): 521–536.

Hecht, Susanna, and Alexander Cockburn. *The Fate of the Forest: Developers, Destroyers, and Defenders of the Amazon*. London: Penguin, 1990.

Heinrich, Michael. *An Introduction to the Three Volumes of Karl Marx's Capital*. New York: Monthly Review Press, 2012.

Herrera, Ramón Vera. "Represión militar en la Amazonía." *La Jornada*, September 19, 2005.

Herzog, Werner. *Conquest of the Useless*. New York: Ecco, 2009.

———, director. *Fitzcarraldo*. DVD. London: BFI 2015.

———. "Interview: Dreams and Burdens." In Flower Films, *The Burden of Dreams*, DVD. Directed by Les Blank. New York: Criterion Collection, 2005.

Holston, James. *The Modernist City: An Anthropological Critique of Brasília*. Chicago: University of Chicago Press, 1989.

Homer, Sean. *Jacques Lacan*. New York: Routledge, 2005.

Howard, Rosaleen. "*Yachay*: The *Tragedia del fin de Atahuallpa*: Evidence of the Colonization of Knowledge in the Andes." In *Knowledge and Learning in the Andes: Ethnographic Perspectives*, edited by Henry Stobart and Rosaleen Howard, 17–39. Liverpool: Liverpool University Press, 2002.

Ikiam. "Code of Ethics for Collaborative Field Research." Unpublished draft, 2015.

———. "Ikiam Amazon University Workshop Memoirs." Unpublished draft, 2012.

"Ikiam fusiona construcción ancestral y tecnología." *El Comercio*, Febuary 1, 2014.

"Ikiam tendrá tres sedes en la Amazonía." *El Ciudadano*, December 3, 2013.

"Ikiam tiene aprobación final del presidente." *El Universo*, December 4, 2013.

Iturralde, Pablo. "Apuntes para pensar la ampliación de la frontera petrolera y minera en Ecuador." In *La alquimia de la riqueza: Estado, petróleo, y patrón de acumulación en Ecuador*, edited by Miguel Ruiz Acosta and Pablo Iturralde, 139–176. Quito: CDES, 2013.

Jackson, Rosemary. *Fantasy: The Literature of Subversion*. London: Routledge, 1981.

Jacobs, Wouter, et al. "Amazon Shipping, Commodity Flows, and Urban Economic Development: The Case of Belém and Manaus." In *Cities, Regions and Flows*, edited by Peter V. Hall and Markus Hesse, 129–148. New York: Routledge, 2013.

Jamasmie, Cecilia. "Ecuador Aims to Attract $750M in Mining Investment Next Year." *Mining.com*, October 27, 2015. http://www.mining.com/ecuador-aims-to-attract-750m-in-mining-investment-next-year/ (accessed June 20, 2018).

———. "Ecuador, Lundin Gold Reach Agreement to Develop Fruta del Norte." *Mining.com*, January 14, 2016. http://www.mining.com/ecuador-lundin-gold-reach-agreement-to-develop-fruta-del-norte/ (accessed June 20, 2018).

Jameson, Fredric. *Archaeologies of the Future: The Desire Called Utopia and Other Science Fictions*. New York: Verso, 2005.

———. "Autobiografía intelectual." Interview, December 9, 2014. https://www.youtube.com/watch?v=60KoW1Gl36s (accessed January 20, 2017).

———. *Marxism and Form: Twentieth-Century Dialectical Theories of Literature*. Princeton: Princeton University Press, 1971.

Kaika, Maria. *City of Flows: Modernity, Nature and the City*. London: Routledge, 2005.

Kapuściński, Ryszard. *Shah of Shahs*. Translated by William R. Brand and Katarzyna Mroczkowska-Brand. 1985. Reprint, London: Penguin, 2006.

Kasarda, John D., and Greg Lindsay. *Aerotropolis: The Way We'll Live Next*. New York: Farrar, Straus and Giroux, 2011.

Kimerling, Judith S. *Amazon Crude*. New York: Natural Resources Defense Council, 1991.

Koepnick, Lutz P. "Colonial Forestry: Sylvan Politics in Werner Herzog's *Aguirre* and *Fitzcarraldo*." *New German Critique* 60 (1993): 133–159.

Kouvelakis, Stathis. "Henri Lefebvre, Thinker of Urban Modernity." In *Critical Companion to Contemporary Marxism*, edited by Jacques Bidet and Stathis Kouvelakis, 711–727. Leiden: Brill, 2008.

Kueffner, Stephan, and Joshua Goodman. "Ecuador May Default on Brazil Loan Tied to Odebrecht (Update 3)." *Bloomberg News*, September 24, 2008.

Labban, Mazen. *Space, Oil and Capital*. New York: Routledge, 2010.

Laboratorio Manta-Manaos. "Consultorio Territorial Amazónico." Quito: Pontifica Universidad Católica de Ecuador. Unpublished draft, 2014.

Larkin, Brian. "The Politics and Poetics of Infrastructure." *Annual Review of Anthropology* 42, no. 3 (2013): 327–343.

Larrea, Ana María. "El buen vivir como contrahegemonía en la Constitución Ecuatoriana." *Utopía y Praxis* 16, no. 53 (2011): 59–70.

Larrea, Carlos. "Extractivism, Economic Diversification and Prospects for Sustainable Development in Ecuador." Paper presented at the conference "Latin America and the Shifting Sands of Global Power," Australia National University, Canberra, September 11–12, 2013.

Lefebvre, Henri. *The Production of Space*. Oxford: Blackwell, 1991.

———. "The Right to the City." In *Henri Lefebvre: Writings on Cities*, edited by Eleonore Kofman and Elizabeth Lebas, 63–184. Oxford: Blackwell, 1996.

———. "Space and Mode of Production." In *State, Space, World: Selected Essays*, edited by Neil Brenner and Stuart Elden, 210–222. Minneapolis: University of Minnesota Press, 2009.

Leiva, Fernando. *Latin American Neostructuralism: The Contradictions of Post-Neoliberal Development*. Minneapolis: University of Minnesota Press, 2008.

"Lenín Moreno: 'No sigan defendiendo a los corruptos.'" *El Comercio*, September 30, 2017.

Lindsay, Greg. "'Divining Providencia' in Venice, Rotterdam, and Quito." *Greg Lindsay Blog*, July 3, 2016. http://www.greglindsay.org/blog/2016/07/divining_providencia_in_venice_rotterdam_and_quito (accessed November 10, 2017).

———. "Rise of the Aerotropolis." *Greg Lindsay Blog*, July 2006. http://greglindsay.org/articles/rise_of_the_aerotropolis/ (accessed October 1, 2020).

Long, Gideon. "Ecuador's Correa Blocked from Return to Presidency." *Financial Times*, February 5, 2018.

Lucero, José Antonio. "Crisis and Contention in Ecuador." *Journal of Democracy* 12, no. 2, (2001): 59–73.

Lund, Henrik Stampe. "The Concept of Phantasmagoria in the *Passagen-Werk*." *Orbis Litterarum* 48 (1993): 96–108.

Maldonado, Pedro. "1000 millones de dólares más de China." *El Comercio*, March 29, 2017.

"Mañana iniciará gira académica." *El Telégrafo*, April 6, 2014.

Mantilla, Sebastián. "Los dilemas de Correa." *El Comercio*, December 21, 2016.

Markus, Gyorgy. "Walter Benjamin on the Commodity as Phantasmagoria." *New German Critique* 83 (2001): 3–42.

Márquez, Cristina, and Valeria Heredia. "División en la provincia de Morona Santiago por la minería." *El Comercio*, November 24, 2016.

Martin, Pamela. "Global Governance from the Amazon: Leaving Oil Underground in Yasuni National Park, Ecuador." *Global Environmental Politics* 11, no. 4 (2011): 22–42.

Martínez, Esperanza. "Ecuador: Contra la globalización de las transnacionales." *OSAL* 17 (2005): 61–66.

Martínez, Javier. *El paraíso en venta: Desarrollo, etnicidad y ambientalismo en la frontera de Yasuní (Amazonía ecuatoriana)*. Quito: Abya Yala, 2015.

Marx, Karl. *Capital*, vol. 1. 1867. Reprint, New York: Random House, 1976.

———. *Grundrisse*. 1971. Reprint, London: Penguin, 1973.

———. *Theories of Surplus Value*, vol. 2. 1951. Reprint, Moscow: Progress, 1968.

Marx, Karl, and Friedrich Engels. *The Communist Manifesto*. 1848. Reprint, London: Penguin, 2002.

Marx Carrasco, Carlos. "La acumulación originaria del socialismo del siglo XXI (Parte 1)." *El Telégrafo*, February 10, 2014.

———. "La acumulación originaria del socialismo del siglo XXI (Parte 2)." *El Telégrafo*, February 17, 2014.

———. "¿Por qué una nueva economía en una nueva constitución?" In *La nueva economía en la nueva constitución del Ecuador*, edited by Alfredo Serrano Mancilla, 73–86. Quito: Servicio de Rentas Internas, 2015.

McNally, David. *Monsters of the Market: Zombies, Vampires and Global Capitalism*. 2011. Reprint, Chicago: Haymarket, 2012.

Medalla, Eva. "The Correa Conundrum." *Business News Americas*, February 13, 2009.

————. "Manta-Manaus Multimodal Corridor to Be Ready in 2011." *Business News Americas*, October 9, 2008.

————. "Pres-Elect: Manta-Manaus Corridor to Be Built by 2011." *Business News Americas*, December 15, 2006.

————. "Times of Crisis Are Times of Opportunities." *Business News Americas*, April 17, 2009.

Memoria Ecuador. "El primer barril del petróleo." Video posted on YouTube, 2009. https://www.youtube.com/watch?v=D9DsiXxxLQI (accessed September 18, 2016).

Merrifield, Andy. *Magical Marxism: Subversive Politics and the Imagination*. London: Pluto, 2011.

Miéville, China. "Symposium: Marxism and Fantasy: Editorial Introduction." *Historical Materialism* 10, no. 4 (2002): 39–49.

Milstein, Mark. "The Private Sector and Sustainable Development." Lecture delivered at the International Conference on Sustainable Development, Quito, June 30, 2015. https://sdsnandes.files.wordpress.com/2015/07/mark-milstein1.pdf (accessed May 10, 2020).

Ministerio de Coordinación de la Producción, Empleo y Competitividad. *Plan comercial bilateral y en tránsito a través del eje multimodal desde el puerto de Manta hasta Manaos*. Quito: Grupo Spurrier, 2011.

————. "Primer viaje de la ruta Manta Manaos—La Morochita 2," March 20, 2012. https://www.youtube.com/watch?v=tQpwyHo1E3E (accessed May 21, 2015).

Ministerio de Relaciones Exteriores. *Manta-Manaos: Eje multimodal bioceánico*. PowerPoint presentation, April 2010. https://docplayer.es/19395365-Manta-manaos-eje-multimodal-bi-oceanico.html (accessed May 10, 2020).

Ministerio de Transporte y Obras Públicas. "Proyecto multimodal Manta Manaos." Unpublished document, 2015.

Moore, Jason W. *Capitalism in the Web of Life: Ecology and the Accumulation of Capital*. London: Verso, 2015.

MPD Sucumbíos. *Las valerosas jornadas de los pueblos del Nororiente Ecuatoriano*. Lago Agrio: Ediciones Opción, 2006.

Muratorio, Blanca. "Introduction: In the Gaze of the Other." In *Retrato de la Amazonia: Ecuador, 1880–1945,* edited by Lucia Chiriboga and Soledad Cruz, 181–197. Quito: Ediciones Libri Mundi, 1992.

Nagera, Humberto. *Basic Psychoanalytic Concepts on the Theory of Dreams.* London: Allen and Unwin, 1969.

Nietzsche, Friedrich. *The Gay Science.* Translated by Thomas Common. 1910. Reprint, Mineola, N.Y.: Dover, 2006.

Nuestro Mar. "Puerto Providencia será el punto de enlace entre Manta y Manaos." March 28, 2008. http://www.nuestromar.org/noticias/puer tos_03_2008_puerto_providencia_sera_el_punto_de_enlace_entre_ manta_y_man_1500 (accessed December 13, 2014).

Obando, Katherine Alexandra. "Dayuma: La construcción del imaginario social de miedo." Master's thesis, Universidad Central, Quito, 2016.

Oppenheimer, Joshua. "Making the Invisible Visible." Interview conducted in Copenhagen, April 2016. https://www.youtube.com/watch?v=b_ dSpzkvVDw (accessed August 4, 2018).

"El Oriente vive dos realidades." *El Universo,* October 6, 2013.

Ortiz, Pablo. "Protestas locales amazónicas y modelo petrolero en Ecuador." *OSAL* 17 (2005): 53–60.

Ortiz, Sara, and El Comercio Data. "Conozca el estado de 18 investigaciones sobre la red de corrupción en Petroecuador." *El Comercio,* December 29, 2016.

Ortiz Durán, René Genaro. "Dinero para carreteras en el oriente ya existe: Afirman petroleras frente al reclamo de las provincias orientales." *El Comercio,* August 2, 2005.

Ospina, Pablo. "Crisis y tendencias económicas en el Ecuador de Rafael Correa: Informe de coyuntura, abril de 2015." *La Línea de Fuego,* April 28, 2015.

———. "La orden de prisión a Rafael Correa y las denuncias de corrupción." *La Línea de Fuego,* July 10, 2018.

———. "¿Por quién doblan las campanas?" *La Línea de Fuego,* March 15, 2016.

"Otro actor entra el mercado de papel higiénico." *El Comercio,* October 18, 2014.

Pacheco, Mayra. "El presidente Lenín Moreno habla de fallas en 640 obras." *El Comercio*, October 24, 2017.

Palacios, William. "Ecuador colocó otros USD 1000 millones en bonos al 10,75%." USFQ, September 29, 2016. https://noticias.usfq.edu. ec/2016/09/ecuador-coloco-otros-usd-1000-millones.html (accessed December 15, 2018).

"Un paro con tácticas militares." *Hoy*, August 19, 2005.

Partlow, Joshua. "Can a Chinese Billionaire Build a Canal across Nicaragua?" *Washington Post*, February 4, 2015.

Perkins, John. *Confessions of an Economic Hit Man*. London: Ebury Press, 2005.

Perreault, Tom, and Gabriela Valdivia. "Hydrocarbons, Popular Protest and National Imaginaries: Ecuador and Bolivia in Comparative Context." *Geoforum* 41 (2010): 689–699.

Petroamazonas. "Consorcio: Petroamazonas EP, Enap Sipetrol y Belorusneft recibe el Bloque 28." April 16, 2015. http://www.petroamazonas.gob. ec/?p=4145 (accessed June 20, 2018).

———. *Proyecto Pañacocha: Un proyecto de Petroamazonas EP.* Quito: Petroamazonas, 2011.

"Petroamazonas paraliza actividad." *El Universo*, October 15, 2008.

"Petroecuador dejó de producir petróleo." *El Comercio*, August 19, 2005.

"Petróleo para el buen vivir de los Ecuatorianos." *El Telégrafo*, October 14, 2013.

"La petrolera estatal firmó un convenio por USD 4 900 millones de Schlumberger." *El Comercio*, December 15, 2015.

Polanyi, Karl. *The Great Transformation: The Political and Economic Origins of Our Time*. Boston: Beacon Press, 2002.

Postone, Moishe. *Time, Labor, and Social Domination: A Reinterpretation of Marx's Critical Theory*. Cambridge: Cambridge University Press, 1993.

Prager, Brad. "Werner Herzog's Hearts of Darkness: *Fitzcarraldo, Scream of Stone* and Beyond." *Quarterly Review of Film and Video* 20, no. 1 (2003): 22–35.

Presidencia de la República. *Constitución de la República de Ecuador* (2008). http://www.unesco.org/culture/natlaws/media/pdf/ecuador/ecuador_ constitucionpo_08_spaorof (accessed September 21, 2017).

"Proyecto Manta-Manaos busca mejorar vida de comunidades." *El Telégrafo*, August 8, 2011.

Puente, Diego. "El fortín electoral de Alianza País cambió en 19 años." *El Comercio*, April 10, 2017.

Purcell, Thomas F., Nora Fernández, and Estefanía Martínez. "Rents, Knowledge and Neostructuralism: Transforming the Productive Matrix in Ecuador." CENEDET Working Papers no. 2, 2015.

Purcell, Thomas F., and Estefania Martínez. "Post-neoliberal Energy Modernity and the Political Economy of the Landlord State in Ecuador." *Energy Research and Social Science* 41 (2018): 12–21.

Quiroz, Gabriela, and Valeria Heredia. "Yachay no pasó el examen en diseño y construcción." *El Comercio*, October 30, 2017.

"Quito y Brasilia discuten integración regional con eje Manta-Manaos." *La Hora*, April 20, 2007.

Ramírez, René. "La disputa política por el sentido del (bio)conocimiento." Keynote speech delivered at the conference "Redes de bioconocimiento: Una alternativa para el desarrollo FLACSO-Ecuador," Quito, May 7, 2015. http://reneramirez.ec/ponencia-la-disputa-politica-por-el-sentido-del-bioconocimiento/ (accessed January 30, 2016).

———. "Entre la transición y la transformación: Conocimiento, rentismo y valor." Blogpost, October 3, 2014. (This post is no longer available online.)

———. "La idea es ir de los recursos finitos a los infinitos." *El Telégrafo*, December 13, 2013.

———. "Interview with Rene Ramirez on the Socialism of Buen Vivir." Interview conducted by Orlando Peréz, translated by Erica Weyer, April 13 2012. http://p2pfoundation.net/Interview_with_Rene_Ramirez_on_the_Socialism_of_Buen_Vivir (accessed February 29, 2016).

———. "Izquierda y 'buen capitalismo': Un aporte critico desde América Latina." *Nueva Sociedad* 236 (2011): 1–13.

———. "Más allá del marxismo y del capitalismo: Más allá del 'valor de uso' y 'valor de cambio.'" *El Telégrafo*, October 23, 2015.

———. "Otra ética para otra sociedad: La de sumak kawsay." In *La nueva economía en la nueva constitución del Ecuador*, edited by Alfredo Serrano Mancilla, 35–72. Quito: Servicio de Rentas Internas, 2015.

————. *Socialismo del sumak kawsay o biosocialismo republicano.* Quito: SE-NESCYT, 2012.

————. *La vida (buena) como riqueza de los pueblos: Hacia una socioecologia política del tiempo.* Quito: IAEN, 2012.

Rancière, Jacques. *Disagreement: Politics and Philosophy.* Minneapolis: University of Minnesota Press, 1999.

————. *The Lost Thread: The Democracy of Modern Fiction.* New York: Bloomsbury, 2017.

Restrepo, Marco. "El proceso de acumulación en la Amazonía ecuatoriana: Una breve visión histórica." In *Amazonía nuestra: Una visión alternativa,* edited by Lucy Ruiz, 105–124. Quito: Abya Yala, 1991.

Robertson, Morgan. "Discovering Price in All the Wrong Places: The Work of Commodity Definition and Price under Neoliberal Environmental Policy." *Antipode* 39, no. 3 (2007): 500–526.

Rosales, Antulio. "Going Underground: The Political Economy of the 'Left Turn' in South America." *Third World Quarterly* 34, no. 8 (2013): 1443–1457.

Rose, Jacqueline. *States of Fantasy.* Oxford: Clarendon Press, 1996.

Ruiz, Miguel. "Parte I." In *La alquimia de la riqueza: Estado, petróleo, y patrón de acumulación en Ecuador,* 1–138. Quito: CDES, 2013.

Rumsey, John. "Ecuador to Seize Brazil's Odebrecht." *Financial Times,* September 24, 2008.

Sacher, William, et al. *Entretelones de la megaminería en el Ecuador.* Quito: Acción Ecológica, 2015.

Sallo, Ángel. "La Asamblea Biprovincial arma los comités del paro." *El Comercio,* August 8, 2005.

————. "El paro toma fuerza en dos provincias." *El Comercio,* August 16, 2005.

Sandoval, Patricia. "Régimen arrancó oficialmente su producción en Pañacocha." *El Universo,* October 22, 2010.

Sawyer, Suzana. *Crude Chronicles: Indigenous Politics, Multinational Oil, and Neoliberalism in Ecuador.* Durham, N.C.: Duke University Press, 2004.

Schaefer, Timo. "Engaging Modernity: The Political Making of Indigenous Movements in Bolivia and Ecuador, 1900–2008." *Third World Quarterly* 30, no. 2 (2009): 397–413.

Scott, James C. *Seeing Like a State: How Certain Schemes to Improve the Human Condition Have Failed*. New Haven: Yale University Press, 1998.

SDSN. *SDSN—Amazonia Launch: Report—Launch Proceedings*, Manaus, Brazil, March 18, 2014. https://irp-cdn.multiscreensite.com/6f2c9f57/files/uploaded/SDSN-Amazonia-launch-event-highlights-conclusions-Final.pdf (accessed November 3, 2020).

"Seis exministros de Estado están en la mira de la Fiscalía o la Contraloría." *El Comercio*, August 24, 2017.

Self, Will. "The Frowniest Spot on Earth." *London Review of Books* 33, no. 9 (2011): 10–11.

SENESCYT. *Yachay: City of Knowledge*. Quito: SENESCYT, 2013.

SENPLADES. *Buen vivir: Plan nacional, 2013–2017, versión resumida*. Quito: SENPLADES, 2013.

———. *Plan nacional de desarrollo, 2007–2010: Planificación para la Revolución Ciudadana*. Quito: SENPLADES, 2007.

———. *Plan nacional para el buen vivir, 2009–2013, versión resumida*. Quito: SENPLADES, 2009.

Sherman, Roger. "Uncovering Providencia: Gensler Goes to Venice Biennale." *Gensler on Cities*, July 15, 2016. http://www.gensleron.com/cities/2016/7/15/uncovering-providencia-gensler-goes-to-venice-biennale.html (accessed November 10, 2017).

Sigcha, Amparo. "Pindo fue reprimida por orden del gobierno." *Red Voltaire*, August 24 2007. http://www.voltairenet.org/article151021.html (accessed June 16, 2017).

———. "Sucumbíos y Orellana: Un paro que se enfrentó al imperialismo." *Red Voltaire*, September 1, 2005. http://www.voltairenet.org/article127239.html (accessed September 22, 2017).

"Si llegan obras, indígenas darán apoyo a explotación en el Yasuní." *El Universo*, October 3, 2013.

Smith, Anthony. *Explorers of the Amazon*. Chicago: University of Chicago Press, 1990.

Smith, Neil. *Uneven Development: Nature, Capital, and the Production of Space*. Oxford: Blackwell, 1984.

Sosa, César Augusto. "El sector externo no cambio en 19 años." *El Comercio*, July 20, 2017.

South America Project. "The IIRSA Workshops." *SAP Network*, 2011. http://www.sap-network.org/p/iirsa-workshops.html (accessed August 1, 2015).

St. Angelo, Steve. "Ecuador Gutted by Low Oil Prices: Rig Count Down to One." *Oil Price*, February 11, 2016. https://oilprice.com/Energy/Energy-General/Ecuador-Gutted-By-Low-Oil-Prices-Rig-Count-Down-To-One.html (accessed June 20, 2018).

Stepan, Nancy Leys. "Tropical Modernism: Designing the Tropical Landscape." *Singapore Journal of Tropical Geography* 21, no. 1 (2000): 76–91.

Stites, Richard. *Revolutionary Dreams: Utopian Visions and Experimental Life in the Russian Revolution*. Oxford: Oxford University Press, 1989.

Stratfor. "Ecuador: An Oil Strike's Present and Future Consequences." Report, August 23, 2005. https://worldview.stratfor.com/analysis/ecuador-oil-strikes-present-and-future-consequences (accessed September 21, 2017).

"Sucumbíos y Orellana en manos de militares." *El Universo*, May 19, 2005.

Swyngedouw, Erik. "Apocalypse Forever? Post-Political Populism and the Spectre of Climate Change." *Theory, Culture & Society* 27 (2010): 213–232.

Taussig, Michael. "Culture of Terror—Space of Death: Roger Casement's Putumayo Report and the Explanation of Torture." *Comparative Studies in Society and History* 26, no. 3 (1984): 467–497.

———. *The Devil and Commodity Fetishism in South America*. 1980. Reprint, Chapel Hill: University of North Carolina Press, 2010.

———. *The Magic of the State*. New York: Routledge, 1997.

"Termina 'larga noche neoliberal.'" *La Hora*, December 9, 2006.

Thompson, Hunter S. *Fear and Loathing in Las Vegas*. 1971. Reprint, New York: Harper Perennial, 2005.

———. *Happy Birthday, Jack Nicholson*. London: Penguin, 2005.

Todorov, Tzvetan. *The Fantastic: A Structural Approach to a Literary Genre*. Ithaca: Cornell University Press, 1975.

Tomšič, Samo. *The Capitalist Unconscious: Marx and Lacan*. London: Verso, 2015.

Torres, Arturo. "El desgaste de Alianza País." *El Comercio*, February 21, 2017.

Trujillo, Jorge Nelson. *Utopías Amazónicas*. Quito: Occidental Exploration and Production Co., 1998.

"2 autoridades con discurso unificado." *El Comercio*, August 31, 2005.

"La Universidad Ikiam conjuga la naturaleza con lo contemporáneo." *El Comercio*, January 18, 2014.

Vallas, Steven Peter, and Daniel Lee Kleinman. "Contradiction, Convergence and the Knowledge Economy: The Confluence of Academic and Commercial Biotechnology." *Socio-Economic Review* 6, no. 2 (2008): 283–311.

Vallejo, Ivette, and Corinne Duhalde. "Chamanismo, petróleo e itinerarios legales inconclusos en la Amazonía de Ecuador." Unpublished paper, 2015.

Villavicencio, Arturo. *Innovación, matriz productiva y universidad: Por qué Yachay es una estrategia equivocada*. Quito: Fundación Hernán Malo, 2014.

Vincent Bowen, Pedro. *Operación Callao: Vida, pasión y muerte de la concesión de Puerto Manta*. Manta: Casa de la Cultura Ecuatoriana Benjamín Carrión, 2010.

"Vinicio Alvarado es uno de los nuevos ricos del gobierno." *El Comercio*, February 6, 2011.

Visión 360. *Ciudades del Milenio: Promesa inconclusa*. Documentary broadcast on November 12, 2017. https://www.youtube.com/watch?v=v8jHGo9d83k (accessed April 12, 2018).

Viteri Toro, Jorge A. *Petróleo, lanzas y sangre*. Quito: La Palabra, 2008.

Walsh, Catherine. "Development as *Buen Vivir*: Institutional Arrangements and (De)colonial Entanglements." *Development* 53, no. 1 (2010): 15–21.

Watts, Michael. "Petro-Violence: Community, Extraction, and Political Ecology of a Mythic Commodity." In *Violent Environments*, edited by Nancy Lee Peluso and Michael Watts, 189–212. Ithaca: Cornell University Press, 2001.

Wikileaks. "Another One Bites the Dust: Hutchison Port Holdings Abandons Manta Concession." *Wikileaks Cable*, March 6, 2009. https://wikileaks.org/plusd/cables/09GUAYAQUIL52_a.html (accessed May 21, 2015).

Wilson, Japhy. *Jeffrey Sachs: The Strange Case of Dr Shock and Mr Aid.* London: Verso, 2014.

———. "Perplexing Entanglements with a Post-Neoliberal State." *Journal of Latin American Geography* 16 no. 1 (2017): 177–184.

Wood, Michael. *Conquistadors: The Spanish Explorers and the Discovery of the New World.* Berkeley: University of California Press, 2000.

Wylie, Lesley. "Introduction to Special Issue on Amazonian Literatures." *Hispanic Issues Online* 16 (2014): 1–16.

Zeller, Christian. "From the Gene to the Globe: Extracting Rents Based on Intellectual Property." *Review of International Political Economy* 15, no. 1 (2008): 86–115.

Zhang, Kathy. "Ecuador's Galapagos Islands to Host International Conference on Sustainable Development." SDSN, May 15, 2015. http://unsdsn. org/news/2015/05/15/ecuadors-galapagos-islands-to-host-international -conference-on-sustainable-development/ (accessed March 1, 2016).

Žižek, Slavoj. *For They Know Not What They Do: Enjoyment as a Political Factor*, 2nd ed. London: Verso, 2008.

———. "Greece: The Courage of Hopelessness." *New Statesman*, July 20, 2015.

———. "The Need to Traverse the Fantasy." *In These Times*, December 4, 2015.

———. "On Utopia." *Maquinas del Fuego*, August 16, 2011. http:// maquinasdefuego.blogspot.com/2011/08/slavoj-žižek-on-utopia.html (accessed August 1, 2015).

———. *The Plague of Fantasies.* 2nd ed. London: Verso, 2008.

———. "The Reality of the Virtual." Interview conducted in London, December 11, 2003. https://www.youtube.com/watch?v=RnTQhIRcrno (accessed May 1, 2017).

———. *The Sublime Object of Ideology.* London: Verso, 1989.

———. *Violence.* London: Profile, 2008.

Index